SIXTH EDITION

STANDARDS
OF PRACTICE
HANDBOOK

1992

 Association for
Investment Management
and Research

Published by

Association for Investment Management and Research
P.O. Box 3668
Charlottesville, Va. 22903
U.S.A.
804/977-6600
Fax 804/977-1103

200 Park Ave., 18th Floor
New York, N.Y. 10166
U.S.A.
212/953-5700
Fax 212/953-5799

AIMR encourages investment and other firms to provide *Standards of Practice Handbook* to all professional staff members. Additional copies are available for purchase. The price is $20 each. A 25 percent discount applies for CFA candidates. Volume discounts are available on orders of 10 or more. Contact: AIMR Publications Sales Department, P.O. Box 7947, Charlottesville, Va. 22906 U.S.A.; 804/977-3647; Fax 804/977-0350.

ISBN:1-879087-26-X

CONTENTS

PREFACE

Experience has shown that the working investment professional can best understand and apply AIMR's Code of Ethics and Standards of Professional Conduct if they are accompanied by practical illustrations describing the application of individual standards. The *Handbook* was first published in 1982 to provide such assistance. A clear understanding of the contents enhances the ability of the securities analyst and investment manager to make ethical decisions and accept responsibility on behalf of the investment profession. Such conduct, in turn, constitutes a basic ingredient for maintaining public trust.

The Code and Standards that appear in this sixth edition of the *Handbook* succeed those first developed in the early 1960s. Since that time, the standards have been reviewed periodically and amended as necessary both to incorporate practical experience and the impact of change in the profession and to facilitate application of the standards in borderline circumstances. Because both the Code and Standards serve as forms of professional consensus, maintaining relevance in the midst of constant change presents a continuing challenge.

AIMR became the primary professional organization for securities analysts, investment managers, and others related to the investment decision-making process on January 1, 1990. The Financial Analysts Federation (FAF) and the Institute of Chartered Financial Analysts (ICFA) combined on that date and each continues as an AIMR subsidiary to accomplish tasks specific to each organization. One of AIMR's first actions was to adopt the Code and Standards that the FAF and the ICFA had long shared. AIMR enforces both the Code and Standards for all three organizations. Responsibility for practicing within the context of the Code and Standards is assumed by members of the three organizations, any CFAs who are not active members of the ICFA and AIMR, and all CFA candidates.

Responsibility for formulating and reviewing the Code and Standards rests with AIMR's Professional Ethics and Responsibility Committee (PERC). The committee scrutinizes the Code and Standards on a continuing basis for areas of potential improvement. This study, initiated by dedicated individual members of the committee and AIMR staff members, inevitably results in proposals both to amend the standards and update the *Handbook*.

Amendments and Updates

This sixth edition of the *Handbook* contains a number of such amendments to the standards and updates of the relevant supporting text material. First, the Performance Presentation Standards are now the basis for a new Standard III F, reconstituted from the original Standard III E, Prohibition Against Material Misrepresentation of Services.

Second, the various subsections of Standard III, in general, and Standard III C, Portfolio Investment Recommendations and Actions, in particular, have been amended as an outgrowth of a special study conducted by the PERC into the application of the standards to quantitative investment practices. Toward that purpose, the PERC wishes to extend its appreciation to an ad hoc committee of our peers for its participation in significant discussions that culminated in numerous changes to the supporting text of Standards III A through D, and especially in the revision of Standard III C. The ad hoc committee consisted of Theodore Aronson, CFA; Patricia Doumas, CFA; William Jahnke, CFA; Charles Lovejoy, CFA; John Nagorniak, CFA; Evan Schulman; and Anthony Spare, CFA.

Third, Standard IV, Priority of Transactions, has been revised to conform with the current Securities and Exchange Commission definition of "beneficial owner." Finally, Standard VI C, Duty to Employer, has been rephrased to tighten the interpretation of what shall be considered to be acceptable professional conduct when one considers engaging in independent practice. Please review carefully the details of all of these changes.

International Issues

Canadian representatives have served on the PERC and its predecessor committees since their inceptions to guide discussions toward making the *Handbook* to be as useful in Canada as in the United States.

Evidence of the growing internationalization of investing is seen in the increasing number of members—and candidates for the CFA designation—residing and practicing overseas, and frequent trips overseas by U.S. and Canadian analysts and investment managers.

PERC is pleased that analyst societies overseas have found the *Handbook* helpful. Copies have been distributed to securities officials in Great Britain. Also, the Security Analysts Association of Japan had the second edition of the *Handbook* (and its supplement) translated into Japanese for the benefit of its more than 2,500 individual and corporate members; subsequently, the

Japanese Association adopted its own Code and Standards. Furthermore, the fifth edition of the *Handbook* has been translated into the Thai language.

Rapid internationalization can at times pose problems for those engaged in international activities. AIMR members should comply at all times with the Code of Ethics and Standards of Professional Conduct as well as with the relevant laws of the countries in which they live. Also, members should be aware that the laws and regulations of their home countries apply to securities trading in foreign markets. The compliance requirements of the SEC, for instance, apply equally to employees of U.S. companies working in other countries and when trading in U.S. securities abroad.

When there is an absence of specific local or other regulatory requirements, the Code of Ethics and Standards of Professional Conduct should govern members' actions. When the Code and Standards impose a higher degree of responsibility or higher duty than local law but do not conflict with local law, the member is held to the higher standard. The AIMR Board of Governors, at its meeting on May 2, 1992, adopted a resolution reinforcing this position. More details appear on pages 180–84.

The disclosure differences among countries and the scope and effectiveness of local securities regulation can sometimes lead to misunderstandings on the part of those participating in foreign markets. Such misunderstandings often relate to the nature and extent of the information available to make investment judgments and to the degree of protection afforded to public investors.

It is incumbent upon investment professionals to inform their clients of significant differences in these areas when discussing investments in foreign markets.

Service to the Investing Public

The goal of AIMR's professional responsibility program is to ensure that membership in the organization is internationally recognized as representing compliance under all circumstances with the highest ethical standards and to encourage the development of homogeneous international standards.

As part of an ongoing discussion about investors' rights, AIMR has established certain basic principles of fair treatment for the investing public and wishes to encourage high ethical and professional standards. AIMR leaders have discussed the possibility of writing, sponsoring, or endorsing what could become an "investors' bill of rights." Still in the formative stages, this effort has progressed to a level where a position on professionalism and service to the investing public has now emerged. Appearing for the first time in this sixth edition of the *Handbook* is a new section entitled "Professionalism and Service to the Investing Public," appearing on pages 185–87. Note that at this time, we refer to "objectives" and not "requirements" in dealing with the matter of fair treatment for high standards of service to the investing public.

As in the previous editions, we also direct your attention to the short discussion of the professional standards program of AIMR, pages ix–xiii, prepared by John G. Gillis, its general counsel.

The PERC recognizes that the mere presence of a Code and Standards can create a false sense of security if these documents are not fully understood, enforced, and made a meaningful part of everyday professional activities. The committee hopes this edition will prove helpful in the AIMR professional standards program and in the professional practice of members.

For their dedication in guiding this sixth edition to completion, we would especially like to thank members of the PERC: Michael Even, CFA; Gay P. Gervin, CFA; Richard P. Halverson, CFA (*ex officio*); Julianne C. Iwersen-Niemann, CFA; Ian Rossa O'Reilly, CFA; Guy G. Rutherfurd, Jr., CFA; Marion Smith; and Linda H. Taufen, CFA.

Darwin M. Bayston, CFA, AIMR President; N. Joy Hilton, Professional Conduct Administrator; and Paul Johnson and Sandy Mawyer, members of the professional conduct staff, also participated in the committee's deliberations and contributed heavily to the *Handbook*'s contents. John Gillis furnished valuable practical and legal advice regarding all of the material in the *Handbook*.

As was noted in the preface to the earlier editions, the development and interpretation of the Code and Standards is an evolving process and will be subject to continuing refinement. It is likely that, in time, this edition will be superseded by another. This book can not cover every contingency or circumstance and it does not attempt to do so. In the last analysis, there is no substitute for integrity.

We hope you will find that this edition of the *Handbook* provides a useful frame of reference that lends substance to the understanding of professional behavior in the investment decision-making process.

Samuel B. Jones, Jr., CFA, Chairman
Professional Ethics and Responsibility Committee
November 1992

PROFESSIONAL STANDARDS PROGRAM

This *Handbook* is an evolutionary development in the program for professional responsibility established and implemented by the Financial Analysts Federation (FAF) and the Institute of Chartered Financial Analysts (ICFA). As of January 1, 1990, the FAF and ICFA combined and a new parent organization, the Association for Investment Management and Research (AIMR), assumed and is responsible for the professional responsibility programs of all three organizations. All FAF and ICFA members are now also members of AIMR. While a Code of Ethics has existed since the early 1960s, it has only been since the mid-1970s, with the expansion of the Code and the accompanying Standards of Professional Conduct, that extensive enforcement of the Code and Standards through disciplinary proceedings was initiated. AIMR, FAF, and ICFA have identical Codes and Standards.

With this expanded program, including active enforcement, numerous specific situations have developed involving members' conduct (differing widely in facts and background circumstances). The desirability of providing further guidance both to members and to those responsible for developing and enforcing the standards became evident. The *Handbook* is an effort to supply such guidance—not only to help members avoid violations, but also to inform and educate them about appropriate standards of professional practice to further improve their professional work and to benefit their clients, customers, and employers as well as the investing public.

Use of the Handbook

This *Handbook* is a combined effort of members, past and present, working through an AIMR committee known as the Professional Ethics and Responsibility Committee (PERC). The committee draws its membership from a broad spectrum of organizations in the securities field including brokers, investment advisers, banks, and insurance companies. In most instances, these members also have important supervisory responsibilities in their firms. Members of the PERC and its predecessor committees wrote most of the material included, drawing on long experience as investment analysts, investment managers, or both.

The *Handbook* is directed to AIMR members, nonmember CFAs and candidates for the professional designation of Chartered Financial Analyst, and other nonmembers. The Code of Ethics is printed on page 2; the Standards of

Professional Conduct, on page 3. A chapter on each standard then follows sequentially.

Since good professional practice obviously should not be limited to AIMR members, Chartered Financial Analysts, or CFA candidates, other investment practitioners also should be interested in the discussion of professional responsibilities.

This *Handbook* is intended to explain the purpose and application of the standards, including their relevance in typical hypothetical situations. The text discusses and amplifies each standard in real life circumstances and suggests procedures to prevent violations.

As a part of this project, the Code and Standards have been expanded and refined over the years with the most recent amendments in May 1992. The code contains the governing principles for members; the standards provide the minimum rules of conduct to which each member, CFA, and CFA candidate must adhere. These are the rules against which a member's conduct will be measured. Because factual circumstances vary so widely in the application of the standards, the explanatory material is not intended to be all-inclusive. It also should be noted that the *Handbook* is not intended to break new ground or set new policy. Rather, it is intended to reflect the experience and guidelines of able and seasoned practitioners.

There naturally will be many situations not covered by the examples that follow, including many in gray areas. Because these often involve standards that have legal counterparts, members, CFAs, CFA candidates, and nonmembers are strongly urged to discuss with their supervisors and legal and compliance departments their general obligations, the content of the Code and Standards, and circumstances under which they might have questions about appropriate conduct.

In order for professionals to understand their obligations, the following is a brief description of the professional standards programs of the three organizations under AIMR's responsibility.

AIMR Professional Standards Programs

All members of AIMR, whether regular members or affiliates, including those who are retired but maintain an active presence within the profession, are included, as are all those who are awarded the CFA professional designation, whether or not they are members of AIMR, and all candidates for the CFA designation.

The definition of financial analyst and financial analysis in the AIMR bylaws is broad. It provides that a financial analyst "is an individual who spends a substantial portion of time collecting, evaluating, or applying financial, economic, and statistical data, as appropriate, in the investment decision-making process. . . . This process is referred to . . . as financial analysis."

Because the definition of a financial analyst is broad, the *Handbook* often employs the term "investment professional" to indicate the variety and complexity of the functions of members, CFAs, and CFA candidates in a changing and increasingly diverse investment environment.

Extensive diversity exists in the occupations of regular members and affiliates of AIMR, both of whom are referred to as members in the *Handbook* and elsewhere. Regular members either have three years' experience and have passed CFA I or have six years' experience and have passed a self-administered examination based on the Code and Standards. Affiliates lack the minimum experience requirement or do not meet the strict definition of financial analyst but are engaged in related activities, such as corporate pension fund sponsorship or consulting, options and futures analysis and management, corporate financial and investor relations activities, bank loan decisions, and real estate analysis and management.

Violations of the Code and Standards

The bylaws of AIMR, FAF, and ICFA provide, in addition to the required compliance by members, that violations of the Code and Standards are grounds for disciplinary sanctions by AIMR, as are other grounds set forth in the respective bylaws.

AIMR has established in its bylaws the basic structure for enforcing the Code and Standards, implemented through Rules of Procedure (Rules) adopted by AIMR. Authorized sanctions, in increasing order of severity, include an administrative sanction, private reprimand, private censure, public censure, suspension, revocation of membership, and in the case of CFAs, suspension or revocation of the CFA charter. With the exception of summary suspension as outlined in Rule VIII, the latter four sanctions can only be imposed by the AIMR Board of Governors. Appropriate notice of disciplinary sanction is also authorized.

Enforcement Procedures

The AIMR Code and Standards are enforced through procedures based on due process that involve staff investigation and peer review on a confidential basis. (The Rules of Procedure for Proceedings Related to Professional Conduct are printed in AIMR's membership directory.) The AIMR designated officer is responsible for administration of the rules. The AIMR Professional Conduct Committee (PCC) consists of a chairman, one or more vice chairmen, and other members who chair ten regional committees. The more than 80 members of these regional committees provide an additional peer review mechanism.

Each member, CFA, and CFA candidate must submit a member's agreement, and an initial Professional Conduct Statement and subsequent annual statements, which require disclosure pertinent to the Code and Standards. Information received by AIMR relating to an individual's professional conduct, including disclosure in his or her statement or from other sources of legal or regulatory proceedings against him or her or complaints by members or nonmembers, may lead to an inquiry. Complaints regarding professional conduct must be in written form.

Inquiries are conducted by staff operating under the supervision of the designated officer and in consultation with legal counsel. When an inquiry is undertaken, the individual against whom a complaint has been filed is requested to submit a written explanation supported by documents when appropriate.

The designated officer, upon reviewing the explanation, may take one of the following steps: (1) dismiss the complaint, with the concurrence of the regional chairman in the case of a nonmember's complaint; (2) impose a private reprimand; (3) enter into a stipulation agreement with the individual, subject to the approval of the AIMR Board of Governors; or (4) submit the matter to a regional committee for further investigation.

The regional committee may submit a statement of charges resulting in the appointment by the PCC chairman of a panel to hear the charges and any defense offered. The hearing panel reports its findings and recommendations to the AIMR member, CFA, or CFA candidate, and to the AIMR Board of Governors if a sanction is recommended. Any proposed sanction must be approved by the board. Notices of sanctions are published in the AIMR newsletter or other publication of the organization.

Amending the Code and Standards

Responsibility for reviewing and recommending amendments to the Code and Standards rests with the PERC. The AIMR Board of Governors must approve all changes to the Code and Standards.

The *Handbook* is the product of the experience of investment professionals over more than 30 years. The initial hope of the volunteers who developed the material and refined it through the various editions was that the work would be beneficial to their coworkers. Requests for reprint privileges and references in legal and other documents show that the *Handbook* has had a further use as a source and guide for the broader investment community and others.

John G. Gillis, Esq.
Counsel to the Professional Ethics and Responsibility Committee
November 1992

AIMR RESOLUTION

Effective January 1, 1990
Amended May 2, 1992

WHEREAS, the profession of securities analysis and investment management has evolved because of the increasing public need for competent, objective, and trustworthy advice with regard to investments and financial management; and

WHEREAS, the Financial Analysts Federation (FAF) and the Institute of Chartered Financial Analysts (ICFA) were organized to advance the profession and its members and for benefit of the investing and general public; and

WHEREAS, the members of the FAF and the ICFA have engaged in the profession of securities analysis and investment management and the term financial analysis has historically been applied to this profession by the FAF, the ICFA and others; and

WHEREAS, both the FAF and the ICFA in the early 1960s adopted a Code of Ethics and Standards of Professional Conduct governing the conduct of their members and holders of and candidates for the professional designation Chartered Financial Analyst; and

WHEREAS, the FAF and ICFA combined, effective January 1, 1990, and all members of the FAF and ICFA became members of the Association for Investment Management and Research (AIMR) as well as continuing to be members of the FAF and ICFA respectively; and

WHEREAS, effective January 1, 1990 members of AIMR are obligated to comply with the AIMR Code of Ethics and Standards of Professional Conduct.

NOW, THEREFORE, The Association for Investment Management and Research hereby adopts the Code of Ethics and Standards of Professional Conduct set forth below.

All members of the Association for Investment Management and Research, the Financial Analysts Federation, and the Institute of Chartered Financial Analysts and the holders of and candidates for the professional designation Chartered Financial Analyst are obligated to conduct their activities in accordance with the following Code of Ethics and Standards of Professional Conduct. Disciplinary sanctions may be imposed for violations of the Code or Standards.

CODE OF ETHICS

A financial analyst should conduct himself[1] with integrity and dignity and act in an ethical manner in his dealings with the public, clients, customers, employers, employees, and fellow analysts.

A financial analyst should conduct himself and should encourage others to practice financial analysis in a professional and ethical manner that will reflect credit on himself and his profession.

A financial analyst should act with competence and should strive to maintain and improve his competence and that of others in the profession.

A financial analyst should use proper care and exercise independent professional judgment.

---

[1]Masculine pronouns, used throughout the Code and Standards to simplify sentence structure, shall apply to all persons, regardless of sex.

STANDARDS OF PROFESSIONAL CONDUCT

I. Obligation to Inform Employer of Code and Standards

The financial analyst shall inform his employer, through his direct supervisor, that the analyst is obligated to comply with the Code of Ethics and Standards of Professional Conduct, and is subject to disciplinary sanctions for violations thereof. He shall deliver a copy of the Code and Standards to his employer if the employer does not have a copy.

II. Compliance with Governing Laws and Regulations and the Code and Standards

A. *Required Knowledge and Compliance*

The financial analyst shall maintain knowledge of and shall comply with all applicable laws, rules, and regulations of any government, governmental agency, and regulatory organization governing his professional, financial, or business activities, as well as with these Standards of Professional Conduct and the accompanying Code of Ethics.

B. *Prohibition Against Assisting Legal and Ethical Violations*

The financial analyst shall not knowingly participate in, or assist, any acts in violation of any applicable law, rule, or regulation of any government, governmental agency, or regulatory organization governing his professional, financial, or business activities, nor any act which would violate any provision of these Standards of Professional Conduct or the accompanying Code of Ethics.

C. *Prohibition Against Use of Material Nonpublic Information*

The financial analyst shall comply with all laws and regulations relating to the use and communication of material nonpublic information. The financial analyst's duty is generally defined as to not trade while in possession of, nor communicate, material nonpublic information in breach of a duty, or if the information is misappropriated.

Duties under the standard include the following: (1) If the analyst acquires such information as a result of a special or confidential relationship with the issuer or others, he shall not communicate the information (other than within the relationship), or take investment action on the basis of such information, if it violates that relationship. (2) If the analyst is not in a special or confidential relationship with the issuer or others, he shall not communicate or act on material nonpublic information if he knows, or should have known, that such information (a) was disclosed to him, or would result, in a breach of a duty, or (b) was misappropriated.

If such a breach of duty exists, the analyst shall make reasonable efforts to achieve public dissemination of such information.

D. *Responsibilities of Supervisors*

A financial analyst with supervisory responsibility shall exercise reasonable supervision over those subordinate employees subject to his control, to prevent any violation by such persons of applicable statutes, regulations, or provisions of the Code of Ethics or Standards of Professional Conduct. In so doing the analyst is entitled to rely upon reasonable procedures established by his employer.

III. Research Reports, Investment Recommendations and Actions

A. *Reasonable Basis and Representations*
1. The financial analyst shall exercise diligence and thoroughness in making an investment recommendation to others or in taking an investment action for others.
2. The financial analyst shall have a reasonable and adequate basis for such recommendations and actions, supported by appropriate research and investigation.
3. The financial analyst shall make reasonable and diligent efforts to avoid any material misrepresentation in any research report or investment recommendation.
4. The financial analyst shall maintain appropriate records to support the reasonableness of such recommendations and actions.

B. *Research Reports*
1. The financial analyst shall use reasonable judgment as to the inclusion of relevant factors in research reports.
2. The financial analyst shall distinguish between facts and opinions in research reports.
3. The financial analyst shall indicate the basic characteristics of the investment involved when preparing for general public distribution a research report that is not directly related to a specific portfolio or client.

C. *Portfolio Investment Recommendations and Actions*
   1. The financial analyst shall, when making an investment recommendation or taking an investment action for a specific portfolio or client, consider its appropriateness and suitability for such portfolio or client. In considering such matters, the financial analyst shall take into account (a) the needs and circumstances of the client, (b) the basic characteristics of the investment involved, and (c) the basic characteristics of the total portfolio. The financial analyst shall use reasonable judgment to determine the applicable relevant factors.
   2. The financial analyst shall distinguish between facts and opinions in the presentation of investment recommendations.
   3. The financial analyst shall disclose to clients and prospective clients the basic format and general principles of the investment processes by which securities are selected and portfolios are constructed and shall promptly disclose to clients any changes that might significantly affect those processes.
D. *Prohibition Against Plagiarism*
   The financial analyst shall not, when presenting material to his employer, associates, customers, clients, or the general public, copy or use in substantially the same form, material prepared by other persons without acknowledging its use and identifying the name of the author or publisher of such material. The analyst may, however, use without acknowledgment factual information published by recognized financial and statistical reporting services or similar sources.
E. *Prohibition Against Misrepresentation of Services*
   The financial analyst shall not make any statements, orally or in writing, which misrepresent (1) the services that the analyst or his firm is capable of performing for the client, (2) the qualifications of such analyst or his firm, and/or (3) the expected performance of any investment.
   The financial analyst shall not make, orally or in writing, explicitly or implicitly, any assurances about or guarantees of any investment or its return except communication of accurate information as to the terms of the investment instrument and the issuer's obligations under the instrument.
F. *Performance Presentation Standards*
   1. The financial analyst shall not make any statements, orally or in

writing, which misrepresent the investment performance that the analyst or his firm has accomplished or can reasonably be expected to achieve.

2. If an analyst communicates directly or indirectly individual or firm performance information to a client or prospective client, or in a manner intended to be received by a client or prospective client ("Performance Information"), the analyst shall make every reasonable effort to ensure that such Performance Information is a fair, accurate, and complete presentation of such performance.

3. The financial analyst shall inform his employer about the existence and content of the Association for Investment Management and Research's Performance Presentation Standards (see Appendix A), and this Standard III F, and shall encourage his employer to adopt and use the Performance Presentation Standards.

4. If Performance Information complies with the Performance Presentation Standards, the analyst shall be presumed to be in compliance with III F 2 above.

5. An analyst presenting Performance Information may use the following legend on the Performance Information presentation, but only if the analyst has made every reasonable effort to ensure that such presentation is in compliance with the Performance Presentation Standards in all material respects:

    "This report has been prepared and presented in compliance with the Performance Presentation Standards of the Association for Investment Management and Research."

This standard shall take effect January 1, 1993.

G. *Fair Dealing with Customers and Clients*
    The financial analyst shall act in a manner consistent with his obligation to deal fairly with all customers and clients when (1) disseminating investment recommendations, (2) disseminating material changes in prior investment advice, and (3) taking investment action.

IV. Priority of Transactions

The financial analyst shall conduct himself in such a manner that transactions for his customers, clients, and employer have priority over transactions in securities or other investments of which he is the beneficial owner, and so that transactions in securities or other investments in which he has such beneficial ownership do not operate adversely to their interests. If an analyst decides to make a recommendation about the purchase or sale of a security or other investment, he shall give his customers, clients, and employer adequate opportunity to act on this recommendation before acting on his own behalf.

For purposes of these Standards of Professional Conduct, a financial analyst is a "beneficial owner" if he directly or indirectly, through any contract, arrangement, understanding, relationship or otherwise, has or shares a direct or indirect pecuniary interest in the securities or the investment.

V. Disclosure of Conflicts

The financial analyst, when making investment recommendations, or taking investment actions, shall disclose to his customers and clients any material conflict of interest relating to him and any material beneficial ownership of the securities or other investments involved that could reasonably be expected to impair his ability to render unbiased and objective advice.

The financial analyst shall disclose to his employer all matters that could reasonably be expected to interfere with his duty to the employer, or with his ability to render unbiased and objective advice.

The financial analyst shall also comply with all requirements as to disclosure of conflicts of interest imposed by law and by rules and regulations of organizations governing his activities and shall comply with any prohibitions on his activities if a conflict of interest exists.

VI. Compensation

A. *Disclosure of Additional Compensation Arrangements*

The financial analyst shall inform his customers, clients, and employer of compensation or other benefit arrangements in connection with his services to them which are in addition to compensation from them for such services.

B. *Disclosure of Referral Fees*

The financial analyst shall make appropriate disclosure to a prospective client or customer of any consideration paid or other benefit delivered to others for recommending his services to that prospective client or customer.

C. *Duty to Employer*

The financial analyst shall not undertake independent practice which could result in compensation or other benefit in competition with his employer unless he has received written consent from both his employer and the person for whom he undertakes independent employment.

VII. Relationships with Others

A. *Preservation of Confidentiality*

A financial analyst shall preserve the confidentiality of information communicated by the client concerning matters within the scope of the confidential relationship, unless the financial analyst receives information concerning illegal activities on the part of the client.

B. *Maintenance of Independence and Objectivity*

The financial analyst, in relationships and contacts with an issuer of securities, whether individually or as a member of a group, shall use particular care and good judgment to achieve and maintain independence and objectivity.

C. *Fiduciary Duties*

The financial analyst, in relationships with clients, shall use particular care in determining applicable fiduciary duty and shall comply with such duty as to those persons and interests to whom it is owed.

VIII. Use of Professional Designation

The qualified financial analyst may use, as applicable, the professional designation "Member of the Association for Investment Management and Research," "Member of the Financial Analysts Federation," and "Member of the Institute of Chartered Financial Analysts," and is encouraged to do so, but only in a dignified and judicious manner. The use of the designations may be accompanied by an accurate explanation (1) of the requirements that have been met to obtain the designation, and (2) of the Association for Investment Management and Research, the Financial Analysts Federation, and the Institute of Chartered Financial Analysts, as applicable.

The Chartered Financial Analyst may use the professional designation "Chartered Financial Analyst," or the abbreviation "CFA," and is encouraged to do so, but only in a dignified and judicious manner. The use of the designation may be accompanied by an accurate explanation (1) of the requirements that have been met to obtain the designation, and (2) of the Association for Investment Management and Research and the Institute of Chartered Financial Analysts.

IX. Professional Misconduct

The financial analyst shall not (1) commit a criminal act that upon conviction materially reflects adversely on his honesty, trustworthiness, or fitness as a financial analyst in other respects, or (2) engage in conduct involving dishonesty, fraud, deceit, or misrepresentation.

STANDARD I
I. OBLIGATION TO INFORM EMPLOYER OF CODE AND STANDARDS

The financial analyst shall inform his employer, through his direct supervisor, that the analyst is obligated to comply with the Code of Ethics and Standards of Professional Conduct, and is subject to disciplinary sanctions for violations thereof. He shall deliver a copy of the Code and Standards to his employer if the employer does not have a copy.

Purpose of the Standard

The purpose of the standard is to state the responsibility of AIMR members and nonmember holders of, and candidates for, the CFA designation to inform their employers that they are obligated to comply with the Code and Standards in their professional activities and are obligated to deliver a copy of such to their employer. AIMR believes that such knowledge may help to avoid actions in conflict with the Code and Standards and, thereby, potential embarrassment and possible disciplinary action against a member.

The responsibility required by this standard is considered an integral part of professional practice. It is viewed as a minimum rule of conduct exceeding legal requirements and contributes to professional honesty and respect. Individual analysts and investment managers, their employers and clients, and the participants and beneficiaries of accounts all benefit from this standard.

Conduct Affected by the Standard

The standard requires that each member initiate action to notify his employer of the Code and Standards that control his professional practice. "Employer" means "immediate supervisor." Thus, a member can satisfy his obligation under the standard by informing his immediate supervisor. A member need not take action if his supervisor notifies the member that he is aware of the existence and content of the Code and Standards and the member's obligations thereunder.

Members who are supervisors have a greater responsibility, especially those supervised in turn by nonmembers. In larger organizations, therefore, the process becomes more complicated and, possibly, more crucial. The ultimate responsibility for this standard, in most cases, falls on the most senior member (in organizational responsibility) who reports to a nonmember.

Organizational decisions that might result in a violation of the Code or Standards would most frequently occur at a senior level. Thus, it is important that all senior management and the legal and compliance departments of organizations that employ AIMR members and all nonmember CFAs and candidates be aware of the Code and Standards. Further, since the legal department in any organization serves in an important advisory capacity to senior management, that department might be an appropriate source of appeal for analysts and managers with lower organizational status should senior management appear to make decisions that might appear to violate the Code or Standards.

The combined simplicity of this standard and the potentially serious problems that could result from noncompliance emphasize its importance.

Members are encouraged to recommend that employers adopt the Code and Standards as their own or use them as the basis for developing their own standards or internal guidelines. (See Exhibit A.)

Application of the Standard

Example 1: Jones, President of XYZ Trust Company, was contacted by a partner of a brokerage firm and asked to sell XYZ's large holding of Ajax Corporation bonds at a substantial premium over market, but with a severe time limit on the transaction. Jones called in Smith, the director of the investment department and a CFA. Jones and Smith agreed the price was attractive considering the economic conditions and value to the accounts. They concluded, however, that there was not enough time to contact all consult accounts. They decided, consequently, that none should be contacted and that the bonds would be sold for the discretionary accounts only. Brown, a portfolio manager, complained to Smith regarding the consult accounts and was told to "forget it or speak to Jones." Brown informed Jones that the action might violate Standards III A, III G, and VII C. Jones replied that he was unaware of what standards Brown was talking about but would check them out later. However, in the interim, the discretionary bonds were sold.

Comment: Standard I was violated in this case by Smith because he did not take steps to ensure that Jones was aware of the existence and content of the Code and Standards. Jones should have been provided with a copy of the Code and Standards and informed of Brown's (and Smith's) compliance obligation under penalty of disciplinary sanctions. Brown would have violated the standard if he had not reminded Smith about this obligation even though Smith was a CFA and subject to it himself. A subordinate employee cannot assume that his supervisor is aware of the obligation, even if he is a member. (See also III A and VII C.)

Failure to contact nondiscretionary accounts could have been a violation of Standard III G, which requires members to deal fairly with all customers and clients when taking investment action.

If Standard III G was violated, Smith was also in violation of Standard II B by knowingly participating in or assisting any acts in violation of the Code or Standards.

Complying with Standard I might not have prevented what occurred, but it certainly would have provided a valid reason to appeal Jones' decision. If XYZ's legal department had been made aware of the existence and content of the Code and Standards before the incident, Brown could have appealed through it. This course of action might have been easier for Brown and of greater influence on Jones.

Example 2: Johnson, senior partner of ABC Securities, a small brokerage firm, learned that his firm would be a participant in a large stock offering. He told Black, his analyst, to update his last report on the stock (which was somewhat unfavorable) and that there would be nothing wrong in making it more exciting and more favorable. Black followed Johnson's instructions. He rewrote the report and changed his opinion.

Comment: Black violated Standard I if Johnson believed "there would be nothing wrong" in Black's action. Johnson probably was unaware of the existence of the Code and Standards and certainly was unaware of their content. He should have been provided a copy of the Code and Standards and informed of Black's compliance obligation under penalty of disciplinary sanctions.

By writing a "more exciting" and "more favorable" report, Black may have violated Standards III A 1 and III A 2, which require an exercise of diligence and thoroughness and a reasonable and adequate basis in making an investment recommendation to others.

Procedures for Compliance

Standard I probably offers the greatest gain for the least effort of all the standards. Despite this, Standard I is probably the most overlooked and accordingly the most often violated standard. Because most members are supervised by other members, or are one of several members being supervised, it is often assumed that "someone else will take care of it." The potential ramifications of noncompliance are so serious, however, that each member must assume personal responsibility for Standard I.

The procedure is simple. Make an oral or written request to your supervisor to find out whether your employer complies with Standard I. A written memorandum is the most certain evidence (see Exhibit B). Many organizations have established procedures whereby the most senior member (in organizational status) or most senior official distributes a memorandum annually on this subject (see Exhibit C and Exhibit D).

In organizations where size or other factors make such procedures impractical, copies of the Code and Standards can be posted on a bulletin board or other suitable place. (A pamphlet containing the Code and Standards is available from AIMR.)

Supervisors in many organizations periodically (usually annually) circulate copies of the Code and Standards to members of their departments. The need to be familiar and comply with these documents is stressed, and often a written response is required from each recipient indicating a current review of the materials.

An increasing number of organizations also circulate supplemental information on areas covered by the Code and Standards. Many employers also conduct seminars and refresher programs for employees on standards of professional responsibility in their activities.

Given the rapidity of change in investment instruments and methods of dissemination of information, and the increasing overall complexity of fiduciary duty and investment management, it is particularly important that new employees be alerted to the expectation that their conduct meet high ethical standards. The Code and Standards should be called to the attention of new employees who are AIMR members, nonmember CFAs, or CFA candidates during briefing procedures. Other new employees might be informed of the Code and Standards and the existence of an AIMR Self-Administered Standards of Practice Examination so that they may test their understanding of professional conduct and ethical behavior and, having passed the examination, show proof of their knowledge. (See Appendix B for sample.)

Additional copies of the *Handbook* are available through AIMR.

EXHIBIT A
SAMPLE MEMORANDUM

THE XYZ TRUST COMPANY
(Interoffice Communication)

To: All Investment Personnel   August 29, 1992
Subject: Association for Investment Management and
            Research Code of Ethics and Standards of
            Professional Conduct

The XYZ Trust Company has adopted the Code of Ethics and the Standards of Professional Conduct of the Association for Investment Management and Research. XYZ is keenly aware of potential conflicts of interest that may arise in any investment counseling or money management organization. Although no guidelines can adequately cover every situation that might arise, these guidelines, I believe, will minimize or eliminate potential conflicts of interest and, in turn, will contribute to our goal of placing the interests of our clients first.

Louis Lipp
Chairman and CEO

EXHIBIT B
SAMPLE MEMORANDUM

THE XYZ TRUST COMPANY
(Interoffice Communication)

To: Bill Smith   August 29, 1992

Do you know whether we have complied with AIMR Standard I by sending a copy of the Code and Standards to John Jones?

If not, would you like me to do it, or would you prefer to handle it?

Possibly, we should include the Trust Legal Office.

Bob

EXHIBIT C
SAMPLE MEMORANDUM

THE XYZ TRUST COMPANY
(Interoffice Communication)

To: John Jones, President   August 29, 1992
Subject: Association for Investment Management and
            Research Code of Ethics and Standards of
            Professional Conduct

Enclosed is a copy of the AIMR Code of Ethics and Standards of Professional Conduct. According to Standard I, members are required to take steps to ensure that their employer is informed of the members' obligation to comply with the Code and Standards under penalty of disciplinary sanctions and to deliver copies of such to their employer.

I am sure you will agree it is in the interest of XYZ and its staff that all members strictly adhere to the Code and Standards as well as all company regulations on these subjects.

                                                William Smith
                                                Senior Vice President

cc: Trust Legal Office
     All Division Heads
     All Research Analysts
     All Portfolio Managers

EXHIBIT D
SAMPLE MEMORANDUM

THE XYZ TRUST COMPANY
(Interoffice Communication)

To: All Investment Personnel   August 29, 1992
Subject: Association for Investment Management and
            Research Code of Ethics and Standards of
            Professional Conduct

The Trust Legal Office and all senior trust personnel should read and retain copies of the above Code and Standards. All investment personnel are expected to be familiar with their requirements and adhere strictly to them in their professional practice.

John Jones
President

cc: Trust Legal Office
     All Division Heads

Standard I
Reference Material

1. Office of Comptroller of Currency, *Comptroller's Handbook for National Trust Examiners* (January 1981).
2. Securities and Exchange Commission, *Guide to Broker–Dealer Compliance: Report of the Broker–Dealer Model Compliance Program Advisory Committee* (November 13, 1974).
3. Address by Bevis Longstreth to the 1987 Annual Conference of the Financial Analysts Federation, "Fiduciaries, Capital Markets and Regulation—the Current Challenge" (May 12, 1987).
4. Remarks by Richard C. Breeden, SEC Chairman, at Pre-Commencement Program, New York University School of Business, "A Celebration of Ethics" (May 15, 1991).

II. COMPLIANCE WITH GOVERNING LAWS AND REGULATIONS AND THE CODE AND STANDARDS

A. Required Knowledge and Compliance

The financial analyst shall maintain knowledge of and shall comply with all applicable laws, rules, and regulations of any government, governmental agency, and regulatory organization governing his professional, financial, or business activities, as well as with these Standards of Professional Conduct and the accompanying Code of Ethics.

Purpose of the Standard

The purpose of the standard is to state the responsibility of AIMR members and nonmember holders of, and candidates for, the CFA designation to comply with the laws and rules of governments, governmental agencies, and self-regulatory organizations, as they carry out their professional, financial, or business activities. AIMR believes that as a matter of professional responsibility and minimum professional conduct, each investment professional should be aware of, and comply with, laws and rules governing their conduct. Thus, in addition to other minimum standards of conduct expected, which in many cases may exceed the law, it is considered axiomatic that each investment professional comply with the law.

Conduct Affected by the Standard

The Standards of Professional Conduct cover many important areas. However, because financial analysts engage in a wide variety of professional, financial, and/or business activities, the standards cannot provide a guide to proper conduct in every circumstance they may encounter. Therefore, Standard II A sets forth minimum standards of conduct in areas not covered by other standards and requires compliance with laws, rules, and regulations governing conduct.

A financial analyst will come into conflict with this standard if he violates a law, rule, or regulation governing his professional, financial, or business activities.

Application of the Standard

A financial analyst should learn about laws and rules that govern his conduct. Depending on individual circumstances, these could include: the U.S. federal and state laws, Canadian federal and provincial laws, administrative regulations of U.S. federal and state and Canadian federal and provincial agencies, and the rules of self-regulatory organizations such as the National Association of Securities Dealers, the Investment Dealers Association of Canada, the New York Stock Exchange, and the Toronto Stock Exchange,[1] if they govern his professional, financial, or business activities.[2] The broad anti-fraud prohibitions of the Securities Act of 1933[3] and the Securities Exchange Act of 1934[4] affect the activities of almost all U.S. investment professionals and, for this reason, analysts should be familiar with the requirements and prohibitions of these laws.

When members are working abroad and/or are advising investors about foreign securities, the requirement to be informed of the laws and rules governing their conduct may include the need to be familiar with the securities laws and regulations of governments and self-regulatory bodies in overseas countries. (See "International Application of the Code and Standards," pages 180–84.)

Example 1: Green is employed in the trust department of a Boston national bank and invests the assets of trusts of which the bank is a trustee.

Comment: Green should familiarize himself with the limitations and requirements imposed by federal and Massachusetts laws on the bank's investment duties and powers with respect to the trusts. (See also Standards III A, III C, and VII C.)

Example 2: Johnson is the research director for a brokerage firm in Toronto and must approve research reports prepared for use within the firm and for public dissemination.

Comment: Johnson should become familiar with the portions of Ontario and other applicable provincial securities laws and regulations, stock exchange rules, and the rules of the Investment Dealers Association of Canada that define his general supervisory responsibilities and that govern the preparation and dissemination of research reports. (See also Standards II D, III A, III B, and III E.)

Example 3: Mendez, a portfolio manager for an investment adviser in New York City, invests funds for several institutional clients, including a union pension fund.

Comment: Mendez should be familiar with the Investment Advisers Act of 1940, SEC rules and regulations, state and statutory and judicial law governing fiduciaries, the Employee Retirement Income Security Act, the rules and regulations interpreting ERISA, and any applicable labor laws as they affect his work and responsibilities. (See also Standards III A, III C, and VII C.)

Example 4: Smith is employed by a Denver broker–dealer that is a market maker in several over-the-counter stocks and regularly handles transactions in those stocks.

Comment: Smith should be familiar with the statutes and regulations that govern market-making transactions, including the rules of the National Association of Securities Dealers, since all federally registered broker–dealers are required to be members.

Example 5: Jones, a CFA, is a vice president of a medium-sized corporation. Although his business activities do not include any form of investment, he is often informed of valuable material nonpublic information in the course of his management duties.

Comment: Because improper disclosure of this information could subject Jones and his company to liability under SEC Rule 10b-5, he should familiarize himself with the applicable provisions of the securities laws and avoid making such disclosure.

Example 6: Roe is a financial analyst who conducts an investment business in his individual capacity. He knowingly does not include $250,000 of income in his federal tax return.

Comment: Roe has violated Standard II A by filing a false tax return, which is a financial activity covered by this standard. (See also Standard IX.)

Example 7: Doe works as an analyst in a venture capital firm. Without informing her firm, she privately sells oil and gas limited-partnership interests of the type purchased by her firm. Doe sells interests in a partnership, representing it as having a substantial number of leases when she knows that it has none.

Comment: Doe has violated Standard II A in her business activities by making material misrepresentations violating federal securities laws. She also has violated Standard VI C, which requires disclosure of outside compensation arrangements with regard to competing business activities.

Example 8: Brown is a U.S.-domiciled investment analyst employed by the United Kingdom subsidiary of an international stock brokerage and securities underwriting firm in New York City. He specializes in U.K. food and beverage stocks listed on the London Stock Exchange.

Comment: In addition to complying with all SEC requirements, Brown must follow the laws set by the Financial Services Act of the United Kingdom and administered by the Securities and Investments Board as well as the rules of the London Stock Exchange.

Example 9: Black is an AIMR member and president of Black Asset Management. The firm holds discretionary authority over some client funds. Black asked Jones to prepare the firm's Form ADV, the 1940 Investment Adviser Act registration form, for his signature. He told Jones to gloss over disclosure of a heavy fine levied against the firm for regulatory violations because payment of the fine placed the firm in a precarious financial position. Jones decided not to mention the violation or fine. Black signed the form without reading it.

Comment: Black's order to gloss over the disciplinary action and the firm's precarious financial condition violates both federal rules and many states' rules. These require reports to clients of fines of more than $2,500 and, in the case of a firm with discretionary authority, custody of client funds, or certain prepayment of fee requirements, reports of any precarious financial condition.[5] The order also violates Standard II A. Black also is in violation of Standard II D because he failed to supervise Jones properly.

Example 10: Harris, a financial analyst and CFA, recently joined Internationale Ltd. as a partner. Internationale is the largest brokerage firm in its country. During recent interviews with executives of Acme Mines Ltd., Harris received detailed information about a discovery of low-cost, high-quality gold ore. The finding carried the potential for multiplying Acme's earnings many times over. Harris was aware that the information had not been made public and that, for political reasons, it would not be for at least two months. Nonetheless, he discussed the information with his partners. He was surprised when they purchased a substantial number of shares for their own accounts as well as for the firm's. When he questioned the purchases, he was told that the country had no law prohibiting investment on the basis of material nonpublic information and that such trades were considered part of normal compensation. Because there was no law against the transaction, Harris also bought shares in Acme Mines.

Comment: Although Harris did not violate any laws or regulations governing investing in the country, he violated Standard II C, Prohibition Against Use of Material Nonpublic Information. And although all details of the case are not available, Harris may also have violated Standards III G, Fair Dealing with Customers, and IV, Priority of Transactions.

A financial analyst should seek the advice of counsel when in doubt concerning the requirements of the law in a particular case. In some circumstances, reliance on the advice of counsel is a defense to violations of securities law.

Example 11: Allen works for a brokerage firm and is responsible for an underwriting of securities. A company official gives her information indicating that the financial statements filed with the registration statement may overstate the issuer's earnings. She seeks the advice of the brokerage firm's general counsel.

Comment: Allen can defend herself against allegations that she violated the Securities Act[6] if she reveals to her attorney all the facts believed to be relevant[7] (and all the facts her attorney requests), has reason to believe that her attorney is both competent to render the advice sought and sufficiently unbiased to make the advice reliable, obtains the advice in writing,[8] and then follows it without any material variation.[9] (See Standards II B and II C.)

Example 12: O'Neil is employed in the trust department of a bank. He learns from an acquaintance in the financial department of A-Z Corporation that it has suffered disastrous losses for the second quarter and will make a public announcement within a week, after establishing the magnitude of the loss. One of the trusts O'Neil administers holds a large block of A-Z Corporation stock. He knows this is material nonpublic information. He asks the bank's counsel, who is not a securities lawyer, whether he can sell the stock and is told he can.

Comment: O'Neil cannot rely on advice of counsel here because he knows the opinion of counsel is clearly erroneous.[10] (See Standard II C.)

A financial analyst and his employer may discharge their obligations to comply with some securities laws by establishing and implementing internal procedures designed to prevent legal violations.[11] A financial analyst who is not responsible for establishing or implementing internal compliance procedures should carefully follow those procedures established by his employer.[12] A supervisor should take the initiative to establish and implement such procedures. Other provisions of the securities laws provide a defense to persons who make a good-faith effort to discharge their obligations under the law.[13]

Example 13: Schmidt, a member of AIMR, is a principal in a small brokerage firm. An account which represents 1 percent of all account holdings is generating 4.7 percent of the total commission income. Schmidt, who is responsible under the firm's procedures to monitor such matters, investigates the account, suspecting excessive transactions or "churning." He finds that all of the transactions were specifically requested by the customer, the trustee of a private trust. The member takes no further action. The trust beneficiaries later sue the trustee and the brokerage firm, alleging the trustee made frequent transactions of trust investments to increase commissions of the broker handling the account, who is the trustee's brother-in-law.

Comment: Schmidt can assert that he acted in good faith in supervising his employee by investigating the account. Other steps might also be appropriate, such as written confirmation of instructions and trades and disclosure of family or family equivalent relationships with clients and customers.[14] (See Standard II D.)

Example 14: In a large brokerage firm, the corporate finance department may have adverse material nonpublic (inside) information about an issuer, which it cannot communicate to the research or sales department because of procedures to prohibit the dissemination of inside information. At the same time, the corporate finance department possessing the information may wish to stop the research or sales department from recommending or soliciting purchases of the stock in order to protect the firm's customers. A firm should be able to avoid violating the inside information prohibition and carry out its duty to its other customers by using a restricted list, which contains securities of companies about which the firm has nonpublic information or a special relationship. Companies are placed on a restricted list so no recommendations are made and no sales are solicited when the firm, for example, possesses material nonpublic information (whether favorable or adverse) or commences a potential underwriting.[15] (See Standards II C, II D, and VII B.)

Procedures for Compliance

Members can acquire and maintain knowledge about applicable laws, rules, and regulations via the following actions:

■ *Maintain current files.* Maintaining, or encouraging their employers to maintain current reference copies of applicable statutes, rules, regulations, and important cases that are readily available to individual members. The employer might be encouraged to distribute such information to members for this purpose.

■ *Keep informed.* Establishing a procedure under which members are regularly informed about changes in applicable laws, rules, regulations, and case law. In many instances, the employer's counsel can provide such information in the form of memoranda distributed to each member in the organization.

■ *Review procedures.* Regularly reviewing written compliance procedures to ensure that they reflect current law and provide adequate guidance to employees concerning what is permissible conduct under the law. Compliance procedures for specific problem areas are discussed in the sections of this *Handbook* interpreting relevant standards.

Footnotes

1. Note: Private professional organizations that do not have statutory responsibility, such as the Investment Counsel Association of America, are not included in this standard.
2. Ignorance of the requirements of the law is not a defense in an action alleging violation of securities laws even if the violations are only technical transgressions. See *Harry L. Whitmer, Jr.*, SEC Rel. No. 34-18734 (May 12, 1982). Conscious avoidance of knowing the facts, sometimes called "recklessness in not knowing," is also not a defense. See *SEC v. Musella*, 678 F.Supp. 1060 (S.D.N.Y. 1988).
3. Securities Act of 1933, §17(a).
4. Securities Exchange Act of 1934, §10(b) and Rule 10b-5. See also the anti-fraud provisions under the Investment Advisers Act of 1940,1 §206.
5. SEC Rel. No. IA-1083, Rule 206(4)-4, *Financial and Disciplinary Information that Investment Advisers Must Disclose to Clients* (September 25, 1987). Also NASAA Uniform Rule 102(a)(4)-1, *Dishonest or Unethical Practices* (October 9, 1988).
6. Securities Act of 1933, §11.
7. See *Stephens v. Stinson*, 292 F.2d 838 (9th Cir. 1961).
8. *In re John R. Brick*, SEC Rel. No. 34-11763 (October 24, 1975).
9. *SEC v. Geon Industries*, 531 F.2d 39 (2d Cir. 1976).
10. See *SEC v. Lum's*, 365 F.Supp. 1046 (S.D.N.Y. 1973) and *U.S. v. Crosby*, 294 F.2d 928, 942 (2d Cir. 1961); see also reference material at end of this chapter for articles on reliance on advice of counsel.
11. See Securities Exchange Act of 1934, §15(b)(4)(E); Investment Advisers Act of 1940, §203(e)(5), and footnote 37.
12. Securities Exchange Act of 1934, §15(b)(4)(E) and Investment Advisers Act of 1940, §203(e)(5) limit the defense to cases where procedures are regularly followed. See *SEC v. Geon Industries*, 531 F.2d 39 (2d Cir. 1976).
13. Securities Exchange Act of 1934, §20(a).
14. Cf. *Hecht v. Harris, Upham & Co.*, 430 F.2d 1202 (9th Cir. 1970) (interpreting the good faith defense of the Securities Exchange Act of 1934 §20(a)).
15. *Slade v. Shearson, Hammill*, 356 F.Supp. 304 (S.D.N.Y. 1973) and 517 F.2d 398 (2d Cir. 1974). The restricted list also prevents the firm from violating its fiduciary duty to its brokerage customers under state law by advising them on less than the best available information.

Standard II A
Reference Material

1. *In re Patterson Capital Corp., and Joseph B. Patterson,* SEC Administrative Proceeding No. 3-7349 (June 25, 1990) describes the need to file Form ADV in accord with requirements of federal securities laws.
2. Securities and Exchange Commission, *Broker–Dealer Policies and Procedures Designed to Segment the Flow and Prevent the Misuse of Material Nonpublic Information, A Report by the Division of Market Regulation* (March 1990).
3. Securities and Exchange Commission, *Financial Planners: Report of the Staff of the United States Securities and Exchange Commission to the House Committee on Energy and Commerce's Subcommittee on Telecommunications and Finance,* Appendix B, "The Operation of the Investment Advisers Act" (February 1988).
4. North American Securities Administrators Association, Inc., Model Amendments to Uniform Securities Act (1956).
5. Gillis and Cohn, "Legal Aspects of Professional Standards," *Financial Analysts Journal* (January/February 1978).
6. Gillis and Earp, "Interpretations of Professional Conduct," *Financial Analysts Journal* (March/April 1979).
7. Hamermesh, "The Reliance on Counsel Defense," 18 *Review of Securities Regulation* 22 (December 18, 1985).
8. Hawes and Sherrard, "Advice of Counsel, 9 *Review of Securities Regulation* 14 (August 18, 1976).
9. Longstreth, "Reliance on Advice of Counsel as a Defense to Securities Law Violations," 37 *Business Lawyer* 1185 (April 1982).
10. Address by David S. Ruder, Chairman, Securities and Exchange Commission, before the Securities Industry Association, "Securities Industry Operations Responsibilities Following the October Market Break . . ." (December 2, 1987).

II. COMPLIANCE WITH GOVERNING LAWS AND REGULATIONS AND THE CODE AND STANDARDS

B. Prohibition Against Assisting Legal and Ethical Violations

The financial analyst shall not knowingly participate in, or assist, any acts in violation of any applicable law, rule, or regulation of any government, governmental agency, or regulatory organization governing his professional, financial, or business activities, nor any act which would violate any provision of these Standards of Professional Conduct or the accompanying Code of Ethics.

Purpose of the Standard

The purpose of this standard is to state the responsibility of AIMR members and nonmember holders of, and candidates for, the CFA designation to avoid participating in legal and ethical violations committed by others.

Conduct Affected by the Standard

Standard II B applies when a financial analyst knows or should know that his conduct may contribute to a violation of applicable laws, rules, regulations, the Code of Ethics, or the Standards of Professional Conduct. Members are presumed to be aware of applicable laws, rules, and regulations under Standard II A, as well as the requirements of the Code and the Standards. If a member does not have such knowledge, as required by Standard II A, he is held responsible for participating in illegal acts in instances where violation of the law is evident to anyone who knows the law.[1]

Standard II B acknowledges that members who know the requirements of applicable laws and regulations may not recognize violations if they are not aware of all the facts giving rise to the violations. A member is only responsible for violations he knowingly participants in or assists. Knowledge of an abuse, when no action is taken to prevent it or dissociate from it, is a violation of Standard II B.[2]

This standard does not require that members report legal violations to the appropriate governmental or regulatory organizations, but such disclosure may be prudent under certain circumstances. Because of issues outside of this standard, advice of counsel should be sought when legal or regulatory violations occur. There are other steps, mentioned below, that can be taken to avoid participating in or assisting illegal or unethical acts.

Application of the Standard

Investment professionals who know of planned or ongoing illegal or unethical acts can take a number of steps to avoid the inference that they knowingly participated in, or assisted in, illegal or unethical acts. One step might include reporting evidence to superiors in their organization, to officials of other involved organizations, or to the appropriate governmental or self-regulatory organizations.

Example 1: Brown's employer, an investment banking firm, is the principal underwriter for an issue of convertible debentures by Courtney Company. He discovers that Courtney Company has concealed severe third quarter losses in its foreign operations in the prospectus. The red herring prospectus has already been distributed.

Comment: Knowing that the prospectus is misleading and thus violates the Securities Act of 1933, Brown should report his findings to the appropriate supervisory persons in his firm. Presumably, the firm will notify Courtney Company of the steps to be taken to correct the prospectus and to carry out other remedial action. If Courtney Company does not comply, the firm should withdraw from the underwriting. However, if the matter is not remedied and Brown's employer does not dissociate his company from the underwriting, Brown should sever all his connections with the underwriting.[3] Brown should also seek legal advice to determine whether additional reporting or other action should be taken.

Example 2: Cohen is employed by an Ottawa union as a portfolio manager for its pension fund. One of the union's officers tells him that an employee of a company whose stock is held by the pension fund has divulged in a private conversation the fact that the company will announce several plant closings the following day. The price of the stock has been steadily rising for several months. The officer directs Cohen to sell the stock. Cohen believes that this would violate laws forbidding use of material nonpublic information.

Comment: Cohen should explain to the union officer that this violates provincial securities laws and should refuse to sell the stock until the plant closings are announced.[4]

Example 3: Bio is a development stage biotechnology company of limited financial resources. Its single product, Bysol, is a single-sniff antiviral agent which could be a blockbuster if it passes FDA efficacy tests. Lucas, who provides research to several portfolio managers, overhears two analysts discussing rumors of eminent approval. Lucas feels that the rumors are unfounded and unverifiable and passes them along to a portfolio manager that way. Based solely on these rumors, however, the portfolio manager takes a large position in Bio.

Comment: Lucas felt that the hasty action on the part of the portfolio manager violated Standard III A 1, which requires reasonable basis for taking investment actions. He should report his concern to the management of his firm.

Example 4: Murray is a financial analyst and a director of Allied Corporation. The board of directors learns that management has made foreign political contributions without disclosing them in its financial statements to the SEC or the stockholders. Murray consults his employer's counsel and determines that these unreported foreign political contributions will result in illegally misleading financial statements. Despite his urging at meetings with directors and management, the board of directors votes not to disclose the secret contributions.

Comment: Murray should promptly dissociate himself from Allied Corporation's actions by resigning as a director and, with advice of counsel, consider making the SEC aware of the situation.[5]

Example 5: Jackson is the Chief Financial Officer of a medium-sized commercial bank. At the quarterly loan review meeting, some loan officers told him about a substantial amount of loans that had deteriorated, for which repayment seemed highly unlikely. Jackson decided not to disclose the weakening loan quality because it might threaten an impending securities offering by the bank.

Comment: Failure to disclose the change in portfolio quality in the offering prospectus would violate the antifraud provisions of the Securities Act of 1933. The loan officers should notify bank management of the indiscretion and, with advice of counsel, consider notifying the SEC about the misinformation if the misleading prospectus is fitted.[6]

Example 6: Green, a financial analyst and a principal with Jones Financial Services, is responsible for assisting the firm's treasurer in the preparation of its annual federal income tax return. Although Green has reason to believe he is violating the Internal Revenue Code, he helps the treasurer alter certain documents to increase the amounts Jones may take as business deductions.

Comment: Green has violated not only federal tax laws but also Standard II B. Financial analysts who encounter evidence of illegal activities, even if they are not directly involved, are encouraged to report this evidence to the appropriate governmental or self-regulatory organization. It should be noted that in certain circumstances, it may be required by law or by the rules of self-regulatory organizations to report such information.

Example 7: Allen, a portfolio manager with an investment adviser, learns from a middle level officer of one of her clients, ABC Corporation, that officers of the corporation have been selling ABC stock for two weeks on nonpublic information concerning the loss of a contract that had accounted for 75 percent of the Corporation's revenue and earnings. Neither Allen nor his employer has any special or confidential relationship with the issuer except that their accounts hold substantial positions in ABC stock. In fact, Allen purchased ABC stock for some accounts during the two-week period.

Comment: This information should be reported to Allen's supervisors, the client should be informed, and presumably with advice of counsel, the information reported to the appropriate governmental and self-regulatory organizations.

Example 8: Ford is employed in the mergers and acquisitions department of an investment banking firm. He learns that employees under his supervision have been illegally tipping friends with material nonpublic information about pending mergers and acquisitions. He has followed his employer's supervisory procedures, which are designed to detect such trading by employees, and he has not violated Standard II D.

Comment: Ford should report this to his supervisor. If the firm is a member of the New York Stock Exchange, it will be required to report the matter to the Exchange.[7] (See Standard II C.)

Procedures for Compliance

When a financial analyst suspects a client or an employee of planning or engaging in ongoing illegal activities, the financial analyst should take these actions:

■ *Determine legailty.* Consult his supervisor or his employer's counsel to determine whether the conduct is, in fact, illegal. (See Standard II A.)

■ *Take appropriate action.* If the financial analyst has reasonable grounds to believe that imminent or ongoing client or employee activities are illegal, he should dissociate himself from these activities and urge his firm to attempt to persuade the perpetrator(s) to stop the illegal activities. If the firm is unsuccessful, it should dissociate itself from the activities and take action against any perpetrating employee.[8] The financial analyst can dissociate himself from the illegal activities by reporting them to the appropriate authorities. Inaction combined with continuing association with those involved in illegal conduct might be construed as participation, or assistance, in the illegal conduct.[9]

Footnotes

1. Three elements are necessary to establish aiding and abetting violations under the antifraud provisions of the federal securities laws: (1) the commission of a securities law violation by a primary violator, (2) the rendering of substantial assistance to the primary violator by the aider and abettor in the commission of the violation, and (3) knowledge or awareness by the aider and abettor that his role was part of an activity that was improper. *In re Prudential-Bache Securities, Inc.*, SEC Rel. No. 34-22755, Fed. Sec. L. Rep. (CCH) ¶83,948 (January 2, 1986).
2. *SEC v. Chatham*, [1979] Fed. Sec. L. Rep. (CCH) ¶96,911 (D. Utah, 1979); *In re Nielsen*, SEC Rel. No. 34-16479, [1979–80] Fed. Sec. L. Rep. (CCH) ¶82,446 (January 10, 1980).
3. Failure to do so will subject the member to liability under the securities laws. See *SEC v. Frank*, 388 F.2d 486, 489 (2d Cir. 1968). Cf. (Ontario) Securities Act, R.S.O. 1980, c. 466, §126(3)(b).
4. See (Ontario) Securities Act, R.S.O. 1980, c. 466, §75(1), trading where undisclosed change. See also *Dupont v. Atlas*, No. 500-27-047-70-871 (September 24, 1987) for first case prosecuted under provisions of Quebec Securities Act, §178, effective April 1983.
5. See *In re Melrose*, [1978] Fed. Sec. L. Rep. (CCH) ¶81,578 (May 1, 1978).
6. See *In re Hodgin*, SEC Rel. No. 34-16225, [1979-80] Fed. Sec. L. Rep. (CCH) §82,334 (September 27, 1979).
7. New York Stock Exchange, Rule 351, Reporting Requirements.
8. For a discussion of the requirement that employers maintain procedures designed to monitor the actions of their employees in the law firm context, see *In re Keating, Muething and Klekamp*, No. 34-15982, [1979] Fed. Sec. L. Rep. (CCH) ¶82,124 (July 2, 1979).
9. *In re Carter*, SEC Rel. No. 34-17597, Fed. Sec. L. Rep. (CCH) ¶82,847 (February 28, 1981).

Standard II B
Reference Material

1. SEC Rel. No. 33-6344, [1981-82] Fed. Sec. L. Rep. (CCH) ¶83,026. On September 21, 1981, the SEC solicited public comments on the proposed standard of conduct for lawyers relating to potential illegal activities of clients. No further action has been publicly announced. For the American Bar Association committee response, see 37 *Business Lawyer* 915 (April 1982).
2. New York Stock Exchange, Rule 351, Reporting Requirements.
3. American Bar Association, *Model Code of Professional Responsibility*, DR 7-102, DR 1-103 and DR 4-101 (1980); *Model Rules of Professional Conduct*, Rules 1.2, 1.6, 3.3, and 8.3 (adopted 1983, amended 1987); American Institute of Certified Public Accountants, *Statement of Auditing Standards*, Illegal Acts by Clients, April 1988.
4. Gillis and Cohn, "Legal Aspects of Professional Standards," *Financial Analysts Journal* (January/February 1978).
5. Gillis and Durrell, "Duty to Report Illegal Acts," *Financial Analysts Journal* (September/October 1980).
6. Sonde, "The Responsibilities of Professionals under the Securities Laws," 68 *Northwestern University Law Review* 1 (1973).
7. Longstreth, "Reliance on Advice of Counsel as a Defense to Securities Law Violations," 37 *Business Lawyer* 1185 (April 1982).
8. Address by David S. Ruder, Chairman, Securities and Exchange Commission, before the Securities Industry Association, "Securities Industry Operational Responsibilities Following the October Market Break . . . " (December 2, 1987).

II. COMPLIANCE WITH GOVERNING LAWS AND REGULATIONS AND THE CODE AND STANDARDS

C. Prohibition Against Use of Material Nonpublic Information

The financial analyst shall comply with all laws and regulations relating to the use and communication of material nonpublic information. The financial analyst's duty is generally defined as to not trade while in possession of, nor communicate, material nonpublic information in breach of a duty, or if the information is misappropriated.

Duties under the Standard include the following: (1) If the analyst acquires such information as a result of a special or confidential relationship with the issuer or others, he shall not communicate the information (other than within the relationship), or take investment action on the basis of such information, if it violates that relationship, (2) If the analyst is not in a special or confidential relationship with the issuer or others, he shall not communicate or act on material nonpublic information if he knows, or should have known, that such information (a) was disclosed to him, or would result, in a breach of duty, or (b) was misappropriated.

If such a breach of duty exists, the analyst shall make reasonable efforts to achieve public dissemination of such information.

Purpose of the Standard

The purpose of the standard is to state the responsibility of AIMR members and nonmember holders of, and candidates for, the CFA designation to comply with the laws relating to material nonpublic information, sometimes referred to as inside information, and the activity known as insider trading. As a matter of professional responsibility and minimum professional conduct, investment professionals should be aware of and comply with laws governing their conduct. This is especially true in the area of inside information and insider trading because of the potential exposure to nonpublic information through the investment professional's frequent contacts with corporate management and others relating to an issuer and the market for its securities. Thus, in addition to other minimum standards of conduct expected of every investment professional, it is considered axiomatic that each comply with the laws regulating the use of material nonpublic information.

Conduct Affected by the Standard

Judicial and Securities and Exchange Commission decisions interpreting Section 10(b) of the Securities Exchange Act of 1934, and Rule 10b-5 thereunder, make it unlawful for certain persons to trade, or recommend trading in, securities on the basis of material nonpublic (inside) information. Moreover, these decisions also make it unlawful to communicate inside information in certain circumstances.[1] The SEC also adopted in 1980 Rule 14e-3 under the Exchange Act specifically prohibiting trading on or communicating material nonpublic information about proposed tender offers.

Prior to 1980, almost everyone, with some limited exceptions, who possessed inside information was prohibited from trading on it or communicating it. Since 1980 and the Supreme Court decision in *Chiarella v. U.S.*,[2] the traditional theory of insider trading liability has provided that a securities trader commits fraud by violating Section 10(b) and Rule 10b-5 only if he fails to disclose material information prior to the consummation of a transaction when he is under a duty to do so. This duty to disclose or abstain from trading only arises from a fiduciary or similar relation of trust and confidence between the parties to the transaction—that is, typical insiders of a corporation and its shareholders. Moreover, the duty does not arise from the mere possession of nonpublic information.

In 1983, this concept was extended by the Supreme Court in *Dirks v. SEC*,[3] to hold that liability of a tippee (a person who receives the information from the corporate insider) is imposed only when an insider has breached his fiduciary duty to the shareholders by disclosing the information to the tippee and the tippee knows or should have known that there has been a breach.

A second theory for Rule 10b-5 liability developed in the 1980s is called the misappropriation theory. It was first utilized in the influential Second Circuit Court of Appeals (which includes Manhattan and which decided the recent *Chestman* case, discussed below) and subsequently adopted in three other circuits.[4] This theory provides that a person violates Rule 10b-5 when he misappropriates material nonpublic information in breach of a fiduciary duty or similar relationship of trust and confidence owed to an employer or other person which is not the issuer corporation, and uses that information in a securities transaction or communicates it to others who then use it. It is not necessary, as it is in the traditional theory, that a buyer or seller of securities be shareholders of the corporation to whom the insider's duty is owed.

No statutory definition of insider trading has been adopted; instead, the courts and the SEC have developed a definition in a long series of cases over a period of more than 25 years. In recent years there have been attempts in Congress to create a legislative definition. A legislative proposal to define insider trading based on the concept of trading while in possession of material nonpublic information was introduced in 1987. It was not adopted, and no new proposals have since been filed.[5] Congress did, however, adopt in 1988 the Insider Trading and Securities Fraud Enforcement Act and the Securities Enforcement Remedies and Penny Stock Reform Act of 1990 discussed in detail beginning on page 38.

Material nonpublic information is often defined as any information about a company, or the market for the company's securities, that has not been generally disclosed to the marketplace, the dissemination of which is reasonably certain to have a substantial impact on the market price of the company's securities, or that is substantially likely to be considered important by reasonable investors in determining whether to trade in such securities.[6] In this context, the specificity of the information as well as the extent of its difference from public information, its nature, and its reliability are important factors.

Though the investment professional should not ask for, nor be provided with, material nonpublic information, the courts and the SEC have recognized the importance of encouraging market analysis and the flow of information from issuers to financial analysts and from analysts to the marketplace.[7] Accordingly, where knowledge of a corporate action or event is arrived at by a perceptive analysis of material public information or nonmaterial nonpublic information, the courts and the SEC have generally recognized that there has been no violation of Rule 10b-5. Financial analysts are free to act under this "mosaic theory," as nonmaterial nonpublic information does not fall within the insider trading doctrine. A financial analyst may arrive at and use significant conclusions from analysis of public and nonmaterial nonpublic information—conclusions that would be material inside information if the company had communicated them to the financial analyst or other individuals selectively.[8]

Fiduciary Trust Theory. The Supreme Court decision in *Dirks* reaffirmed the previously held position (*Chiarella*) that a relationship of trust and confidence, not mere possession, was a prerequisite for imposing a duty to disclose or abstain from trading on the basis of inside information. The Court indicated that the prohibition against using material nonpublic information applies to outside recipients of information from corporate insiders, such as financial analysts, only if the communicator of the information breached a fiduciary duty to the shareholders of the corporation.[9] The test of whether a fiduciary duty has been breached is whether the insider personally benefits directly or indirectly from the disclosure. If there has been no such personal gain, then there has been no breach of duty to the shareholders. If there is not a breach by the insider, then there is no derivative breach by the recipient.

There are three types of personal benefits discussed by the Court. The first is a pecuniary benefit or a reputational benefit that will translate into future earnings. The second is a relationship between the insider and the recipient that suggests a *quid pro quo* from the latter, or an intention to benefit the recipient. Finally, there is the gift of confidential information, for example, to a relative.

Misappropriation Theory. Lower courts have applied a misappropriation theory to insider trading cases, finding both criminal liability and imposing injunctions in SEC enforcement actions. (In the *Carpenter* case, the Supreme Court affirmed the misappropriation theory by an equally divided Court.) Such cases involve breaches of duty to an employer or others, but not to the corporation whose securities are traded, by trading on or communicating confidential material nonpublic information misappropriated from that employer or illegally obtained. Employers involved have been investment banks, financial printers, and newspapers, among others.[10]

In October 1991, the entire court of the Second Circuit Court of Appeals, in *U.S. v. Chestman,*[11] endorsed the misappropriation theory but imposed a substantial standard of proof, which it held had not been met in this case involving criminal convictions of a stockbroker who was a remote tippee.[12] For a discussion of the potential pitfalls in selectively disclosing issuer information see Phillips and Nojeim "Disclosures to Securities Analysts: The Drafty Exposure of the Open-Door Policy," 4 *Insights* 5 (May 1990). However, the Court upheld the convictions for tender offer fraud under Rule 14e-3(a).

This case involved the communication of material nonpublic information by a Waldbaum family member (nephew-in-law Loeb) to his stockbroker, the defendant Chestman, about a sale of the family business. The president and controlling shareholder of the Waldbaum grocery chain decided to sell in a proposed tender offer at a price almost double the market price of its shares. This decision was conveyed to the president's sister, who conveyed it to her daughter, who conveyed it to her husband—the nephew-in-law. Each communication included a caution about the confidential nature of the information. Finally the nephew-in-law Loeb spoke with his stockbroker Chestman.

There was a dispute about when and what information Loeb conveyed to the defendant but the defendant purchased a large number of shares in the grocery chain, some for Loeb. After an SEC investigation, Loeb settled civilly with the SEC, agreeing to an injunction, disgorgement of profits, and an additional fine. A criminal action was later brought against the stockbroker Chestman. He was convicted on counts of securities fraud in violation of Section 10(b) and Rule 10b-5, fraud in connection with a tender offer under Section 14(e) and Rule 14e-3(a), mail fraud, and perjury.

A three-judge panel of the Court of Appeals for the Second Circuit reversed all of the convictions including those under Section 10(b) and Rule 10b-5, which were based on the premise that the broker was a tippee liable under the misappropriation theory.

In rehearing before the full court, the court upheld Chestman's conviction on the Rule 14e-3(a) counts, acquitted on the 10b-5 and mail fraud counts (by a 6-5 vote), and upheld the reversal of the conviction on the perjury count. As to the 10b-5 reversals, the court held that Chestman's criminal convictions could not be sustained unless (1) Loeb breached a duty owed to his wife or the family based on a fiduciary or other similar relationship of trust and confidence, and (2) Chestman knew that Loeb had done so.

The court stated that a securities trader commits Rule 10b-5 fraud only if he fails to disclose material information prior to the consummation of a transaction when he is under a duty to do so. A duty to disclose or abstain arises only when there is a fiduciary or other similar relationship of trust and confidence between the two parties. In particular, the court stated that two factors do not of themselves create the necessary relationship: (1) a fiduciary duty cannot be imposed unilaterally by entrusting a person with confidential information; and (2) marriage and kinship do not, of themselves, create a fiduciary relationship. Any more elastic concept of a confidential relationship, the court added, has no place in the criminal law. The court found that there was no fiduciary relationship, or its functional equivalent, between Loeb and the Waldbaum family. Loeb was not a member of the inner circle of the

Waldbaum family, which ran the business. He was neither an employee nor a confidant of this controlling faction. In fact, the government failed to show that the disclosure to Loeb of the information pertaining to the tender offer was in any way in the interests of the family or its business. The relationship between Loeb and the Waldbaums was not characterized by any influence exercised by Loeb or reliance by the Waldbaums. Loeb was an outsider, and the information was gratuitously communicated to him.

Nor did Loeb's relationship with his wife exhibit the necessary influence and reliance to establish that Loeb breached a fiduciary duty or similar duty of trust. His wife's disclosure of the information to him served no business purpose. Her admonition "not to tell anyone" was merely a unilateral entrusting which cannot serve to elevate the standard by which Loeb's conduct is measured. Absent Loeb's predicate act of fraud, Chestman could not be derivatively liable as Loeb's aidor and abettor or as a tippee under Rule 10b-5.[13]

With regard to the 14e-3(a) convictions, the Second Circuit held that the SEC had the authority to define fraud expansively in the tender offer context so as to remove the requirement of a fiduciary duty owed by the defrauding party to the defrauded party. These convictions, therefore, were upheld.

Three New Securities Acts.   In the decade ending in 1990, Congress enacted three new and extensive securities acts to prevent insider trading and to expand the SEC's enforcement capabilities.

The *Insider Trading Sanctions Act* was enacted in 1984. This amendment to the Securities Exchange Act (Section 21(d) and other sections) came in response to suggestions that existing remedies did not have sufficient deterrent effect. The Act provides for new civil monetary damages of up to three times the profit (or the loss avoided) on insider trading transactions and increased fines for criminal violations to $100,000 from $10,000. (These penalties were increased again in 1988 in the Insider Trading and Securities Fraud Enforcement Act discussed below.) The Act applies to persons "purchasing or selling a security while in possession of material nonpublic information" and those "aiding and abetting the violation of such person" (i.e., tippers). Despite many requests to Congress during consideration of the Act, there is no definition of the term "material nonpublic information," and there are continuing interpretative issues regarding that and other provisions.[14] The Act also provides, however, that persons who aid and abet an insider trading transaction, other than by communicating material nonpublic information, are not subject to the sanction. In addition, brokerage and other firms are not liable under the Act solely by reason of employing a person who violates the law.

The Act also provides a definition to determine the amount of profit or loss that would be used as the basis for the treble damages penalty and a five-year statute of limitations on actions.

The SEC has initiated and been successful in numerous actions under the Act.[15]

Finally, the Act extends insider trading liability to persons communicating or trading while in possession of material nonpublic information in transactions involving a put, call, straddle, option, privilege, or group or index of securities. (Section 20(d).)[16]

The SEC reviewed the legal developments since *Dirks* in a report to the Committee of the House of Representatives responsible for securities matters when it was considering the Insider Trading Sanctions Act.[17] The Commission stated that it believed the *Dirks* decision "has not adversely affected, to a significant degree, the Commission's enforcement program against insider trading" in the two years following the decision. The SEC reiterated the conclusion in hearings on the Insider Trading Proscriptions Act in 1987.

It also noted that the misappropriation theory, which it had been advocating, was approved by lower courts, including the important Second Circuit Court of Appeals in the *Materia* case, confirmed in the Supreme Court *Bateman Eichler* opinion and affirmed in *Carpenter*.[18] Although there will be instances in which it is difficult to apply the theory to particular factual situations, the principle now seems to be well accepted.[19]

While the Senate Securities Subcommittee was holding hearings intensely debating a new insider trading bill (which slowed down, among other reasons, because of disputes about the definition of insider trading), the House moved quickly and enacted, without an insider trading definition, the *Insider Trading and Securities Fraud Enforcement Act* (ITSFEA), which became effective in November 1988. The Act contains a number of far-reaching provisions.

ITSFEA increases the penalties for criminal securities law violations as follows: (1) the maximum jail term is increased from five to ten years, (2) the maximum criminal fine for individuals is increased from $100,000 to $1 million, and (3) the maximum fine for entities other than individuals is increased from $500,000 to $2.5 million. (Section 32(a) of the Securities Exchange Act.)

ITSFEA retains the civil penalty structure adopted in the Insider Trading Sanctions Act, and it expands both the penalties and enforcement methods in a revised Section 21 and a new Section 21A. Among other things, it authorizes the SEC to award bounty payments to persons who provide information leading to the successful prosecution of insider trading violations. The SEC has discretion to award an amount up to 10 percent of any penalty imposed.[20]

ITSFEA authorizes the SEC, under amended Section 21(a)(2) of the Exchange Act, to cooperate with foreign governmental bodies by conducting investigations to assist a foreign authority to determine whether a violation of its laws has occurred. ITSFEA also directs the Commission to conduct a broad review of the adequacy of existing laws to protect investors.

Several provisions in new Section 21A of the Exchange Act and other new sections have a direct impact on participants in the securities industry. First, the Exchange Act and the Investment Advisers Act are amended by adding new sections (Section 15(f) and Section 204A, respectively) to require brokers, dealers, and investment advisers to "establish, maintain and enforce written policies and procedures reasonably designed, taking into consideration the nature of such [broker's, dealer's, or adviser's] business, to prevent the misuse of material nonpublic information by such [broker, dealer, or adviser] or any person associated with such [broker, dealer, or adviser]."

Second, new Section 21A makes controlling persons—that is, those who at the time of the violation directly or indirectly controlled the person who committed a violation—subject to the civil penalties. In awarding such penalties, the court, in its discretion, may award a sum not to exceed the greater of $1 million or three times the profit gained or loss avoided as a result of the illegal transaction.[21] However, the mere employment of a controlled person who has violated ITSFEA, by itself, is not enough to impose liability on a controlling person. There are two standards applicable to the imposition of liabilities and penalties on controlling persons: (1) For registered broker–dealers and investment advisers, the SEC must prove that the registrant "knowingly or recklessly failed to establish, maintain or enforce" a required policy or procedure and that "such failure substantially contributed to or permitted the occurrence of the act or acts constituting the violation."[22] (2) For all other controlling persons, the standard is that such person "knew or recklessly disregarded the fact that [the] controlled person was likely to engage in the act or acts constituting the violation and failed to take appropriate steps to prevent such act or acts before they occurred."[23]

Third, a new Section 20A of the Exchange Act creates a new private right of action for "contemporaneous traders"[24] when insider trading violations occur. Tippers are subject to joint and several liability for the violations of their tippees who gained profits or avoided losses. Damages are limited to the profit gained or loss avoided, and the award is reduced by any amount disgorged in related actions by the SEC.[25]

The *Securities Enforcement Remedies and Penny Stock Reform Act of 1990* (the "Remedies Act") amends the Securities Act, the Securities Exchange Act, the Investment Company Act of 1940 and the Investment Advisers Act of 1940 (the 1940 Acts) to provide the SEC with additional remedies which the commission can seek from those who have violated the provisions of these acts and the rules and regulations promulgated thereunder. These additional remedies are civil penalties in administrative proceedings, money penalties in civil proceedings, and temporary and permanent cease and desist orders.[26]

The SEC is now empowered to impose civil penalties in its administrative proceedings. Under the Exchange Act and both of the 1940 Acts, the SEC or other appropriate regulatory agency can impose a civil penalty on a person in an administrative proceeding if it finds willful violations, willful aiding or abetting, willful material misrepresentations or omissions in a filing with the SEC, or failure to reasonably supervise.

The SEC may award penalties according to a three-tier system. If the violation involved fraud, deceit, manipulation, or deliberate or reckless disregard of a regulatory requirement, and such violation directly or indirectly resulted in substantial losses or created a significant risk of substantial losses to other persons, for each violation the amount of the penalty shall not exceed the greater of $100,000 for an individual or $500,000 for an entity, or the gross amount of pecuniary gain to such defendant as a result of the violation. If the violation did not result in substantial losses or create a significant risk of substantial losses to other persons, for each violation the amount of the penalty shall not exceed the greater of $50,000 for an individual or $250,000 for an entity, or the gross amount of pecuniary gain to such defendant as a result of the violation. If the violation did not involve fraud, deceit, manipulation, or deliberate or reckless disregard of a regulatory requirement, for each violation the amount of the penalty shall not exceed the greater of $5,000 for an individual or $50,000 for an entity, or the gross amount of pecuniary gain to such defendant as a result of the violation.[27]

The SEC may also commence a court proceeding to impose civil penalties. If the SEC determines that any person has violated any provision under the Securities Act, the Exchange Act or either of the 1940 Acts (except Section 21A of the Exchange Act), the rules promulgated thereunder or any cease and desist order entered into by the SEC, the SEC may bring an action in federal district court for a civil penalty to be paid by the violator. The court may award such penalties in its discretion, subject to the three-tiered system as described in the preceding paragraph. Additionally, under the Securities Act and the Exchange Act, if the SEC can demonstrate the violators' unfitness, the court can prohibit violators from serving as officers or directors of any issuer of securities registered pursuant to the Exchange Act.[28]

Finally, the SEC may issue permanent and temporary cease and desist orders. Under all four acts, the SEC can issue permanent cease and desist orders if the SEC finds that a person has violated, is violating, or will violate, by an act or omission, any provision of the Acts. The SEC may order such affirmative steps which it deems necessary to effect compliance with law.

Moreover, under all four acts, the SEC can issue temporary cease and desist orders against brokers, dealers, investment advisers, or their associated persons if the SEC determines that the violation or threatened violation is likely to result in significant dissipation or conversion of assets, significant harm to investors, or substantial harm to the public interest. Such orders would remain in effect pending formal proceedings to determine whether such violation has actually been committed by the respondent.

Enforcement. The SEC has achieved notable and increasing success in its enforcement program both in the U.S. and internationally notwithstanding isolated judicial setbacks such as the insider trading reversal in *Chestman*.

The Santa Fe International Corporation litigation was a significant development not only in the context of inside information but also in light of the increasing globalization of the securities markets and the establishment of means to protect the emerging internationalized markets from fraud. As a result of discussions begun in 1982, the SEC in 1984 obtained an agreement with the Swiss government to order Swiss banks to disclose the identity of customers alleged to have traded securities of Santa Fe International Corporation before Kuwait Petroleum Corporation's 1981 tender offer. It took nine additional months, overall a little more than three years after the SEC began its search for evidence, before the SEC received documents regarding the accounts. As a result, the SEC obtained a judgment, by consent, from the U.S. District Court in Manhattan ordering disgorgement of $7.8 million in profits from the illegal trading. The judgment also enjoined the several defendants from future violations of Section 10(b) and Rule 10b-5 of the Securities Exchange Act.[29]

Most of the defendants were nationals of the Middle East residing in Europe who allegedly received the inside information from a director of Santa Fe and who used Swiss bank accounts for their trading. The director who traded on the information consented to an injunction and disgorgement in 1982, pled guilty, and was imprisoned in 1987 for his activities. Several other individuals involved in Santa Fe trading were the subject of successful SEC civil actions and criminal convictions.

An additional example of the increased ability of U.S. enforcement officials to obtain trading information from foreign countries occurred in 1986 when the Bahamian Attorney General ruled that it was not in a violation of Bahamian law for a branch of a Swiss bank located there to disclose the identity of, and details about, an account holder and his transactions.[30] The information eventually resulted in obtaining a criminal guilty plea by the investment banker involved, who had specialized in mergers and acquisitions,[31] and in turn led to several guilty pleas by other securities professionals involved with the trader.[32] A vigorous SEC enforcement program has discovered numerous other instances of the use of material nonpublic information, usually about proposed tender offers or acquisitions. A significant number of criminal prosecutions have resulted.

Finally, the SEC and the Justice Department have achieved a substantial measure of success in obtaining settlements in the United States in the insider trading and general antifraud enforcement program.[33] Foremost among these were the settlements in 1989 of civil and criminal charges against the brokerage firm of Drexel Burnham Lambert (DBL) for $650 million in fines and penalties and in 1990 against Michael R. Milken, head of the DBL high yield department, for $600 million, of which $200 million was in criminal fines and $400 million in a civil disgorgement payment.

Among the scores of civil and criminal cases brought and resolved for insider trading and related violations in the past few years against investment bankers, arbitrageurs, or brokers were those involving Dennis B. Levine, Ivan Boesky, Martin A. Siegel, Boyd L. Jefferies, Marcus Schloss & Co., Inc., and Robert Freeman.

Summary. The AIMR standard requires any financial analyst or investment manager who is not in a special or confidential relationship with an issuer to evaluate the materiality of any nonpublic information he may receive and whether the disclosure violates the communicator's fiduciary duty. If the analyst or manager determines that the information is material and disclosed in breach of a duty, he should make reasonable efforts to achieve public dissemination of the information. This usually means encouraging the issuer corporation to make the information public. If public dissemination is not possible, the analyst or manager should not communicate the information except to designated supervisory and compliance personnel within the firm, nor take any investment action on the basis of that information. (See also Standards II A and II B.)

Application of the Standard

By way of example, violations of the insider trading rule have occurred when persons traded on nonpublic information that:

- A company had made a rich ore find.
- A company had cut its dividend.
- A company had sustained its first and unexpected substantial loss.
- Earnings projections showed a substantial increase.
- Earnings projections showed a substantial decrease.
- A tender offer was to be made for a company's securities above the market price.

Legal sanctions have been applied to:

- Persons inside a company who traded the stock.
- Persons outside the company who traded the stock.
- Persons inside the company for the act of telling persons outside the company who traded the stock.
- Persons outside the company for the act of telling other persons outside the company who traded the stock.

Recent cases have applied the rule to persons in the investment community who received such information from sources in a confidential relationship with a company that proposed to make a tender offer. The sources were persons employed by investment banks and law and accounting firms, among others.[34]

The securities laws have also been applied to persons who used inside information to acquire significant holdings in a target company in a tender offer and "parked" stock to avoid net capital or disclosure rules.[35]

Standard II C recognizes two divergent sets of circumstances under which a financial analyst may receive material nonpublic information as well as correspondingly different duties regarding the financial analyst's obligation to achieve public disclosure of the information.

First, a financial analyst may receive the information when in a special or confidential relationship with an issuer. In that event, he may use it for that purpose (assuming it is lawful) and obviously need not encourage disclosure. Examples include receiving the information as a representative of the underwriter of the issuer (where the issuer is obligated to disclose it to the underwriter) or receiving it as a financial consultant, rating agency, or lender to the issuer. Such relationships very likely make the analyst and his firm constructive or temporary insiders of the issuer.

Second, a financial analyst may receive information from an issuer although no special or confidential relationship exists between them. In the absence of such a relationship with the issuer, the financial analyst should usually make an effort to achieve public disclosure. For example, if a financial analyst inadvertently hears an officer tell an outsider by telephone of a significant corporate event, such as a large unannounced quarterly loss, he should encourage the officer to make a public announcement.

Procedures for Compliance

AIMR has long advocated that members and members' firms adopt compliance procedures to prevent insider trading violations and the misuse of material nonpublic information, and this encouragement has received a sharp impetus since the enactment of ITSFEA in late 1988. Registered brokers, dealers, and investment advisers are now required to "establish, maintain and enforce written policies and procedures" to prevent violations.

The SEC Division of Market Regulation, pursuant to rulemaking authority granted under ITSFEA, made a comprehensive study of compliance procedures of major New York broker–dealers. Its report released in March 1990, entitled *Broker–Dealer Policies and Procedures Designed to Segment the Flow and Prevent the Misuse of Material Nonpublic Information*, concludes that no immediate rulemaking by the SEC is appropriate. Rather, the necessary improvements that it believes should occur in the compliance systems would best be effectuated by vigorous self-regulatory examination programs (e.g., the stock exchanges and the National Association of Securities Dealers) with SEC oversight.

Although noting improvements since its last review in 1987, the Division found that certain areas still need improvement. Cited were such areas as reviewing employee and proprietary trading, memorialization and documentation of firm procedures, and supervision of interdepartmental communications.

The Report noted minimum elements of so-called "Chinese Wall" compliance systems, which are designed to prevent the communication of material nonpublic information between departments. The minimum elements include: (1) substantial control (preferably by the compliance department) of relevant interdepartmental communications; (2) review of employee trading through effective maintenance of some combination of watch, restricted, and rumor lists; (3) dramatic improvement in the memorialization of Chinese Wall procedures and documentation of actions taken pursuant to those procedures; and (4) heightened review or restriction of proprietary trading while the firm is in possession of material nonpublic information.

Brokerage and investment advisory firms must adopt compliance procedures designed and implemented to prevent misuse of material nonpublic information and should adopt them to avoid other legal and regulatory violations. Compliance procedures must suit the particular characteristics of a firm, such as its size and the nature of its business. Most compliance procedures should contain the following basic provisions to ensure their effectiveness.[36]

The most common and widespread approach to prevent insider trading violations by employees, and to protect the firm against potential liability, is the information barrier usually referred to as a Chinese Wall.[37] The purpose is to prevent communication of material nonpublic information and other sensitive information from one department of a firm, which, for example, learned the information in its representation of a client in a prospective tender offer, to other departments. An information barrier is the minimum procedure a firm should consider.

Additional procedures, used typically in conjunction with an information barrier, include (1) restrictions or prohibitions on personal employee trading, (2) careful monitoring of firm and personal employee trading, (3) placing securities on a restricted list when the firm has or may have material nonpublic information, and (4) use of a stock watch list in the foregoing circumstances to monitor transactions in specified securities. The watch list is usually known only to a limited number of people. It is gaining wider use, because broad distribution of a restricted list within a firm often triggers the very problems the list was developed to avoid.[38]

Written policies and guidelines should be circulated to all employees and firm members. Persons who are particularly likely to encounter inside information problems include research analysts, portfolio managers, venture capitalists, pension sponsors, investor relations executives, rating agencies, persons in commercial loan departments of banks or in underwriting departments of investment banks, trust officers, and others who make or recommend investment decisions. These policies and guidelines should be coupled with a program of seminars and refresher courses for employees.[39] Many firms have a policy of continually informing their employees of developments in areas affecting compliance with regulatory and professional responsibilities, and they also conduct regular programs for maintaining knowledge of these issues.

Exhibit A contains typical compliance guidelines and Exhibit B summarizes some pertinent legal cases.

EXHIBIT A
COMPLIANCE GUIDELINES

The basic components of typical compliance guidelines are the following:[40]

1. *Define material nonpublic information.* The leading cases, notably the most recent Supreme Court decision in *Chestman*, provide a definition for material nonpublic information which is described above.

2. *Require communication.* Provide that anyone who receives information that is known or reasonably believed to be material nonpublic information should communicate that information to a designated supervisor or compliance officer without otherwise discussing the information with his co-workers. The recipient should then be required to refrain from trading on the information or from discussing the information inside or outside the firm until a supervisor decides the information either is not material or has been made public. Constant review and improvement of control mechanisms are required especially because of technological advances such as electronic mail networks and cellular telephones. Separate procedures should be adopted and implemented for safeguarding information received in a special or confidential relationship.

3. *Establish training and compliance procedures.*[41] Although one court has suggested that guidelines should call for a supervisor's approval before securities personnel may contact companies, a more practical approach would be extensive and intensive training and continuing education programs for employees designed to develop the ability to recognize material nonpublic information and firm procedures designed and implemented to prevent misuse of such information. In addition, many firms have agreements requiring confidentiality of information that employees are required to reaffirm annually.

4. *Review accounts.* Require regular review of customer or client accounts and investigation of patterns of heavy trading by all employees and firm members in particular securities. A pattern of trading on inside information can be more easily detected if employees and firm members are required to make periodic reports of their transactions on their own behalf or on behalf of members of their families. It is recommended that, to the extent such reporting is not already required (for example by Rule 204-2(a)(12) under the Investment Advisers Act and Rule 17j-1 under the Investment Company Act), a firm adopt procedures to make it mandatory. New York Stock Exchange (NYSE) Rule 342.21(a), effective May 1988, requires member firms to engage in extensive review procedures relating to trades for their own

accounts and for the accounts of associated and allied members, employees, and their families in NYSE-listed securities and related financial instruments. In addition, insofar as possible, the firm should separate, or establish an information barrier between, the people who are likely to obtain inside information (because of their involvement in acquisitions, tender offers, mergers, underwritings, commercial lending, venture capital, or similar activities) and those who make investment recommendations to the public or to specific customers, or who invest client funds.[42] In particular, the written policy statement should include a prohibition on soliciting or accepting disclosure of inside information from fellow employees or soliciting or accepting access to files that could contain inside information. The guidelines should designate a supervisor or compliance officer who will have the specific authority and responsibility to decide whether information is sufficiently public or is sufficiently lacking in materiality or for other reasons may be used as a basis for investment recommendations or decisions.

For example, the investment banking and corporate finance departments of a brokerage firm should be segregated from the sales and research departments. The segregation usually means that there should be no overlap of personnel. If possible, even the supervisor or compliance officer who approves communication of information to the research and brokerage departments should not be a member of those departments. The primary objective is to establish a reporting system within a department in which authorized persons review and approve communications between departments.

A bank's commercial lending department should be similarly segregated from its trust department and its research operation.

EXHIBIT B
SUMMARY OF LEGAL CASES

The cases summarized below were selected to illustrate the requirements that Section 10(b) of the Securities Exchange Act and Rule 10b-5 thereunder, the most often applied of the antifraud provisions, place on financial analysts, their employers and issuers:

1. *Dirks v. SEC*, 463 U.S. 646 (1983), *rev'g*, 681 F.2d 824 (D.C. Cir. 1982), SEC Rel. No. 34-17480 (January 22, 1981). A financial analyst, Dirks, received information from a former vice president of Equity Funding that there was widespread fraud at the company. Dirks confirmed this information with one current and several former Equity Funding employees and communicated it to five investment advisers. The five investment advisers sold or directed

the sale of large blocks of Equity Funding stock without disclosure of the information they had received from Dirks. The SEC found that once Dirks had confirmed the information by contact with a number of former insiders, it had a reasonable probability of being true and was, for that reason, material nonpublic information. The SEC also held that Dirks aided and abetted violations of Section 10(b) on the part of the investment advisers who were his tippees. The decision was upheld by the Court of Appeals but reversed by the Supreme Court on the grounds that the insider did not breach his fiduciary duty by disclosure of the information because there was no benefit to the insider, and thus Dirks did not breach any duty.

2. *SEC v. Geon Industries*, 381 F.Supp. 1063, (S.D.N.Y. 1974), *aff'd*, 531 F.2d 39 (2d Cir. 1976). A registered representative employed by a broker received inside information from an officer of Geon concerning a possible acquisition and traded for his own account and the accounts of family members. The court found the registered representative had clearly violated Section 10(b), but exonerated his employer. The employer had a policy of disseminating written guidelines on material nonpublic information and testing its employees for familiarity with the guidelines.

3. *SEC v. Bausch & Lomb, Inc.*, 420 F.Supp. 1226 (S.D.N.Y. 1976), *aff'd*, 565 F.2d 8 (2d Cir. 1977). The chairman of Bausch & Lomb, in an interview with a securities analyst, revealed that sales had not increased as much as expected, new products would be delayed, and that another analyst's earnings projections were optimistic. The analyst, who was very knowledgeable about the company and the industry, then changed his own earnings projections and changed his buy recommendation, and trading ensued. (The analyst had anticipated making these changes before the interview.) The appeals court held that the sales and new product information was public and that none of the other information was material. Thus the court found that the analyst had utilized nonpublic nonmaterial information in his mosaic without violating the inside information prohibition.

However, when the chairman subsequently gave the analyst an estimate of earnings per share, he was communicating material nonpublic information. The court did not find that the chairman had violated Section 10(b) because he attempted to achieve public dissemination of the information through an interview with a financial columnist. The court indicated, however, that a prompt press release would have been superior disclosure. Nonetheless, there was no evidence of trading on the inside information before it was made public.

Footnotes

1. See also (Ontario) Securities Act, R.S.O. 1980, c. 466, §74, requiring disclosure of material changes by the issuer, and §75, trading where there is a material undisclosed change; and also "Other Standards," (3) and (4), of *Standards of Professional Conduct for Security Analysts*, adopted by the Security Analysts Association of Japan (July 29, 1987).
2. *Chiarella v. U.S.*, 455 U.S. 222 (1980).
3. *Dirks v. SEC*, 463 U.S. 646 (1983); see 8 *The Canadian Business Law Journal* 4, "Of Secretaries, Analysts and Printers; Some Reflections on Insider Trading," by Stanley M. Beck, February 1984, for comments on *Dirks* and *Chiarella* from the perspective of the Canadian Business Corporations Act and the Ontario Securities Act.
4. In 1987, the Supreme Court in *Carpenter v. U.S.*, 484 U.S. 19, affirmed, by an equally divided court, the criminal convictions under the securities laws of R. Foster Winans, a former Wall Street Journal columnist, and two others, and affirmed unanimously their convictions under the mail and wire fraud statutes. The three had been convicted in the trial court, *U.S. v. Winans*, 612 F.Supp. 827 (S.D.N.Y. 1985), and the convictions affirmed by the Court of Appeals, 791 F.2d 1024 (2d Cir. 1986). See also *SEC v. Cherif*, 933 F.2d 403 (7th Cir. 1991), *cert. denied*, 112 S.Ct. 966 (January 27, 1992) (a terminated bank employee was convicted for surreptitiously acquiring and using confidential bank records to trade on proposed tender offers); *SEC v. Clark*, 915 F.2d 439 (9th Cir. 1990) (president of an acquiring company was held liable for buying stock in tender offer target companies); *Rothberg v. Rosenbloom*, 771 F.2d 818 (3d Cir. 1985) (an insider tipped by another insider was held liable for purchasing stock in his company).
5. Legislation entitled "The Insider Trading Proscriptions Act" (S. 1380) was introduced in Congress in June 1987 to define and prohibit insider trading. Several hearings were held, and in November the SEC submitted its version of a bill to correct perceived problems in the Senate bill. In February 1988, the SEC submitted proposed legislative report language to accompany its revised bill. No further action was taken on these bills.
6. The "market impact" test has been cited in the following insider trading decisions among others: *Elkind v. Liggett & Myers, Inc.*, 635 F.2d 156 (2d Cir. 1980); *SEC v. Bausch & Lomb*, 565 F.2d 8 (2d Cir. 1977); and *SEC v. Texas Gulf Sulphur Co.*, 401 F.2d 833 (2d Cir. 1968), *cert. denied*, 394 U.S. 976 (1969). A "reasonable investor" test derived from *TSC Industries, Inc. v. Northway, Inc.*, 426 U.S. 438 (1976), which involved proxy violations and provides a lower threshold of materiality, has also been cited in insider trading cases.
7. For a collection of references that recognizes the value of analysts' role and functions, see the Written Statement of the Financial Analysts Federation to the Senate Securities Subcommittee of the Senate Banking, Housing and Urban Affairs Committee regarding S. 1380, August 28, 1987, at page 25.
8. *SEC v. Bausch & Lomb, Inc.*, 420 F.Supp. 1226 (S.D.N.Y. 1976), *aff'd*, 565 F.2d 8 (3d Cir. 1977); *In re Dirks*, SEC Rel. No. 34-17480 (January 22, 1981), *aff'd*, 681 F.2d 824 (D.C. Cir. 1982), *rev'd*, 463 U.S. 646 (1983). For analysts' role and functions see the Written Statement of the Financial Analysts Federation to the Senate Securities Subcommittee of the Senate Banking, Housing and Urban Affairs Committee regarding S. 1380, August 28, 1987, at page 25.
9. *Dirks v. SEC*, 463 U.S. 646 (1983). In *Bateman Eichler, Hill Richards, Inc., v. Berner*, 472 U.S. 299 (1985), the principles relating to insider trading announced in *Dirks* were

discussed and confirmed and, in addition, the Court endorsed the misappropriation theory discussed in this chapter.

10. U.S. v. Newman, 664 F.2d 12 (2d Cir. 1981), *aff'd after remand*, 722 F.2d 729 (2d Cir.), *cert. denied*, 464 U.S. 863 (1983) (investment banker and stockbroker); *SEC v. Materia*, [1983-84] Fed. Sec. L.Rep. (CCH) ¶99,583 (S.D.N.Y. 1983), *aff'd*, 745 F.2d 197 (2d Cir. 1984), *cert. denied*, 105 S.Ct. 2112 (1985) (employee of financial printer); *Carpenter v. U.S.*, 108 S.Ct. 316 (1987) (financial columnist); *U.S. v. Grossman*, 843 F.2d 78 (2d Cir. 1988) (member of law firm); *U.S. v. Reed*, 601 F.Supp. 685 (S.D.N.Y.), *rev'd on other grounds*, 773 F.2d 477 (2d Cir. 1985) (son of corporate director); *SEC v. Musella*, 578 F.Supp. 425 (S.D.N.Y. 1984) (manager of office services for law firm). This concept was initially suggested by Chief Justice Burger in his dissent in *Chiarella*.

11. 947 F.2d 551 (2d Cir. 1991), 903 F.2d 75 (2d Cir. 1990), 704 F.Supp. 451 (S.D.N.Y. 1989), *cert. denied*, 112 S.Ct. 1759 (April 27, 1992).

12. See Pitt and Groskaufmanis, "Family Ties, Tippees and the *Chestman* Decision: Time for a Principled Definition of Insider Trading," 4 *Insights* 7 (July 1990).

13. For an analysis of the full court decision see Groskaufmanis, "Chestman Revisited: The Slow Death of Fraud," 6 *Insights* 1 (January 1992), and Frankhauser, "Chestman II," 25 *Securities and Commodities Regulation* 5 at 63 (March 11, 1992).

14. Miller, "The Insider Trading Sanctions Act" 17 *Review of Securities Regulation*, 821 (1984). Many commentators on the Senate's 1987 proposed Insider Trading Proscriptions Act (S. 1380) advocated a definition of material nonpublic information. The Financial Analysts Federation in its three submissions recommended that if an Act is passed it should contain the market impact definition. See *supra*, notes 5 and 6.

15. See, for example, *Report of the Securities and Exchange Commission to the House Committee on Energy and Commerce on Dirks v. Securities and Exchange Commission*, August 23, 1985. For a comprehensive review of the history and policy of insider trading prohibitions, see American Bar Association, Committee on Federal Regulation of Securities, *Report of the Task Force on Regulation of Insider Trading*, July 1, 1985, *reprinted in* 41 *Business Lawyer* 223 (1985). The first ITSA penalty against a defendant after trial was *SEC v. Clark*, (D.W.D. Wa.), *The SEC Today*, May 31, 1989, *aff'd*, 915 F.2d 439(9th Cir. 1990).

16. The Commodity Futures Trading Commission has adopted several regulations to prevent the disclosure of material nonpublic information. See *AIMR Standards of Practice Handbook*, 401–41 (Fifth Ed. 1990). For trading prohibitions, see American Bar Association, Committee on Federal Regulation of Securities, *Report of the Task Force on Regulation of Insider Trading*, July 1, 1985, reprinted in 41 *Business Lawyer* 223 (1985). The first ITSA penalty against a defendant after trial was *SEC v. Clark*, (D.W.D. Wa.), *The SEC Today*, May 31, 1989, *aff'd*, 915 F.2d 439 (9th Cir. 1990).

17. See *supra*, note 15.

18. See *supra*, notes 9, 10 and 11. However, as noted in the text, the *Chestman* decision imposes significant new standards of proof, at least in criminal cases, brought under the misappropriation theory.

19. All versions of an insider trading bill submitted to the Senate in 1987 included the misappropriation theory.

20. The SEC subsequently approved rules on its bounty program (Rules 61-68 of its Rules of Practice, SEC Rel. No. 34-26994, June 30, 1989), and issued a brochure about the program, 80 *The SEC Today* 136, July 19, 1989. See also Shaw, "Awards to Informers Under the 1988 Insider Trading Act," 3 *Insights* 11 (November 1989).

21. Exchange Act §21A(a)(3).
22. Exchange Act §21A(b)(1)(B).
23. Exchange Act §21A(b)(1)(A).
24. Liability is provided to a "contemporaneous trader" as follows: Any person who violates any provision of the Exchange Act or any of the rules and regulations thereunder by purchasing or selling a security while in possession of material nonpublic information shall be liable to any other person who contemporaneously with the purchase or sale of securities which is the subject of the violation, has sold or purchased, as the case may be, securities of the same class. Exchange Act §20A(a).
25. For a detailed analysis of ITSFEA, see Lavoie, "The Insider Trading Securities Fraud Enforcement Act of 1988," 22 *Securities and Commodities Regulation* 1 (January 11, 1989); Pitt and Groskaufmanis, "An Analysis of the Insider Trading and Securities Fraud Enforcement Act of 1988," 3 *Insights* 1 (January 1989).
26. For a review of actions under this Act see DeTore and Gilber, "Recent Enforcement Developments," 25 *Securities and Commodities Regulation* 15 (September 9, 1992).
27. See Exchange Act §21B; Investment Company Act §9(d); and Investment Advisors Act §203(i).
28. See Securities Act §§20(d) and 20(e); Exchange Act §§21(d)(2) and 21(d)(3); Investment Company Act §42(e); Investment Advisers Act §209(e); and Advisors Act §203(i).
29. *SEC v. Certain Unknown Purchasers of the SEC Common Stock of, and Call Options for the Common Stock of Santa Fe International Corp.*, (S.D.N.Y.) SEC Rel. No. LR 11012, [1985-86] Fed. Sec. L. Rep. (CCH) ¶92,484 (February 26, 1986); see also *In the Matter of Evidence Proceedings Act of 1975*, Order of Mr. Justice Drake, February 23, 1984, *reprinted in* 34 *International Legal Materials* 511, 515. *A Memorandum of Understanding* between the U.S. and Switzerland signed August 31, 1982 ("MOU") and Convention XVI of the Swiss Banker's Association were the first in a series of memoranda and other agreements providing for the exchange of information and other mutual assistance in the enforcement of national securities laws. (Since the Swiss MOU dealt exclusively with insider trading, it was superseded when Switzerland passed laws outlawing all forms of insider trading.) Comparable or similar documents were subsequently signed with the Securities Bureau of the Japanese Ministry of Finance, the United Kingdom's Department of Trade and Industry (1986), the Securities Commissions of Ontario, Quebec, and British Columbia, the Comissao de Valores Mobilarios of Brazil (1988), the French Commission des Operations de Bourse, the Italian Commissione Nazionale per le Societa e la Borsa, and the Government of the Kingdom of the Netherlands (1989). In 1987 the SEC formally ratified a resolution of the International Organization of Securities Commissions providing for reciprocal assistance to the extent permitted by law among the 13 member signers—Brazil, Chile, Colombia, France, Great Britain, Hong Kong, Italy, Mexico, Norway, Ontario, Panama, Peru, and Quebec. In a related matter in November 1989 the Council of the European Communities issued a directive coordinating regulations on insider trading in the EC. See also *SEC v. Wang* (S.D.N.Y. July 10, 1990), SEC Rel. No. LR 12191, where a Hong Kong investor consented to an order for an injunction, an ITSA penalty, and disgorgement of $25 million, and *SEC v. Fondation Hai* (S.D.N.Y. July 3, 1990), 22 *Securities Regulation and Law Reporter* 1036 (July 13, 1990), where a Swiss investor consented to disgorgement.
30. *The Wall Street Journal*, May 28, 1986.
31. *Securities Regulation and Law Reporter* 18 The investment banker, Dennis B. Levine, also implicated Ivan Boesky.

32. 18 *Securities Regulation and Law Reporter* 1341 (September 19, 1986) (Ira B. Sokolow and David S. Brown); 18 *Securities Regulation and Law Reporter* 1498 (October 17, 1986); *The Wall Street Journal*, October 10, 1986 (Ilan K. Reich); 16 *Securities Regulation and Law Reporter* 19 (January 2, 1987) at 16, *The Wall Street Journal*, December 23, 1986 (Robert M. Wilkis).
33. For recent enforcement actions and settlements see the article cited in note 26.
34. See Levine, *The Financial Analyst's Handbook*, chapter by Gillis on "Insider Trading" at 1765 (1988), and *supra*, notes 4, 10, 11 and 18.
35. *U.S. v. Bilzerian* (S.D.N.Y. June 12, 1989), the first conviction in a jury trial for parking securities; *U.S. v. Jeffries* (S.D.N.Y. July 6, 1989); and *U.S. v. Milken* (S.D.N.Y. April 24, 1990).
36. See In re Faberge, Inc., SEC Rel. 34-10174, [1973] Fed. Sec. L. Rep. (CCH) ¶79,378 (May 23, 1973). For a discussion of various types of compliance programs, see Phillips, "Insider Trading Controls for Law Firms," 23 *Securities and Commodities Regulation* 12 (June 20, 1990); Phillips and Nojeim, "Disclosures to Securities Analysts: The Drafty Exposure of the Open-Door Policy." 4 Insights 5 (May 1990); Phillips and Nojeim, "Insider Trading Liability for Publicly Held Companies," 23 *Securities and Commodities Regulation* 3 (February 14, 1990); Poser, "Chinese Walls in the U.S. and the U.K.," 21 *Securities and Commodities Regulation* 21 (December 7, 1988); Weiss and Spolan, "Preventing Insider Trading," 19 *Securities Regulation and Law Reporter* 19 (November 5, 1986).
37. The SEC first required such a barrier in a Statement of Policy in *Merrill Lynch, Pierce, Fenner and Smith Inc.*, SEC Rel. No. 34-8459 (1968). An early recognition of the information barrier by the Financial Analysts Federation is contained in "Trouble at Quigby," *Financial Analysts Journal* (July/August 1969). An example of a required statement of policy for an investment manager is contained in *SEC v. Lums, Inc.*, (S.D.N.Y. 1972), [1972-73] Fed. Sec. L. Rep. (CCH) ¶93,659. More extensive undertakings were part of a broker's settlement with the SEC in *In re Kidder Peabody & Co., Inc.*, SEC Rel. No. 34-24543 (June 4, 1987), 38 SEC Docket 9 at 602 (June 17, 1987). An example of an information barrier that did not work appears in *SEC v. First Boston Corporation* (S.D.N.Y. 1986), SEC Rel. No. LR 11092 (May 5, 1986), 35 SEC Docket 13 at 858 (May 20, 1986). Compliance procedures are required or are the basis for exemptions from liability in numerous other contexts: Investment Company Act Rule 17j-1 (required codes of ethics for investment company access persons); Securities Exchange Act §20(a) (exemption from liability of controlling persons); Securities Exchange Act Rule 14e-3(b) (exemption from liability of multiservice firms); Securities Exchange Act §21(d) (exemption from aiding and abetting liability under the Insider Trading Sanctions Act); Securities Exchange Act §15(b)(4)(E) (regarding supervisory responsibilities); and Investment Advisers Act §203(e)(5) (exemption from supervisory sanctions).
38. See Miller, "Preventing Misuse of Information by Financial Institutions," 1 *Insights* 5 (November 1987).
39. In *SEC v. Geon Industries*, 381 F. Supp. 1063, 1070 (S.D.N.Y. 1974), *aff'd*, 531 F.2d 39, 53 (2d Cir. 1976), the court exonerated a brokerage firm (which was the employer of a registered representative who traded on inside information) from responsibility for the employee's trading on material nonpublic information because it had disseminated written guidelines and tested him on his understanding of the contents of the guidelines. See also *In re Faberge, Inc.*, *supra* note 36, in which the SEC recommends written compliance procedures and educational programs designed to ensure that employees recognize material nonpublic information

40. A form of Policy Statement as to Confidential Information is contained in Brown, "Disclosure and the Corporate Issuer," 21 *Securities and Commodities Regulation* 4 (February 24, 1988). See also the articles cited in note 36.
41. In *SEC v. Geon Industries*, 531 F.2d 39 at 52 (2d Cir. 1976), the court noted that this was a desirable procedure for preventing violations of Rule 10b-5. The New York Stock Exchange received SEC approval in May 1988 for a series of rule amendments that require the member firm to (1) establish proprietary and employee trading reviews (Rules 342.21(a) and (b)), (2) prepare an annual compliance report (Rule 342.30), (3) report additional information about compliance (Rules 351(d) and (e)), (4) have its compliance supervisors pass a special examination (Rule 342.13(b)), and (5) satisfy new procedural compliance requirements (Rules 342.20, 476(a)(11) and 476A). SEC Rel. No. 34-25763 (May 27, 1988), 41 SEC Docket 1 at 30.
42. See *Slade v. Shearson, Hammill & Co., Inc.*, 356 F.Supp. 304 (S.D.N.Y. 1973), and 517 F.2d 398 (2d Cir. 1974), approving such a so-called Chinese Wall in a brokerage firm. A restricted list and watch list of securities are also useful techniques. This segregation of functions is also useful to prevent premature use of information or recommendations developed by a research department. (See Standards III E and IV.)

Standard II C
Reference Material

1. Alboini, "Insider Trading and Self Dealing," Part XX of *Ontario Securities Law* (1980).
2. Anisman, *Insider Trading in Canada: Recommendations and Guidelines on Boardroom Practice* (1988).
3. Anisman, "Insider Trading Under the Canada Business Corporations Act," *The Meredith Memorial Lectures* (1975).
4. "New Guidelines on Insider Information," *Financial Analysts Journal* (January/February 1974).
5. Gillis and Ciotti, "Insider Trading Update," *Financial Analysts Journal* (November/December 1992).
6. Gillis, "Two Years After Dirks," *Financial Analysts Journal* (January/February 1986).
7. Gillis, "After Dirks," *Financial Analysts Journal* (January/February 1984).
8. Gillis, "Equity Funding Finale," *Financial Analysts Journal* (September/October 1983).
9. Gillis, "Dirks Redeemed," *Financial Analysts Journal* (July/August 1983).
10. Gillis, "SEC Warnings on Use of Inside Information," *Financial Analysts Journal* (November/December 1981).
11. Gillis, "Equity Funding—A Continuing Saga," *Financial Analysts Journal* (May/June 1981).
12. Gillis, "The Supreme Court and Market Information," *Financial Analysts Journal* (November/December 1980).
13. Gillis, "Inside Information Developments," *Financial Analysts Journal* (March/April 1980).
14. Gillis, "Equity Funding Revisited—Once Again," *Financial Analysts Journal* (November/December 1978).
15. Gillis, "Inside Information Review," *Financial Analysts Journal* (May/June 1978).
16. Gillis, "Inside Information," *Investment Management and the Law*, Financial Analysts Federation (1978).
17. Gillis, "Equity Funding Revisited," *Financial Analysts Journal* (March/April 1977).
18. Gillis, "Bausch & Lomb: Analytical Judgment and Inside Information," *Financial Analysts Journal* (November/December 1976).
19. Gillis, "Inside Information and Accountants: Scope of Liability," *Financial Analysts Journal* (May/June 1976).
20. Gillis, "Mandatory Use of Inside Information," *Financial Analysts Journal* (March/April 1975).
21. Gillis, "Inside Information: Are Guidelines Possible?" *Financial Analysts Journal* (May/June 1974).
22. Gillis, "Equity Funding," *Financial Analysts Journal* (July/August 1973).
23. Gillis, "Growing Spectre of Inside Information," *Financial Analysts Journal* (January/February 1973).
24. Gillis, "Metamorphosis of Inside Information," *Financial Analysts Journal* (November/December 1972).
25. Gillis, "Bausch & Lomb and Analytical Judgment," *Financial Analysts Journal* (May/June 1972).
26. Gillis, "The Tippee in Transition," *Financial Analysts Journal* (January/February 1971).
27. Goelzer, Macey, Phillips & Zutz, Aldave, and Fischel, "Symposium on Insider Trading," 13 *Hofstra Law Review* 1 (1984).

28. Johnston, Chapter 6, "Insider Trading," *Canadian Securities Regulation* (1977 with 1982 supplement).
29. Langevoort, "Insider Trading Under State Law," 2 *Insights* 2 (February 1988).
30. Levine, *The Financial Analyst's Handbook*, chapter by Gillis on "Insider Trading," at 1765 (Second Ed. 1988).
31. Levine, *The Investment Manager's Handbook*, chapter by Gillis on "Regulation of Investment Managers Under Federal Securities Laws," at 638–43 (1980).
32. "Loomis on Inside Information," *Financial Analysts Journal* (May/June 1972).
33. Security Analysts Association of Japan, *The Healthy Development of Securities Markets and the Sales of Security Analysts* (1989).
34. Williams, Reilly, and Houck, *Ethics and the Investment Industry*, at 96–100, 101–20 and 162–68 (1989).

II. COMPLIANCE WITH GOVERNING LAWS AND REGULATIONS AND THE CODE AND STANDARDS

D. Responsibilities of Supervisors

A financial analyst with supervisory responsibility shall exercise reasonable supervision over those subordinate employees subject to his control, to prevent any violation by such persons of applicable statutes, regulations, or provisions of the Code of Ethics or Standards of Professional Conduct. In so doing the analyst is entitled to rely upon reasonable procedures established by his employer.

Purpose of the Standard

The purpose of the standard is to state the responsibility of AIMR members and nonmember holders of, and candidates for, the CFA designation to prevent violations of law and violations of the Code and Standards by persons acting under their supervision.

Conduct Affected by the Standard

Any investment professional who has subordinate employees subject to his control—whether or not they are AIMR members, nonmember CFAs, or CFA candidates—exercises supervisory responsibility. The conduct that constitutes reasonable supervision depends on the number of employees supervised by the analyst or manager and the work performed by those employees. Some investment analysts and managers who supervise large numbers of subordinates must delegate most supervisory duties; they exercise reasonable supervision by establishing written supervisory procedures and by ensuring that those procedures are followed through periodic review. Their responsibility includes instructing those to whom supervision is delegated about methods to prevent and detect violations. Other investment professionals must evaluate the conduct of their subordinates on a continuing basis, relying on employer procedures where available, and establishing and implementing such procedures if none exist.

Supervisory responsibility exists whether or not the underlying conduct is covered by the Code and Standards, if it is otherwise covered by governmental laws or regulations or rules of self-regulatory organizations.[1] Under this standard, members who have supervisory responsibility must exercise it with all employees, including those who are not AIMR members, nonmember CFAs, or CFA candidates.

The analyst or investment supervisor is not expected to have extensive legal knowledge, but is expected to know basic legal requirements in his area and to know when to submit questionable issues to legal advisers or other compliance personnel.[2] The member–supervisor is expected to have in-depth knowledge of the Code and Standards and to apply this knowledge in discharging his responsibilities.

The supervisor is also expected to understand what constitutes an adequate compliance system for his firm and to make reasonable efforts to see that appropriate procedures are adequately established, documented, and communicated to covered personnel and to the legal, compliance, and auditing departments. The requirement for the procedures and implementation is one of reasonableness. The supervisor must make every effort to detect fraudulent or deliberately misleading statements or practices as well as other improper or inadequate work or conduct, but in most cases he is not legally liable if unable to do so despite reasonable procedures and efforts. However, a supervisor should bring an inadequate compliance system to the attention of management and recommend corrective action. If it is clear that the analyst or investment manager cannot discharge supervisory responsibilities because of the absence of a compliance system, or because of an inadequate compliance system, the supervisor should not continue to accept supervisory responsibility until reasonable procedures permitting him to exercise reasonable supervision are adopted. (See Standards II A and II C.)

If an employer authorizes a supervisor to establish compliance procedures, it is his responsibility under the standard to do so. Thus, reference in the standard to procedures established by an employer includes procedures established by the member–supervisor.

Application of the Standard

It is not the purpose of this standard to set forth the details of proper conduct under other substantive standards. That is done in standards such as Standard

III G, relating to the fair treatment of customers and clients in disseminating recommendations and in taking investment action; Standard II C, relating to the prohibition against the use of material nonpublic information; Standards III A and III B, relating to the preparation and content of research reports; and Standard VII C, which discusses fiduciary duties.

In this section, several standards are cited to illustrate a supervisor's responsibility under Standard II D and the steps that should be taken to exercise that responsibility.

Example 1: Mattock, senior vice president and head of the research department of H&V, Inc., a regional brokerage firm, has decided to change his recommendation on Timber Products from buy to sell. In line with H&V's procedures, he orally advises certain other H&V executives of his proposed actions before the report is prepared for publication. As a result of a conversation with Mattock, Frampton, one of the executives of H&V accountable to Mattock, immediately sells Timber's stock from his own account and from certain discretionary client accounts. In addition, the firm's research department and other personnel inform certain institutional customers of the changed recommendation before it is printed and disseminated to H&V customers who have received previous Timber reports.

Comment: Mattock failed to supervise reasonably and adequately the actions of those accountable to him because he did not prohibit, or establish reasonable procedures designed to prohibit, dissemination of the information or trading on the information by those who knew of his changed recommendation. His firm did not have procedures for reviewing trading in the stock of any corporation, such as Timber, which was the subject of an undisseminated material change in recommendation; such a procedure would have informed the subordinates of their duties and detected sales by Frampton and selected customers. As a result of this failure to establish supervisory procedures, Frampton violated Standard IV, Priority of Transactions, and he and other employees violated Standard III G, which requires fair treatment of all customers and clients in disseminating material changes in prior investment advice.

Example 2: Miller was the research director for Jamestown Investment Programs. The portfolio managers were critical of Miller and his staff because the Jamestown portfolios did not include any stock that had been the subject of a merger or tender offer. Ginn, a member of Miller's staff, told Miller that he had been studying a local company, Excelsior, Inc., and that he recommended its purchase. Ginn added that it was widely rumored that the company had been the subject of a merger study by a well-known conglomerate and discussions were between them under way. Miller directed Ginn to prepare a memo recommending the stock, which he did. Miller passed along Ginn's memo to the portfolio managers, noting that he had not reviewed it and was leaving town for a week. As a result of the memo, the portfolio managers bought Excelsior stock immediately. The day Miller returned to the office, Excelsior reported a sharp decline, and the exchange suspended trading because of an influx of sell orders following a public announcement of declining earnings.

Upon questioning Ginn, Miller learned that Ginn's only sources were his brother, an acquisitions analyst with Acme Industries, the "well-known conglomerate," and that the merger discussion had been planned but not held.

Comment: Miller did not exercise reasonable supervision when he disseminated the memo without checking it to ensure that Ginn had a reasonable and adequate basis for his recommendations as required by Standard III A, and that he was not relying on material nonpublic information in violation of the federal securities laws as prohibited by Standard II C.

Example 3: Edwards, a trainee salesman at Wheeler & Co., a major national brokerage firm, assists a customer in paying for the securities of High, Inc., using anticipated profits from the immediate sale of the same securities. Despite the fact that High is not on Wheeler's recommended list, a large volume of its stock is traded through Wheeler in this manner. Mason is a Wheeler vice president responsible for supervising compliance with the securities laws in the sales department. Part of his compensation from Wheeler is based on commission revenues from the sales department. Although noticing the increased trading activity, he does nothing to investigate or halt it.

Comment: Mason's failure to review and investigate purchase orders adequately in High stock executed by Edwards and his failure to supervise the trainee's activities properly violate Federal Reserve Board Regulation T as well as Standard II D. Supervisors should be especially sensitive to actual or potential conflicts between their own self-interest and their supervisory responsibilities.

Procedures for Compliance

A supervisor complies with Standard II D by identifying situations in which legal violations or violations of the Code and Standards are likely to occur, by establishing compliance procedures, and by reviewing the actions of employees to prevent such violations and to enforce the procedures. Incorporating an annual professional conduct review as part of the employee's performance review is also recommended. The following compliance procedures are illustrative and are designed to point out problem areas and help supervisors prevent violations. Specific procedures should conform to each firm's individual circumstances and applicable regulatory requirements. Exhibit A concerns research reports and detailed matters to be satisfied with regard to appropriate procedures. Exhibit B concerns portfolio management. Exhibit C concerns analyst contacts with issuers. Supervisors should also identify areas of their practice where employee violations of the law and the Code and Standards are likely and find further help in formulating compliance procedures. Exhibit D summarizes pertinent legal cases.

EXHIBIT A
RESEARCH REPORTS

General Considerations

1. Provisions of all relevant securities acts and regulations are met.
2. Rules of self-regulatory organizations such as stock exchanges, the National Association of Securities Dealers, and the Investment Dealer's Association are followed.
3. Compliance with the AIMR Code and Standards is achieved.
4. All appropriate sources of information are used.
5. Conclusions are based on reasonable and adequate research.
6. Facts are clearly distinguished from opinions.
7. Any part of the report appearing to indicate a definite assurance of gain is deleted; the tone of the report is not too promotional and avoids exaggeration, unwarranted superlatives, and flamboyant or promissory language.

Administrative Process

1. Report is dated and all significant information is reasonably current.
2. Current price, indicated dividend yield, and price–earnings ratio of all recommended securities are given.
3. All opinions, projections, predictions, and estimates are labeled as such, not as facts.
4. Supporting data for recommendations is provided with the legend "Additional Information Available Upon Request" or "Report on Basic Characteristics Available Upon Request" prominently indicated.
5. The supervisor checks calculations on a test basis.
6. The report discusses appropriate relevant factors and the basic characteristics of the investment.
7. The analyst completes any applicable stock exchange or other related checklists.
8. The firm's ownership as a principal or intended ownership of the stock or related securities is disclosed. (See Standard V.)
9. Any relevant firm underwritings within the last three years are disclosed in which the dealer was manager or co-manager. (See Standard V.) The firm's market-making activities are disclosed.
10. The security is checked to verify it is not on a restricted list or in registration.
11. Provisions are made for simultaneous dissemination of all initial copies of the report. (See Standard III G.)

Ethical and Professional Considerations
1. An adequate investigation is made, and the analyst is thorough in his analysis.
2. Reasonable steps are taken to evaluate the accuracy of the data when the analyst's judgment is based on historical information received from third-party sources, that is, commercially available data bases maintained by outside vendors.
3. The analyst is properly prepared for corporate interviews.
4. If the analyst or any associated analyst is on loan to the firm's underwriting department at any point this fact is disclosed and special care is taken regarding nonpublic information. (See Standard II C.)
5. The personal securities transaction reports to the firm are checked for the analyst or supervising analyst and his immediate family. (See Standard V.)
6. The analyst has no special relationship with the issuer. (See Standards V and VII B.)
7. The supervisor's firm has no partners or directors who are also directors of the recommended company. (See Standards V and VII B.)
8. The analyst or supervising analyst receives from the recommended companies no material gratuities or hospitality that affect his objectivity. If gratuities are received, they are specified. (See Standards V and VII B.)
9. The analyst or supervising analyst should not accept from financial intermediaries such as brokers or dealers through whom the firm may either trade securities and derivatives or receive services of value related to the investment process any material gratuities or hospitality that affect his objectivity.
10. If the report is not prepared under the firm's direct supervision, outside authors are identified and given credit. (See Standard III D.)
11. Special commissions, research, soft dollar arrangements, performance or incentive fees, and commitments are reviewed to determine whether any of these require steps to be taken for legal compliance. Disclosure requirements and appropriate disclosures are made.

EXHIBIT B
PORTFOLIO MANAGEMENT

Overall Responsibility

1. The portfolio manager is not influenced in his decision or decisions by excessive entertainment or other incentives. (See Standard VII B.)
2. The portfolio manager is objective in his judgment in buying or selling a security or group of securities.
3. The portfolio manager gives priority to portfolio trading over his own trading.
4. The portfolio manager conforms with the investment objectives and policy guidelines established by the client and/or the employer. (See Standard III C.)

Supervisory Activities

1. The portfolio manager provides the supervisor (that is, the firm) with a list—quarterly or more often—of trading (with dates) of securities and commodities for his account and that of his immediate family. (See Investment Advisers Act Rule 204-2(a)(12).)
2. Portfolio decisions are not influenced by excessive entertainment or other incentives. The portfolio manager at all times gives priority to portfolio trading over his own.
3. The portfolio manager receives no other compensation or income that might conflict with his duties. (See Standard VI C.)
4. No material nonpublic information is received or used.
5. The portfolio manager personally or through his business expenditures (e.g., through the brokerage) has paid out no amounts that might directly influence the receipt of other business by the firm.
6. Special commissions, research, other soft dollar arrangements, performance fees, and commitments are examined to determine whether any of these require that steps be taken for legal compliance. Disclosure requirements and appropriate disclosures are made.
7. Adequate managerial controls are provided over the supervising function to protect both the supervisor and the portfolio managers.
8. Care is taken to determine the portfolio manager's fiduciary duty to his clients. The employer has written guidelines or a policy for voting proxies and the portfolio manager follows it if he is accountable for voting proxies. (See Standard VII C.) A record of the vote is maintained.

9. Investment decisions are consistent with the employer's investment process and with the clients' investment policies and objectives. (See Standard III C).

EXHIBIT C
ANALYST CONTACTS WITH ISSUERS, BROKER–DEALERS AND/OR OTHER FINANCIAL INTERMEDIARIES

Supervisors should review any arrangements made by analysts with issuers, broker–dealers, and other financial intermediaries to ensure that, for example, any travel arrangements do not give the appearance of, or are in fact, compromising the analyst's independence and objectivity. The supervisor should also review any arrangements involving gratuities made by issuers or financial intermediaries for the benefit of the analyst or any other covered employee. The supervisor should make sure that the analyst's plans meet the criteria set out in Standard VII B (see also Standards II A and V). In particular, the supervisor should ask the following questions:

1. Who is paying for transportation?
2. Who is paying for meals, lodging, or other services of value?
3. Who initiated the meeting?
4. How frequently in the past have there been meetings between the issuer, or financial intermediaries and the analyst, and who has paid expenses?
5. Is the issuer's or financial intermediaries' hospitality so lavish that it is clearly intended to influence the analyst's judgment?
6. What types of gifts have been given, how frequently, and what is the estimated value?

EXHIBIT D
SUMMARY OF LEGAL CASES

The securities laws impose a duty on employers to establish internal procedures designed to prevent violations of the securities laws. See, for example, Securities Exchange Act of 1934, Section 15(b)(4)(E), Investment Advisers Act of 1940, Section 203(e)(5), and references cited in the chapter on Standard II C, footnote 27. The following cases indicate how the courts and the Securities and Exchange Commission evaluate the adequacy of supervisory procedures.

1. *Petrites v. J. C. Bradford & Co.*, 646 F.2d 1033 (5th Cir. 1981). Petrites instructed Hyde, an employee of J.C. Bradford & Co., to buy stocks and hold them for long-term appreciation. Hyde instead set up a margin account and engaged in speculative transactions resulting in large commissions. The court relied heavily on the fact that the firm's supervisory procedures did not meet the requirements of stock exchange rules in finding J.C. Bradford & Co. liable for Hyde's actions under state law.

2. *In re Alm, Kane, Rogers & Co.*, SEC Rel. No. 34-16639 Fed. Sec. L. Rep. (CCH) ¶82,470 (March 10, 1980). One of Alm, Kane's salesmen solicited trades on the basis of material nonpublic information. The SEC found that Alm, Kane failed to supervise the salesman reasonably, because its procedures were informal and not designed to prevent or uncover the type of conduct described above. In particular, the firm had no objective procedures for determining when a salesman was soliciting large amounts of trading in a security that would trigger an inquiry into the basis for particular solicitations. Moreover, the firm's compliance manual provided no guidelines to salesmen about the basis on which they could solicit trades.

3. *SEC v. Geon Industries*, 531 F.2d 39, 52 (2d Cir. 1976). See the summary in Standard II C.

4. *SEC v. The First Boston Corporation*, (S.D.N.Y. 1986), SEC Rel. No. LR-11092 (May 5, 1986), 35 SEC Docket 13 at 858 (May 20, 1986). CIGNA stock was placed on First Boston's restricted list on the basis of confidential information about a likely addition of major loan loss reserves. Days later, when a decision was imminent, various persons, including the head trader and his supervisor, were confidentially informed. Without checking the restricted list, a trader, who was also informed, sold stock from the firm's account, bought put options, and later repurchased the stock at a lower price and sold the options before the announcement of CIGNA's decision was made. First Boston was fined, ordered to disgorge profits from the transactions, and required to review its restricted list and Chinese Wall procedures to prevent violations of Section 10(b) of the Exchange Act and Rule 10b-5. This prevention could be accomplished by restricting or limiting trading for its own account in any security about which it possessed material nonpublic information or by preventing persons making trading decisions from receiving material nonpublic information concerning entities to which the firm provides investment banking advice or services.

Footnotes

1. National Association of Securities Dealers, *Rules of Fair Practice*, Article III, §27, Supervision, and Article III, §35, Communications with the Public; New York Stock Exchange, Rule 344, Supervisory Analysts, and Rule 472, Communications with the Public. In June 1988 the SEC approved proposed amendments to Rules 342, Offices—Approval, Supervision and Control, 351, Reporting Requirements, and 476, Disciplinary Proceedings Involving Charges Against Members, Member Organizations, Allied Members, Approved Persons, or Employees, to supplement existing internal compliance procedures by imposing additional trade review, inquiry, and reporting requirements.
2. For an example of sanctions imposed on a supervisor for failure to recognize a questionable issue regarding compliance with NASD standards, see *In re Wall Street West, Inc.*, SEC Rel. No. 34-18320, [1981–2], Fed. Sec. L. Rep. (CCH) ¶83,069 (December 9, 1981).

Standard II D
Reference Material

1. Regulations under the (Ontario) Securities Act, Part XII, Conflicts of Interest, 1987.
2. Securities and Exchange Commission, *Guide to Broker–Dealer Compliance: Report of the Broker–Dealer Model Compliance Program Advisory Committee*, Chapters I, "Supervision," VII, "Investment Advisory Services," IX, "Proprietary Trading," and X, "Research and Recommendations" (November 13, 1974).
3. Securities and Exchange Commission, *Broker–Dealer Policies and Procedures Designed to Segment the Flow and Prevent the Misuse of Material Nonpublic Information: A Report by the Division of Market Regulation* (March 1990).
4. National Association of Securities Dealers, *Rules of Fair Practice*, Article III, §27, Supervision.
5. New York Stock Exchange, Rule 344, Supervisory Analysts.
6. Bines, *The Law of Investment Management*, 4.01 et. seq. (1978).
7. Gillis, "Mandatory Use of Inside Information," *Financial Analysts Journal* (May/June 1975).
8. Gillis, "Inside Information: Are Guidelines Possible?" *Financial Analysts Journal* (May/June 1974).

III. RESEARCH REPORTS, INVESTMENT RECOMMENDATIONS AND ACTIONS

A. Reasonable Basis and Representations

1. The financial analyst shall exercise diligence and thoroughness in making an investment recommendation to others or in taking an investment action for others.

2. The financial analyst shall have a reasonable and adequate basis for such recommendations and actions, supported by appropriate research and investigation.

3. The financial analyst shall make reasonable and diligent efforts to avoid any material misrepresentation in any research report or investment recommendation.

4. The financial analyst shall maintain appropriate records to support the reasonableness of such recommendations and actions.

Purpose of the Standard

The purpose of this standard is to state the responsibility of AIMR members and nonmember holders of, and candidates for, the CFA designation to perform diligent and thorough investigation appropriate to the circumstances for an investment recommendation/action, establish a reasonable basis therefore, exercise diligence in avoiding any material misrepresentation therein, and maintain such records and documentation as are appropriate to support that action/recommendation, or process.

Conduct Affected by the Standard

This standard directly concerns all aspects of the investment decision-making process (e.g., asset allocation, security selection, options writing, use of derivative products, etc.) and the requirement to maintain records in support of decisions made.

The interpretation of the standard is meant to provide both for the different relationships between clients and analysts and the different roles each can take in the investment process. For example, an account representative would be in compliance if he recommended an investment transaction on the basis of his firm's research or the research of another party who exercised diligence and thoroughness in arriving at a decision. Other sources might include research reports prepared by a brokerage firm, bank, or investment service for general distribution or quantitatively oriented strategies and research, such as computer-generated screening or ranking of universes of common stocks based on various sets of prescribed criteria. In all these circumstances, the account executive has the responsibility to understand, in a general way, the basic characteristics (as defined in the chapters on Standards III B 3 and III C) of the investment to ensure that it is suitable for the client and to make every reasonable effort to ensure that the client understands the basis for the recommendations.

The portfolio manager, with respect to an individual investment transaction, may rely on the same sources, but he also has the obligation to consider the transaction within the context of the entire portfolio, including client factors. (See Standard III C.)

For part or all of the background information for general recommendations, the research analyst may depend on reliable sources both within and outside his firm. The use of such sources should be disclosed.

The analyst must also make a reasonable and diligent effort to ensure that any research report finding or investment recommendation is accurate and does not involve misrepresentation. The requirements for issuing conclusions on research will vary with the investment style (a list of considerations is included in the sections on Standard III B 1 and Standard III B2). It is the analyst's responsibility, however, to make reasonable efforts to cover all pertinent issues. In the case of fundamental analysis, such an effort normally would include an examination of historical earnings, ownership of assets, and outstanding contracts as well as other business factors. A quantitative analyst should concentrate on using valid statistical analysis techniques and on ensuring, to the greatest possible degree, that his conclusions are based on accurate and meaningful data and on as wide a sample as possible. If the analyst has reason to suspect that any of his information may not be accurate, he should refrain from relying on it. Standard III E prohibits misrepresentations regarding services, qualifications, and investment performance.

The requirement for maintenance of appropriate records similarly reflects the nature of the client relationship, the specific role in the process played by the analyst, and the process itself. The firm's research analysis is an appropriate record for an account executive making a general recommendation. The record for the portfolio manager should refer to the specific research analysis or quantitative system but should also indicate reasons for the specific transaction. The research analyst is required to maintain files, including work papers, indicating the scope of his research and the assumptions behind his conclusions. Files should include details of where the data necessary for the analysis was obtained as well as an account of the method of analysis detailed enough to allow reconstructing it. Quantitative analysts should maintain detailed records that document the development of, and describe the purpose of, algorithms used in any investment decision-making process. In the event of real-time or path-dependent quantitatively driven investment systems, the analyst must have the capability to reconstruct the variables and conditions leading up to and precipitating actual transactions and have a basis for demonstrating that these investment systems are functioning as intended.

The SEC, various stock exchanges, and the National Association of Securities Dealers all have specific record-keeping requirements that should be reviewed and satisfied.

Application of the Standard

The application of these standards is best illustrated by the following examples.

Example 1: Gold, a portfolio manager at Jones & Black, had invested 20 percent of a client's portfolio in Johnson stock with proceeds from some high-yielding securities. The client, White, was dependent on the portfolio for her support. In a memo to the files covering her conversation with White, the portfolio manager stated he would repurchase high-yielding securities after the Johnson stock reflected the favorable merger terms, thereby increasing White's income.

Comment: In this case, Gold was in violation of Standards III A 1 and A 2 in that he had the obligation to consider any specific transaction within the context of the entire portfolio, including client factors. He also violated Standard III B 3 by failing to explain the basic characteristics of the investment to his client, particularly the sizable risk being assumed in relation to the needs of the portfolio.

Example 2: Green, an analyst at Jones Co., an investment counseling firm, is told by the vice president of investor relations of Sky Avionics, a major defense contractor, that the firm is in the final stages of developing a new radar system that represents a major advance over existing Air Force systems. The investor relations officer also indicated that he is optimistic that Sky will prevail over three other companies in obtaining a $1 billion contract to produce the system. In a research report recommending that clients buy large quantities of Sky stock, Green states that the contract will be awarded to Sky.

Comment: In turning the vice president's optimism into certainty, Green has misrepresented the facts in violation of this standard. His misrepresentation is material because it is likely to influence an investor's judgment in deciding whether to purchase Sky stock.

Example 3: Martin, a quantitative analyst at Allen Brothers, an investment counseling firm, has completed an analysis of returns patterns of out-of-favor, low-book-value stocks over the past five years. Based on the study, Martin's report recommends selling this class of stocks out of all portfolios where client objectives allow such a move. Flynn, his boss, suspects that the five-year study is too short, particularly as these five years represent only one type of economic environment, but he approves the recommendations.

Comment: By approving Martin's recommendation, Flynn has misrepresented the research conclusions. The recommendation is not a thorough quantitative work because it needs to be extended over a longer period of time to be comprehensive. The study should be redone or the recommendation issued in such a manner as to make its limitations obvious.

Example 4: Jenner, a CFA, works on the fixed income trading floor of a major investment bank, supporting the sales and trading effort by advising clients and traders about company credit trends and potential rating actions. Noticing that an automotive company was making a large acquisition, he called the company to obtain more information. He also called the rating agencies to gauge their response. With this information in hand, he worked up an advisory for interested clients about the credit implications of the company's action.

Randall, a senior partner of the firm, had a good relationship with the auto company. He exploded when he discovered that Jenner had contacted the company without his knowing it. He told Jenner he never again should contact one of "his" companies without his consent. Jenner felt that the restriction tied his hands in such a way that he could not continue to do his job properly.

Comment: Business considerations are also important in the investment profession, and Jenner should be sensitive to them. At the same time, he has a responsibility to exercise diligence and thoroughness in forming investment judgments. Although he can try to cooperate more effectively with Randall in obtaining needed information, he must also let the firm's clients know when he is "conflicted" or otherwise unable to obtain the information necessary to draw a conclusion.

Procedures for Compliance

In fulfilling the basic provision of this standard, an analyst or investment manager must take into account the analyst– or manager–client relationship, the role of the analyst or manager in the investment decision-making process, and the support the organization provides the investment professional in the performance of his role. These factors in turn will determine the nature of the diligence and thoroughness required by Standard III A 1; the development of a reasonable basis for a recommendation/action required by Standard III A 2; the thoroughness of the research and investigation required by Standard III A 3; and the records in support of such recommendation/action required by Standard III A 4.

The section on Standard II D relating to supervisory responsibilities contains detailed checklists for the preparation of research reports and recommendations.

For illustrative purposes, several specific procedures are listed in the Exhibit A. Exhibit B summarizes legal cases.

EXHIBIT A
GUIDELINE PROCEDURES

1. *Basic characteristics.* An account executive, investment manager, or research analyst, before recommending a specific investment or investment discipline to a broad client group, should investigate (directly or indirectly) its basic characteristics and then communicate this information to the clients to whom he is recommending this action or process. This should allow the prospective purchaser to evaluate these characteristics in relation to his own needs. Further, written records should indicate such characteristics (quality ratings, terms such as "businessman's risk," "speculative issue," etc.) and the basis for the recommendation (quantitative, fundamental, technical, etc.). A research report can serve as a record when referencing a particular issue or group of securities. With respect to a quantitative investment discipline, the process should be illustrated in thorough detail, and any applicable backtesting data be made available for inspection or review.

2. *Implementation of basic characteristics requirement.* The portfolio manager has the obligation to analyze his client's investment needs as well as the basic characteristics of the investments. The analysis of a client's needs and circumstances is not a one-time matter but a continuing responsibility. An extensive discussion of client factors and basic characteristics of investments is found in the chapters on Standards III B 3 and III C.

As for the meshing of client characteristics and investment characteristics, the combination of several different investments is likely to provide a more acceptable level of risk exposure than having all one's eggs in a single basket. Also, the basic characteristics of the entire portfolio will largely determine whether client factors are being served. Thus, the focus should be on the characteristics of the total portfolio rather than on an issue-by-issue review.

As for records, the portfolio manager and his client, at the outset of the relationship, should develop a statement of investment objectives and should review this periodically (annually or when there is a major change in client circumstances). These objectives should be set forth in writing. Then each recommendation/transaction should be made in view of client objectives and the basic characteristics of the investment to be bought and sold.

3. *Files.* The research analyst or investment manager should maintain files to support his recommendations. If recommendations are based on a report from an outside source, the report should be maintained. If original research is undertaken, files should include details of where the analyst obtained the necessary data, plus enough information regarding the method used by the

analyst to allow the process to be reconstructed. In the case of fundamental research, the file should contain company-published data and industry data (either in the company file or a general file), as well as records of all management contact. Records and files may be kept on paper or in electronic form on computer tapes or disks. If kept in electronic form, adequate backup of disks or tapes should be maintained.

Besides furnishing excellent reference materials for future work, research files play a key role in justifying investment decisions under later scrutiny. Files can serve as the ultimate proof that recommendations and actions, good or bad, were made based on the same methodology that drives every one of an analyst's decisions.

EXHIBIT B
SUMMARY OF LEGAL CASES

1. *In the Matter of Merrill Lynch, Pierce, Fenner & Smith Inc.*, SEC Rel. No. 34-14149 (November 9, 1977). The SEC found, by consent without admission of the allegations, that a financial analyst responsible for following Scientific Control Corporation based his research recommendations to Merrill Lynch sales operations largely on information supplied by management without additional investigation and despite current information in his files contradicting management representations concerning new products and financial condition. The SEC stated that a securities broker's recommendation represents that it has conducted a reasonable investigation and holds an adequate and reasonable basis for it and is perceived by the customer to be the product of an independent and objective analysis. This imposes an obligation to go beyond the self-serving statements of management. Ongoing investigation is required when projections made by a company fail to materialize, and adverse information must be communicated to customers.

2. *Hanly v. SEC*, 415 F.2d 589 (2d Cir. 1969). Without obtaining financial data, securities salesmen recommended stock of U.S. Sonics Corporation to customers on the basis of its introduction of a new product. They later obtained unfavorable financial information, such as Sonics's deteriorating financial condition, inability to manufacture its new product, and negative results of negotiations with potential licensees. The court stated that the salesmen had a duty to investigate adverse facts reasonably ascertainable and to disclose such facts. The court also held a salesman who lacks essential information should disclose this fact as well as the risks associated with lack of knowledge.

Standard III A
Reference Material

1. (Ontario) Securities Act, R.S.O., 1980, c. 466, §1(1)(24), Misrepresentation.
2. Securities and Exchange Commission, *Guide to Broker–Dealer Compliance: Report of the Broker–Dealer Model Compliance Program Advisory Committee,* Chapter X, "Research and Recommendations" (November 13, 1974).
3. Securities and Exchange Commission, *Report of Special Study of Securities Markets,* Part I, at 330-87 (1963).
4. National Association of Securities Dealers, *Rules of Fair Practice,* Article III, §35, Communications with the Public.
5. New York Stock Exchange, Rule 472, Communications with the Public.
6. New York Stock Exchange, *Expanded Policy on Timely Disclosure.*
7. Canadian National Policy No. 40, Timely Disclosure (1987).
8. Commission des Valeurs du Quebec, *Policy Statement No. Q-11, Future Oriented Financial Information* (1989).
9. American Institute of Certified Public Accountants, *Guide for Prospective Financial Statements* and *Statement on Standards for Accountants' Services on Prospective Financial Information* (1986 and 1985, respectively).
10. Financial Analysts Federation, *Guidelines for Earnings Forecasts Made by Financial Analysts* (April 27, 1974).
11. Frankel, *The Regulation of Money Managers,* Volume 2, Chapter XV D (1978).
12. Fleischer, Mundheim, and Murphy, "Disclosure of Investment Advice," 6 *Review of Securities Regulation* 16 (September 27, 1973).
13. Peloso, "The Security Analyst," 7 *Review of Securities Regulation* 17 (October 10, 1974).
14. Longstreth, *Modern Investment Management and the Prudent Man Rule,* particularly Chapter 5, "Conclusions and Recommendations" (Oxford University Press 1986).
15. Levine, *The Investment Manager's Handbook* (Dow Jones-Irwin 1980).

III. RESEARCH REPORTS, INVESTMENT RECOMMENDATIONS AND ACTIONS

B.   Research Reports

1. The financial analyst shall use reasonable judgment as to the inclusion of relevant factors in research reports.

2. The financial analyst shall distinguish between facts and opinions in research reports.

Purpose of the Standard

The purpose of these standards is to state the responsibility of AIMR members and nonmember holders of, and candidates for, the CFA designation to include in a research report those key factors that are instrumental to the investment conclusion presented in that report, so that the user of the report is apprised of its basis. As a critical part of this procedure, the research analyst must indicate the difference between opinions and facts (qualitative and probabilistic).

Conduct Affected by the Standards

The standards are specifically limited to research reports or circulated studies. The means of communicating investment information to wide audiences—ranging from practitioners to the least sophisticated clients—is highly varied and includes person-to-person recommendations, telephone conversations, television and radio shows, computer-based recommendations, as well as written reports. Further, the nature of these communications is highly diverse, ranging from one word (either "buy" or "sell") to in-depth reports of more than a hundred pages. The information can range from chartist data to studies on specific projects, brief updates, and the like. As communications technology advances, additional ways of providing investment information will be developed and must be addressed. As the business standards, rules, and regulations required by the public and private sectors change, new kinds of data will be included.

A research report or study may be defined as a prepared document intended to be distributed (or likely to find its way) outside the preparing organization and containing an actual or implied investment recommendation. The analysis may concern itself with a general recommendation about the market, asset allocation, or classes of investments (e.g., stocks, bonds, real estate), or simply relate to a specific security. If recommendations are contained in capsule form (such as a recommended stock list), additional information and analysis should be available to the client, and the client should be so notified. Investment advice based on quantitative research and analysis should be supported by readily available reference material and applied in a manner consistent with previously applied methodology. Any changes in such methodology should also be made available. Furthermore, the financial analyst must outline known limitations of his analysis and conclusions. Discussions with prospective clients outlining a company's or investor's methodology and abilities should conform to the same standards.

Application of the Standards

Standard III A mandates that diligence and thoroughness be exercised either directly or indirectly (by someone in whom the member has reasonable confidence) with respect to an investment recommendation.[1] Analyses can be prepared entirely from outside investment sources (secondary research), from original research, or from a combination of both.

In company analysis, the objective is to determine the nature of the issuer's (or the company's) earning power, cash flow, operating and financial strength and viability, and dividend potential. Earning power considerations may include growth potential, the degree of cyclical sensitivity of the earning power, and the analyst's confidence level in future projections. These considerations should be part of the analytical process whereby the analyst arrives at his conclusion about the basic characteristics of the specific investment security, but disclosure of these factors is not required.

Once the process has been completed, the preparer of the report should select those elements he deems relevant to discuss in his report so that the user can follow and challenge his reasoning. The report writer may emphasize certain areas, touch briefly on others, and omit certain aspects provided the investigation has been done and the writer, in his judgment, deems those aspects unimportant. For instance, a report may dwell on a quarterly earnings release or new product introduction at the sacrifice of examining other fundamental matters in depth as long as the analyst stipulates clearly the limits to the scope of the report.

The selection of the relevant factors is an analytical skill; determination of whether a violation exists would hinge heavily on peer review rather than a specific checklist.

Standard III B 2 requires that opinion be separated from fact. Violations are most likely to occur in failure to separate the past from the future by not indicating that earnings estimates, changes in the outlook for dividends, and future market price opinions are just that and consequently subject to future circumstances. In the case of complex quantitative analysis, it is incumbent upon the analyst to not only clearly separate fact from statistical conjecture but to identify the known limitations of the analysis.

Example 1: Williams, director of marketing for County Technicians, Inc., was convinced he had found the perfect formula for increasing County's income and diversifying its product base. Williams planned to build on County's reputation as a leading money manager and market an exclusive and expensive investment advice letter to high-net-worth individuals. One hitch in the plan was the complexity of County's investment system—a combination of technical trading rules (based on historical price and volume fluctuations) and portfolio construction rules designed to minimize risk. To simplify the newsletter, he decided to include only each week's top five buy and sell recommendations and leave out details of the valuation models and the portfolio structuring scheme.

Comment: Williams's current plans for the letter fail to include all the relevant factors behind the investment advice. Clients need to fully understand County's process and logic in order to effectively implement the advice. Without understanding the basis for the recommendations, the client cannot possibly understand its limitations or the risks inherent in it. In addition to violating Standard III B, Williams may also be violating Standard III C as he is ignoring County's normal portfolio considerations and focusing purely on the recommendations.

Procedures for Compliance

In fulfilling the basic provisions of these standards, a financial analyst must be thorough and diligent in doing the necessary work in preparing a report, include in his report all relevant factors that led to his conclusion, indicate the difference between fact and opinion in discussion, and identify the limitations of the analysis. The analyst should maintain records indicating the nature of the research and should be able to supply additional information to the client (or user) of the report, covering additional factors, if asked to do so.

Exhibit A lists certain basic investigative steps appropriate for a fundamental company analysis. A similar checklist could serve as a guideline for someone who is relying on another's research to determine whether his source of information exercised diligence and thoroughness. The checklist is provided for illustrative purposes only; it is not intended to be all-inclusive nor is it representative of the research necessary for quantitative and other non-fundamentally driven conclusions.

The SEC, various stock exchanges, and the National Association of Securities Dealers have specific requirements relating to research reports that should be reviewed and satisfied. Most firms have developed written compliance procedures incorporating these requirements and other matters deemed desirable. Firms are strongly urged to develop such procedures if they do not have them in place.

The analyst's report and analytical process should be reviewed by his supervisor, or by a peer having supervisory authority in that instance, before general distribution. Further discussion of supervisory procedures is found in the chapter on Standard II D relating to the responsibilities of supervisors.

EXHIBIT A
INVESTIGATIVE STEPS FOR COMPANY ANALYSIS

1. *Macroeconomic factors.* Develop what impact fiscal and/or monetary policies in force domestically as well as overseas, currency exchange rates, and business cycle conditions will have on a company or its industry.

2. *Industry considerations.* Investigate the industry (or, if a diversified company, the principal industries) of the issuer of the security. Considerations should include historic growth and future potential, the nature of worldwide competition, regulatory environment, capital requirements, and methods of distribution, as well as external and internal factors that might change the structure of the industry.

3. *Company's (or issuer's) position in the industry.* Analyze the company's strengths and weaknesses within the industry environment. This analysis should be based not only on discussion with the company's management but should also include investigation with competitors and such trade sources as distributors.

4. *Income statement and statement of cash flows.* Review statements for a period covering two business cycles, and investigate reasons for annual and seasonal changes in areas of volume growth, price changes, operating margins, effective tax rates, capital requirements, and working capital.

5. *Balance sheet.* Investigate the reasons for historic and prospective changes in the company's financial condition and capital structure plus conformance of accounting practices to changes either proposed or implemented by accounting rule-making bodies.

6. *Dividend record and policy.*

7. *Accounting policies.* Determine policies and examine the auditor's opinion.

8. *Management.* Evaluate reputation, experience, and stability. Also evaluate the record and policies toward corporate governance, acquisitions and divestitures, personnel (including labor relations), and governmental relations.

9. *Facilities/programs.* Review plant networks, competitive effectiveness, capacity, future plans, and capital spending.

10. *Research/new products.*

11. *Marketing/distribution.*

12. *Nature of the security.*

13. *Security price record.*

14. *Future outlook.* Examine principal determinants of operating and financial performance, key points of leverage in the future (e.g., new markets and geographic expansion, market share improvement, new products/services,

prospect for profit margin improvement, acquisitions, etc.), competitive outlook, major risks (e.g., competition, erosion of customer base, abbreviated product life cycles, technological obsolescence, environmental hazards, etc.), financial goals (near- and long-term), and level of confidence in achieving them.

15. *Reliance on data bases.* The analyst is likely to use a number of data bases from various sources. It is incumbent that he make an effort to assure himself of the reliability of the data included and of its appropriateness to his purposes. The analyst should incorporate only data which he has reasonable grounds to believe has been accurately gathered. If the data has been processed in any way (e.g., into financial ratios), the analyst should ascertain that such processing has been done in a manner consistent with his analytical purposes. Acknowledgment of the source(s) should be made when appropriate as required under Standard III D.

Footnotes

1. New York Stock Exchange Rule 791, Communications to Customers; National Association of Securities Dealers, *Rules of Fair Practice*, Article III, §35, Communications with the Public. Also see New York Stock Exchange Rule 435(5), Miscellaneous Prohibitions, Circulation of Rumors.

Standard III B 1 and B 2
Reference Material

1. See Reference Material in the chapters on Standard III A, relating to reasonable basis for research reports, and Standard III B 3, relating to basic characteristics of reports for general distribution.
2. National Association of Securities Dealers, *Rules of Fair Practice,* Article III, §35, Communications with the Public.
3. New York Stock Exchange, Rules 435(5), Miscellaneous Prohibitions, Circulation of Rumors, and 791, Communications to Customers.
4. American Institute of Certified Public Accountants, *Guide for Prospective Financial Statements* and *Statement on Standards for Accountants' Services on Prospective Financial Information* (1986 and 1985, respectively).
5. Commission des Valeurs du Quebec, *Policy Statement No. Q-11, Future Oriented Financial Information* (1989).
6. Financial Analysts Federation, *Guidelines for Earnings Forecasts Made by Financial Analysts* (April 27, 1974).
7. Financial Analysts Federation, *Disclosure of Corporate Forecasts to the Investor* (March 1973).
8. Bauman, *Professional Standards in Investment Management,* at 58-62, (Financial Analysts Research Foundation 1980).
9. Levine, *The Investment Manager's Handbook* (Dow Jones-Irwin 1980).
10. Gillis, "A Research Dilemma: Facts or Speculation," *Financial Analysts Journal* (July/August 1981).
11. Gillis, "The SEC on Corporate Projections," *Financial Analysts Journal* (July/August 1980).
12. Gillis and Hewitt, "Suitability," *Financial Analysts Journal* (September/October 1979).
13. Hedberg, "Let's Regulate Investment Advice," *Financial Analysts Journal* (May/June 1973).
14. Zitnik, "Research Report Ethics," *Financial Analysts Journal* (January/February 1966).

III. RESEARCH REPORTS, INVESTMENT RECOMMENDATIONS AND ACTIONS

B. Research Reports

3. The financial analyst shall indicate the basic characteristics of the investment involved when preparing for general public distribution a research report that is not directly related to a specific portfolio or client.

Purpose of the Standard

The purpose of this standard is to state the responsibility of AIMR members and nonmember holders of, and candidates for, the CFA designation to indicate the basic characteristics of an investment in a general way in any reports prepared for general and public distribution containing an investment recommendation.

Conduct Affected by the Standard

In preparing a research report, the financial analyst should determine, and then present in the report, his key conclusions as to the basic characteristics of the security being analyzed. This should allow the user of the report to incorporate this information into his investment decision-making process as he deems appropriate. (See also Standard III C.)

Application of the Standard

The standard requires that every research report containing an investment recommendation include an indication of the investment's basic characteristics.

Items to be considered might include:
- Expected annual rate of return, taking into account income payments and expected price changes during the income period.

- Annual amount of income expected (current and future).
- Current rate of income return or yield to maturity.
- Degree of uncertainty associated with such payments.
- Degree of marketability/liquidity.
- Business, financial, and market risk.

A multitude of quality ranking systems have developed over the years. The most widely recognized are fixed credit ratings, in which the risk of timely payment of interest and principal is indicated by letter (AAA, AA, etc.). For equities, there are numerical quality rating systems and a variety of broad terms such as high risk, high yield, growth, income, and growth/income. Other systems indicate the company's size by the terms large and small capitalization.

Procedures for Compliance

A financial analyst who prepares a research report containing an investment recommendation should include, in some form, an indication of its basic characteristics. If appropriate, a systematic grading system might be used.

As noted in the sections on Standards III A and III B 1 and B 2, the SEC, various stock exchanges, and the National Association of Securities Dealers have specific requirements relating to research reports that should be reviewed and satisfied. Also as noted, there should be employer procedures, preferably in a compliance manual, to meet applicable requirements.

Reference should also be made to the section on Standard II D, which contains checklists to be used by supervisors (and others) in discharging their responsibilities.

Standard III B 3
Reference Material

1. See Reference Material in the chapters on Standard III A, relating to reasonable basis for research reports, Standards III B 1 and B 2, relating to the content of research reports, and Standard III C, relating to portfolio investment recommendations and actions.
2. Bauman, *Guidelines for Communications to Investors* (Financial Analysts Research Foundation 1982).
3. Levine, *The Financial Analyst's Handbook* (Dow Jones-Irwin 1975 and 1988).
4. Phillips and Ritchie, "Suggested Outline for an Analysis of an Industrial Company," *CFA Readings in Financial Analysis,* at 153 (Institute of Chartered Financial Analysts, Charlottesville, Va., Sixth Ed. 1984).

STANDARD III C

III. RESEARCH REPORTS, INVESTMENT RECOMMENDATIONS AND ACTIONS

C. Portfolio Investment Recommendations and Actions

1. The financial analyst shall, when making an investment recommendation or taking an investment action for a specific portfolio or client, consider its appropriateness and suitability for such portfolio or client. In considering such matters, the financial analyst shall take into account (a) the needs and circumstances of the client, (b) the basic characteristics of the investment involved, and (c) the basic characteristics of the total portfolio. The financial analyst shall use reasonable judgment to determine the applicable relevant factors.

2. The financial analyst shall distinguish between facts and opinions in the presentation of investment recommendations.

3. The financial analyst shall disclose to clients and prospective clients the basic format and general principles of the investment processes by which securities are selected and portfolios are constructed and shall promptly disclose to clients any changes that might significantly affect those processes.

Purpose of the Standard

The purpose of the standard is to state the responsibility of AIMR members and nonmember holders of, and candidates for, the CFA designation to consider carefully the appropriateness and suitability of a given investment or course of investment action to the needs and circumstances of the client (or the stated objectives of the fund) for which it is intended and to ensure that the client is fully aware of the investment policies, strategies, and selection procedures that are being applied to the investment of his funds.

Conduct Affected by the Standard

The standard requires that the analyst make a conscientious effort to determine the needs and circumstances, as well as the goals and preferences, of each client (or fund) for whom a particular investment idea or investment course of action is being considered. An effort to gather information with respect to such client factors should ideally take place at the inception of any client relationship but should take place at some point before any specific investment recommendations or decisions are applied. Without the identification of such client factors (or fund objectives), it is not possible to judge whether a particular investment idea or investment course of action is suitable and appropriate.[1]

Because of the rapid growth of synthetic investment vehicles and derivative investment products, the analyst should pay careful attention to the leverage often inherent in such vehicles or products when considering them for application to a client's investment program. Such leverage, depending on the degree to which it is hedged, bears directly on the issue of suitability for the client.

The standard is intended to cover all the broad categories of investment disciplines—e.g., fundamental, quantitative, and technical. For a client to have an adequate understanding of an investment product or service that is being offered, it would be appropriate for the analyst or his firm to disclose the key elements of, and principles behind, the investment process that is used by the firm to select securities or groups of securities and to construct portfolios. Any significant changes to the process, or changes of personnel that might impact the process, must be disclosed accordingly. (See Standard III A.)

Under the Investment Advisers Act of 1940, registered investment advisers may be required to disclose significant changes of their professional staff or of their investment processes. The analyst must comply with all applicable laws and regulations, making required disclosures in, for example, SEC Form ADV. Furthermore, an analyst or his firm must be careful not to misrepresent the services or qualifications of the analyst or firm as described to clients or new business prospects. (See Standard III E.)

Application of the Standard

Preferably the discovery process for establishing client needs, circumstances, and objectives should be completed before making any investment recommendations or taking any investment action.

Because any given financial analyst or investment management firm is likely to have certain limitations, no analyst or firm may be well qualified to serve the needs of all prospective clients in a way that produces a satisfactory relationship. In large organizations, this determination may be made by associates of the financial analyst or investment manager who are involved with sales or business development. Whether made by the investment professional or an associate, an assessment of the likely fit between the established qualifications of the investment firm and the needs of a client should not be made without a reasonable amount of information about the client.[2] Such information should be acquired even in cases where prompt action is required. Exceptions should be limited.

An example of this exception would be a case in which a client relationship has just been established, a portfolio of securities (or other investments) already exists, and the proceeds of a maturing fixed income issue are just available. The prompt reinvestment of these proceeds in some cash equivalent form is likely to be entirely reasonable and would seem desirable under the circumstances. Undoubtedly, there will be other cases that represent variations of this same general theme. However, some information on client factors is necessary to determine whether there is reasonable basis for a satisfactory client relationship.

The effort to determine the needs and circumstances of each client is not a one-time proposition. Investment recommendations or decisions are usually part of an ongoing process that takes into account the diversity and changing nature of considerations that make up client factors. The passage of time is almost bound to produce changes that are important with respect to investment objectives. For an individual client, such changes might include the number of dependents, the amount of wealth beyond that represented in the portfolio, and the extent to which salary income provides for current income needs. With respect to an institutional client, such changes might relate to the magnitude of unfunded liabilities in a pension fund, the withdrawal privileges in an employee's savings plan, or the distribution requirements of a charitable foundation.

Without renewed efforts to update information concerning client factors, it is quite possible that one or more factors can change without the investment manager knowing about it. The proper frequency of such renewed efforts cannot be generalized. However, once a year is desirable unless there are obvious reasons why either a longer or shorter interval is necessary between assessments of client factors.

Perhaps the most important factor to be considered in matching appropriateness and suitability of an investment with a client's needs and circumstances is measuring that client's tolerance for risk. The investment professional must consider the possibilities of rapidly changing investment environments and their likely impact on a client's holdings, both individually and collectively.

Example 1: Smith, an investment adviser, has as clients Roberts, 60 years old, and Lane, 40. Both clients earn roughly the same salary, yet Roberts has a much higher risk tolerance. This is because he has a large asset base, part of which he is willing to invest aggressively; Lane wants only to achieve a steady rate of return with low volatility in order to pay for his children's education.

Comment: In Roberts's case, whether Smith recommends emerging growth stocks, high-yield bonds, buying on margin, or using options strategies, he should acquaint his client with the downside risks along with the upside potential of any recommended transactions. Smith should make sure that Roberts recognizes the higher risks that might be assumed and that he agrees in writing to proceed as planned.

Example 2: Walters, another investment adviser, suggests to a risk-averse client, Crosby, the use of covered call options in her equity portfolio as a means of enhancing income and partially offsetting any untimely depreciation in paper value should the stock market or other circumstances act unfavorably on the holdings. Walters educates Crosby about all possible outcomes, including the risks of incurring added tax liability if a stock rises in price and is called away or, conversely, seeing her holdings unprotected on the downside if prices drop precipitously.

Comment: With the benefit of needed information about client factors, an investment professional is ready to proceed with the application of investment recommendations or to initiate investment actions with respect to a specific portfolio. The analyst or manager needs to understand the basic characteristics of the particular investment being considered. If the manager is using quantitative methods that have been well researched but contain no fundamental research, this should be disclosed to the client. Understanding the basic characteristics of the investment is of great importance in judging the suitability of each investment on a stand-alone basis (which is still the primary focus of prudence under the laws that pertain to personal trusts), but it is especially important in determining the impact that the particular investment will have on the basic characteristics of the whole portfolio. Similarly important is understanding the effects of the investment characteristics of various quantitative strategies on the whole portfolio.[3]

Example 3: Although the characteristics of 1,000 shares of IBM would seem to be the same for any investor if viewed in isolation, the implications of such an investment varies greatly depending on the other investments held. IBM represents 90 percent of Bailey's investments, with the balance in U.S. Treasury bills. The implications of the IBM stock in this individual portfolio are vastly different from the implications of 1,000 shares held by Johnson Corporation's pension fund, a highly diversified common stock portfolio in which the IBM stock represents only 2 percent of the holdings. Furthermore, the incorporation of options-related strategies into the portfolio can potentially alter the risk characteristics of the IBM holding.

Comment: The federal law governing employee benefit funds (ERISA) has made it clear that the primary focus of prudence should be on the characteristics of a client's entire portfolio. Those who follow the case law developments with respect to personal trusts cite examples (cases settled in recent years) that suggest some departure from the earlier preoccupation with an issue-by-issue approach to the determination of prudence. There will probably be further movement in this direction, although progress is likely to be slow.

It is fortunate that the law may now be coming to recognize the advantages of focusing on the total portfolio, because it is the portfolio that provides the only meaningful interface between client factors and particular investment recommendations or actions. The basic characteristics of the entire portfolio will largely determine whether client factors are being served. Therefore, the most important aspects of a particular investment will be those that bear on the characteristics of the total portfolio.

Example 4: Newton has an annual income requirement of $200,000, with $125,000 coming from salary; his investment portfolio is expected to produce about $75,000 per annum. Because Newton's portfolio has a market value of $1,000,000, an average income yield of 7 ½ percent is required. However, in reaching that objective, none of the individual investments need to have a current income yield at that level. Some of the investments might not provide any current income, unless such were prohibited by state law. The only important consideration should be that all of the investments combined should produce Newton's $75,000 annual investment income.

Comment: It has long been recognized that the combination of several different investments is likely to provide a more acceptable level of risk exposure than having all funds represented in a single investment. This idea has been expressed many times through the admonition that it is unwise to have all of your eggs in one basket. As a result, some reasonable amount of diversification has been the norm for many portfolios, especially those managed by individuals or institutions that have some degree of fiduciary responsibility. Federal law (ERISA) makes it clear that fiduciaries should "diversify to minimize the risk of large losses."

Certain things that happen in the diversification process can now be seen with somewhat greater clarity as the practice of modern portfolio theory has advanced. The more unique characteristics (or risks) of an individual investment become partially or entirely neutralized when combined with other individual investments within a portfolio. The risk of many investment strategies can and should be analyzed and quantified in advance.

Example 5: One of the unique characteristics of ACE Home Building Company, is its sensitivity to high interest rates. As a result, the inclusion of ACE stock in a portfolio along with that of a public utility common stock (which also is adversely sensitive to high interest rates) produces certain portfolio characteristics. Such characteristics are different from those of a portfolio combining the ACE stock with the stock of a company that generated most of its revenue from the management of money market funds.

Comment: Other less unique characteristics (or risks) of an individual investment will tend to have an impact on the characteristics of the entire portfolio, somewhat in proportion to the market value of the portfolio. This set of more penetrating perceptions has fortified the notion that the primary focus should be on the characteristics of the total portfolio and has paved the way for somewhat greater use of individual investments that seem risky on a stand-alone basis, but which may be quite suitable within the context of a diversified portfolio.

The basic characteristics of the total portfolio should be considered in terms of both the relevant characteristics of the investments that make up the portfolio (as now constituted and as it might be altered) and the needs and circumstances of the client.[4] It is important to recognize that there are methods for judging the prospects for particular investments in relation to the impact any particular combination of investments might have on the characteristics of the whole portfolio—e.g., portfolio optimization programs. Such tools may be helpful in striving to find the proper balance between such client factors as income requirements, total rate of return aspirations, and risk tolerance.

Example 6: In a regular meeting with Jones, the people at Blue Chip Investment Advisers are careful to allow some time to review his current needs and circumstances. In doing so, it becomes apparent that some significant changes have recently taken place. A wealthy uncle left a portion of his estate to Jones, thereby increasing his net worth fourfold, to $1,000,000.

Comment: The inheritance significantly increased Jones's ability and willingness to assume risk and diminished the average yield required to meet current income needs. Accordingly, a somewhat higher equity ratio is deemed to be appropriate and the specific common stock recommendations are heavily tilted toward low-yield, growth-oriented issues.

Example 7: The investment committee of the Seventh National Bank and Trust Company is reviewing several pension accounts, including that of Quality Food Co. The portfolio manager on the account recommends the purchase of International Airlines common stock in an amount that would create modest overweighing of the airlines industry within the otherwise well-diversified (R^2 of .92 relative to the S&P 500) common stock portfolio.

Comment: The investment committee concludes that the proposal is reasonable in view of the expected impact of the issue on the characteristics of the portfolio. Furthermore, it is satisfied that the 60/40 debt-to-equity ratio is reasonable in relation to the provisions of the plan, its funding status, and the financial circumstances and operating characteristics of the sponsor.

Disclosure of Selection Procedures and Investment Process. The financial analyst should amply and adequately illustrate to clients and prospective clients the manner in which the analyst and his firm conduct the investment decision-making process. Moreover, because the investment process or management style relates to the development of the basis for all investment actions, there is a direct connection with Standard III A on reasonable basis and representations. On an ongoing basis, the financial analyst should keep existing clients and any other interested parties informed with respect to changes to the investment process. Only by thoroughly understanding the nature of the investment product or service for which a client is paying can that client adequately decide whether changes to that product or service would have a material impact on the desired investment returns.

Example 8: May & Associates is an aggressive growth manager that has represented itself since its inception as a specialist at investing in small capitalization stocks. In fact, May included among its selection criteria a maximum capitalization of $250 million for any given issue. After a string of successful years of superior relative performance, May expanded significantly its client base to the point where assets under management exceeded $3 billion. For liquidity purposes, the chief investment officer decided to lift the maximum permissible market cap ceiling to $500 million and changed the company's sales and marketing literature accordingly so as to inform prospective clients and third-party consultants.

Comment: Although May was correct to inform certain potentially interested parties about the investment process change, the firm should also have notified its existing clients. Among the latter group might be a number of clients who had retained May as a small-cap manager alongside mid-cap and large-cap firms in its multiple-manager representation. To such clients, May's change of criteria might be regarded as a style change that could distort the client's overall asset allocation.

Example 9: Assume the same original circumstances above, except that this time May decides to extend its universe of small-cap stocks by including a number of foreign stocks rather than lifting the ceiling from $250 million to $500 million.

Comment: The same guidelines apply for May to advise its clients because it may have been retained by selected clients specifically for its prowess at investing in domestic small-cap stocks. Other variations on the same theme might include introducing derivatives to emulate a certain market sector or relaxing various constraints such as portfolio beta, all without notifying the clients. In any such event, the manager should disclose changes to all interested parties.

Whether an investment manager bases either individual security selection or portfolio construction on the abilities of one person, a committee, or quantitative models, the standard is applicable to all investment disciplines. In effect, all are knowledge-based systems governed by the same rules and guidelines.

Example 10: RJZ Capital Management is a value-style active equity manager that selects stocks using a combination of four multifactor models. Owing to favorable results gained from backtesting the most recent ten years of available market data, RJZ decides to replace a simple price to trailing 12-months earnings model with a new dividend discount submodel which, by the firm's own design, will be a function of projected inflation rates, earnings growth rates, and interest rates.

Comment: Because a new and different valuation model has been introduced to its selection process, RJZ should communicate the change to its clients. Since the firm is moving away from one model that is based on hard data toward a new model that would be at least partially a function of RJZ's forecasting skills, the new submodel could be viewed potentially by some clients as a significant change rather than a mere refinement of RJZ's process.

Example 11: RJZ suffered a loss of the chief architect of its multifactor model valuation system. Without informing its clients, RJZ decided to redirect its talent and resources toward developing a passive equity management product that would emulate the performance of a major market index.

Comment: Not only has RJZ failed to disclose a substantial change to its investment process, but it may still be billing its clients fees that are representative of an active management fee schedule, not competitive with typical passive managers. Therefore, RJZ is not only in violation of Standard

III C, but also possibly Standard III G (Fair Dealing with Customers and Clients) and Standard III E (Misrepresentation of Services).

Example 12: At Fundamental Asset Management, Inc., the responsibility for selecting stocks for addition to the firm's "approved" list has just been shifted from individual security analysts to a committee consisting of the research director and three senior portfolio managers.

Comment: Some of Fundamental's clients might be concerned about the morale and motivation among the firm's best research analysts following the change. Moreover, clients might challenge the stock-picking track record of the portfolio managers and might even want to monitor the situation closely. Fundamental, therefore, should disclose the process change to all interested parties.

Procedures for Compliance

In fulfilling the basic provisions of this standard, a member must take into account the investment objectives and the needs and circumstances of the client in formulating an investment strategy. It is recommended that such investment objectives and the needs and circumstances be put into an investment policy statement for each client. In formulating an investment policy for the client, the items in Exhibit A should be taken into consideration.

The investor's objectives and constraints should be maintained and reviewed periodically to reflect any changes in the client's circumstances. Annual review is reasonable unless there are business or other reasons to review more or less frequently.

EXHIBIT A
INVESTMENT POLICY CONSIDERATIONS

Investor Objectives
1. Return Objectives (income, growth in principle, maintenance of purchase power).
2. Risk tolerance (stability of values).

Investor Constraints
1. Liquidity needs.
2. Investible funds (assets, liabilities or other commitments).
3. Time horizon.
4. Tax considerations.
5. Regulatory and legal circumstances.
6. Investor preferences, circumstances, and unique needs.

Footnotes

1. *Harvard College v. Amory*, 26 Mass. 446 at 461 (1830); *Bank of New York v. Spitzer*, 364 N.Y.S.2d 164 at 168 (1974).
2. *Romano v. Merrill Lynch, Pierce, Fenner & Smith*, 834 F.2d 523 at 529–30 (5th Cir. 1987).
3. *Chase v. Pevear*, 383 Mass. 350, 419 N.E.2d 1358 (1981); *In re Dickinson*, 152 Mass. 184 (1980).
4. *Chase v. Pevear*, 383 Mass. 364 at 364; *In re Dickinson*, 152 Mass. 184 at 187–89.

Standard III C
Reference Material

1. Employee Retirement Income Security Act of 1974 (ERISA), P.L. 93-406, H. Rep. 93-533, 93d Cong. 2d. Sess. *reprinted* in 1974 U.S. Code Cong. and Ad. News, 4639, 4656-660; H.C. Rep. No. 93-1280, 93d Cong. 2d. Sess. *reprinted* in 1974 U.S. Code Cong. and Ad. News, 5038, 5075-106; and S. Rep. No. 93-127, 93d Cong. 2d. Sess., *reprinted* in 1974 U.S. Code Cong. and Ad. News 4838, 4863-71.

2. SEC Rel. No. 34-27160, *Sales Practice Requirements for Certain Low-Priced Securities,* requires written suitability statements to customers before certain transactions (August 22, 1989).

3. 29 C.F.R. Part 2550, Rules and Regulations for Fiduciary Responsibility (1981).

4. Financial Executives Research Foundation, *Pension Asset Management: The Corporation Decision* (1980).

5. Financial Analysts Research Foundation, *Evolving Concepts of Prudence* (1976).

6. Bauman, *Guidelines for Communications to Investors* (Financial Analysts Research Foundation 1982).

7. Bines, *The Law of Investment Management,* 4.01-4.03 2b (1978).

8. Maginn and Tuttle, eds., *Managing Investment Portfolios: A Dynamic Process,* (Second Ed., Warren, Gorham & Lamont 1990).

9. Longstreth, *Modern Investment Management and the Prudent Man Rule* (Oxford University Press 1986).

10. Krikorian, *Fiduciary Standards in Pension and Trust Fund Management* (Butterworth Legal Publishers 1989).

11. Block, "Elements of Portfolio Construction," *Financial Analysts Journal* (May/June 1969).

12. Mennis, Valentine, and Mennis, "New Perspectives on Pension Fund Management," *Journal of Portfolio Management* (Spring 1981).

13. Walters, "The Law and Modern Portfolio Theory," *Investment Management and the Law,* (Boston Security Analysts Society, Inc. and the Financial Analysts Federation 1979).

14. Gillis and Hewitt, "Suitability," *Financial Analysts Journal* (September/October 1979). See also this article for citations to various suitability requirements of the Securities and Exchange Commission, the New York Stock Exchange, and the National Association of Securities Dealers, among others.

15. Gillis, "Measurement of Prudence," *Financial Analysts Journal* (January/February 1977).

16. Gillis and Weld, "Fiduciary Responsibility Under the 1974 Pension Act," *Financial Analysts Journal* (May/June 1975).

17. Hansen and Delphey, "Recent Developments in Broker–Customer Litigation," *Securities and Commodities Regulation* (January 27, 1988).

18. Modigliani and Pogue, "An Introduction to Risk and Return—Concepts and Evidence," *Financial Analysts Journal* (March/April 1974).

19. Sharpe, "Evolution of Modern Portfolio Theory" based on a talk at Wells Fargo Bank on June 18, 1979.

20. "Ruder Questions Wisdom of Selling Risky Products to Individual Investors" *Securities Regulation and Law Reporter* (Bureau of National Affairs, January 18, 1988).

21. "NASSA Customer Hotline Raises Disclosure, Suitability Issues" *Securities Regulation and Law Reporter* (Bureau of National Affairs, November 27, 1987).

III. RESEARCH REPORTS, INVESTMENT RECOMMENDATIONS AND ACTIONS

D. Prohibition Against Plagiarism

The financial analyst shall not, when presenting material to his employer, associates, customers, clients, or the general public, copy or use in substantially the same form, material prepared by other persons without acknowledging its use and identifying the name of the author or publisher of such material. The analyst may, however, use without acknowledgment factual information published by recognized financial and statistical reporting services or similar sources.

Purpose of the Standard

The purpose of this standard is to state the responsibility of members and nonmember holders of, and candidates for, the CFA designation to avoid plagiarism in the preparation of material for distribution to an employer, associates, customers, clients, or the general public. Plagiarism is defined as copying or using, in substantially the same form, materials prepared by others, without acknowledging the source of the material or identifying the author and publisher of such material. The only permitted exception is the use, without acknowledgment, of factual information published by recognized financial and statistical reporting services or similar sources.

Plagiarism is abhorrent because it is dishonest to steal the ideas and work of others and pass them off as one's own. In ethical terms, a financial analyst indulging in plagiarism does not conduct himself with integrity.

Conduct Affected by the Standard

By its very nature, the practice of financial analysis makes use of myriad financial, economic, and statistical data in the investment decision-making process. Through various publications and presentations, the practicing financial analyst is constantly exposed to the work of others and to the temptation to use it for his own purposes without proper acknowledgment.

Plagiarism in financial analysis can take various forms. Years ago, one of the simplest (and most flagrant) examples was to take a research report or study done by another firm or person, change the names, and release the material as one's own original analysis. Fortunately, this kind of malpractice is not prevalent today because of the development of stock exchange rules, government regulations, and the monitoring efforts of private professional organizations such as AIMR in the investment field.[1]

More subtle (but no less abhorrent) practices include using excerpts from articles or reports prepared by others, either verbatim or with only slight change in wording, without acknowledgment; citing specific quotations said to be attributable to "leading analysts," "investment experts," or similar designations, without specific reference; presenting statistical estimates of forecasts prepared by others with the source identified but without hedge statements or caveats that may have been used; using charts and graphs without stating their source; and copying proprietary computerized spreadsheets or algorithms without seeking the cooperation or authorization of their creators.

By plagiarizing, the analyst is not only stealing the ideas and words of others, but is also exposing himself to violations of Standards III A and III B by making recommendations that may not have a reasonable basis and may not avoid material misrepresentations. By copying someone else's work, the analyst may be copying serious deficiencies and attaching his name and approval to them.

The following statement pertaining to Standard III D was adopted and published by the Board of Directors of the Financial Analysts Federation in 1980 and reaffirmed by the AIMR Board of Governors in 1990:

Statement of Board of Governors on Plagiarism. "The Board of Governors calls to the attention of all members the seriousness with which it views plagiarism. Standard III D of the Standards of Professional Conduct provides that a financial analyst who prepares material for distribution must not copy or use in substantially the same form material prepared by others without due acknowledgment. Failure to abide by Standard III D is plagiarism. Plagiarism is an offense to the profession and the public; in many cases, it is also a violation of the copyright laws and will expose the offender to civil suit. A writer who quotes from another writer must in most cases obtain permission and give proper attribution for the quotation. A writer must not only avoid verbatim copying without acknowledgment, but must also avoid using passages with alterations that seek to disguise or conceal the origin but which do not materially change the form of expression.

"The terminology of the standard easily gives the impression that it is directed at written materials. However, the standard also applies to plagiarism in oral communications such as through group meetings; visits with associates, clients, and customers; use of the audio/video media (which is rapidly increasing), and telecommunications such as through electronic data transfer and the outright copying of electronic media.

"One of the insidious practices in the investment field has been the preparation of research reports based on multiple sources of information without acknowledging the sources. Such information would include, for example, ideas, statistical compilations, and forecasts combined to give the appearance of original work. Of course, there is no monopoly on ideas, but the fair financial analyst should give credit when it is clearly due. Analysts should be warned against the use of undocumented forecasts, earning projections, asset values, and the like. Sources should be revealed or at least the research studies should state, 'Our analysis indicates (or shows) that...,' to bring the responsibility directly back to the author of the report or the firm involved. Statements of fact should be documented.

"The standard provides, however, that 'factual information published by recognized financial and statistical reporting services or similar sources' can be used without an acknowledgment. This provision was introduced to eliminate laborious references to information already in the public realm."

Application of the Standard

Example 1: Grant, a research analyst for a Canadian brokerage firm, has specialized in the Canadian mining industry for the past ten years. He read an extensive research report on Deep Shaft Mining, Ltd., by Barton, another analyst. Barton provided extensive statistics analyzing the mineral reserves, production capacity, selling rates, and marketing factors affecting Deep Shaft's operations. He also noted that initial drilling results on a new ore body, which had not been made public, might show the existence of mineral zones that could increase the life of Deep Shaft's main mines but cited no specific data as to the initial drilling results. Grant called an officer of Deep Shaft who read excerpts of the report of the initial drilling results to him over the telephone. This report indicated that the expected life of the main mines would be tripled. Grant added these statistics to Barton's report and circulated it as his own report within his firm.

Comment: Grant plagiarized Barton's report by reproducing large parts of it in his own report without acknowledgment. Moreover, if the Barton report were copyrighted, Grant very likely violated that copyright. He may also have violated Standard II C by including material nonpublic information in the report that could have caused some employees of the firm to make purchases on the basis of the information before the information was made public.

Example 2: Swanson is a senior analyst in the investment research department of Ballard and Company. Ballard was asked by Apex Corporation to assist in acquiring the stock of Campbell Company, a financial consulting firm, and to prepare a report recommending that stockholders of Campbell agree to the acquisition. Another firm, Davis and Company, had already prepared a report for Apex that analyzed both Apex and Campbell and recommended an exchange ratio.

Apex gave the Davis report to Ballard officers who passed it on to Swanson, who reviewed the Davis report together with other available material on Apex and Campbell companies. From her analysis, she concluded that the common stock of both Campbell and Apex represented good value at their current prices; however, she felt that the Davis report did not consider all of the factors a Campbell stockholder would need to know to make a decision. Swanson reported her conclusions to the partner in charge and was told to "use the Davis report, change a few words, sign your name and get it out."

Comment: If Swanson did as requested, she would violate Standard III D. She could refer to those portions of the Davis report she agreed with, if she identifies Davis as the source, and add her own analysis and conclusions to the report before signing and distributing it. If she did not add her analysis including additional relevant factors, she violated Standard III B. If the Davis report were copyrighted, the propriety of using it without permission should be questioned. If the partner was an AIMR member, he violated Standard II B by assisting in the violation of the Standards of Professional Conduct and he violated Standard II D by rendering inappropriate supervision.

Example 3: Chippendale, a quantitative analyst for Double Alpha, Inc., returns from a seminar very excited. In that seminar, Jorrely, a well-publicized quantitative analyst at a national brokerage firm, discussed one of his new models in great detail, and Chippendale is intrigued by the new concepts. He proceeds to test this model, making some minor mechanical changes but retaining the concept, until he produces some very positive results. He quickly announces to his supervisors in the firm that he has discovered a new model and that clients and perspective clients alike should be informed of this positive finding as ongoing proof of Alpha's continuing innovation and value added.

Comment: Although Chippendale tested Jorrely's model on his own and even slightly modified it, he must still acknowledge the original source of the idea. Chippendale can certainly take credit for the final, practical results; he can also support his conclusions with his own test. The credit for the innovative thinking, however, must be awarded to Jorrely.

The permission to use recognized sources of factual information without acknowledgment is susceptible to abuse, and it must be employed with careful discretion. The term "recognized" is both deliberately broad but its implication is that the source will be both worthy of confidence and reliable. It is generally accepted in the profession that factual materials supplied by Standard & Poor's and Moody's have these attributes. Publications of the federal government and Federal Reserve System are similarly recognized. Clearly there are other sources that deserve such recognition. However, this is a matter of experience and good judgment. Financial analysts should be wary of using without acknowledgment materials supplied by sources that have not established a credible record over a considerable period or by sources that do not have a clearly identifiable staff of professionals who prepare financial and statistical reports.

Procedures for Compliance

In preparing research reports or conclusions of analysis, analysts should take these steps:

■ *Make copies.* Keep copies of all research reports, articles containing research ideas, material with new statistical methodology, or other materials that were relied upon in preparing the research report.

■ *Attribute sources.* Attribute to their sources any direct quotations, including use of projections, tables, statistics, model/product ideas, or new methodologies prepared by persons other than recognized financial and statistical reporting services or similar sources.

■ *Attribute summaries.* Attribute to their sources paraphrases or summaries of material prepared by others. For example, the author of a research report on Brown Company may summarize the report of another analyst on Hogan Corp., Brown's chief competitor, in the course of his report in order to support his analysis of Brown's competitive position. The analyst should acknowledge his reliance on the report on Hogan in his report on Brown.

■ *Determine the proper use of copyrighted materials of other authors.* Analysts who review research reports have a responsibility to make sure that all of the analysis in a research report is thorough and supported by adequate research. (See Standard II D.) In the course of reviewing a research report, the supervisor should make sure that there are work papers in the file supporting the reasonableness of the analyst's conclusions. (See Standard III A.) In the course of this review the supervisor should also ask these questions:

1. Does the author's investigation, including his analysis of financial reports and factual information published by recognized financial and statistical reporting services, support all of his analysis and conclusions? If not, are there materials prepared by others in the file supporting his conclusions?

2. If the file contains materials prepared by others, but the analyst's report is based solely on his own investigation and analysis, what use did the author make of the materials prepared by others?

Footnotes

1. New York Stock Exchange, Rule 472, Communications with the Public.

Standard III D
Reference Material

1. Securities and Exchange Commission, *Report of the Special Study of the Securities Markets,* Part I, at 330-87 (1963).
2. National Association of Securities Dealers, *Rules of Fair Practice,* Article III, §35, Communications with the Public.
3. New York Stock Exchange, Rule 472, Communications with the Public.

III. RESEARCH REPORTS, INVESTMENT RECOMMENDATIONS AND ACTIONS

E. Prohibition Against Misrepresentation of Services

The financial analyst shall not make any statements, orally or in writing, which misrepresent (1) the services that the analyst or his firm is capable of performing for the client, (2) the qualifications of such analyst or his firm, or (3) the expected performance of any investment.

The financial analyst shall not make, orally or in writing, explicitly or implicitly, any assurances about or guarantees of any investment or its return except communication of accurate information as to the terms of the investment instrument and the issuer's obligations under the instrument.

Purpose of the Standard

The purpose of this standard is to state the responsibility of AIMR members and nonmember holders of, and candidates for, the CFA designation to avoid misrepresentation with regard to either the services, qualifications, or the expected performance of any investment, and to prohibit inappropriate assurances about any investment or its return. If a misrepresentation appears in a research report or as part of an investment recommendation, it will also violate Standard III A 3.[1]

Conduct Affected by the Standard

Misrepresentation can be defined as the act of representing improperly or imperfectly or giving a false impression. Although the standard is intended to apply to misrepresentation that is material—which in context can be broadly defined as important, significant, or consequential—it does not condone inconsequential or inadvertent misrepresentation. A material misrepresentation includes any untrue statement of a material fact or any statement that is otherwise materially false or misleading.

The standard applies whether a single major misrepresentation or a series of lesser misrepresentations is involved.

Willful misrepresentation is probably easier to spot than instances of unintended carelessness by financial analysts or firms, but penalties are involved in either case.[2] (See also Standard III A 3.)

Care should be taken to ensure that misrepresentation does not occur in either oral representations, advertising, whether in the press or through brochures, or in written materials, whether publicly disseminated or not.[3] Written materials for a general audience include, but not limited to, research reports, market letters, newspaper columns, and books. Truthful statements of fact, adequately supported, can of course be made.

The standard prohibits statements or assumptions that an investment is "guaranteed,"[4] or that superior returns can be expected based on the assumption that an analyst's past success shall or may be repeated in the future. This does not preclude truthful statements that some investments are in fact guaranteed in one way or another or that they have guaranteed returns, such as certain types of insurance contracts, short-term Treasury securities, and insured bank deposits.

The standard also prohibits inferences that an analyst's membership affiliation with the AIMR or his achievement of any or all three levels of the CFA examination process, including award of the CFA designation itself, empower the analyst with a) the ability to produce superior investment results or b) any special or unique knowledge or expertise with regard to financial and investment matters (see also Standard VIII).

In an attempt to minimize the downside risk to asset values or to change expected returns, the concept of "hedging" and/or the use of other strategies have gained prominence. These strategies may involve sacrificing a degree of upside reward during rising stock markets in exchange for obtaining a measure of protection in declining markets. Investment professionals must be careful to point the positive and negative attributes of these strategies.

Application of the Standard

The following are examples of applications of the standard in various areas.[5]

Example 1: Rogers is a partner in the firm of Rogers, Black and Co., a small firm offering investment advisory services. She assures a prospective client, Goff, who has just inherited a million dollars, that "we can perform all the financial and investment services you need." In fact, Rogers, Black is well equipped to provide investment advice but cannot provide a full array of financial and investment services.

Comment: Rogers has violated Standard III E by orally misrepresenting the services her firm can perform for the prospective client. She should have limited herself to describing the range of investment advisory services Rogers, Black and Co. could provide, offering to help Goff obtain the financial and investment services that her firm could not provide.

Example 2: Brooks, a trainee at a brokerage firm, represents himself to several of his employer's clients as a "portfolio management specialist." Relying on his representations and advice, clients purchased securities and held them while they were declining in value.

Comment: Brooks misrepresented his qualifications and, in addition to violating Standard III E, violated Section 10b of the Securities Exchange Act of 1934.[6]

Example 3: White, a securities salesman for Johnson & Co., sells securities of Bland Development Co. stating that "this strongly recommended investment will give you a 100 percent capital gain within six months and much more in the longer term." All that White knows about the company is that it has just licensed a patent to a major manufacturer of food containers for a new form of packaging.

Comment: White's assurances are unsupported by the facts and are in violation of this standard and Standard III A 3. He should have more information about the company before making any recommendation; he should disclose to clients that the gain cannot be assured; and he should warn investors of the risks. (See Standards III A and III C.) By making unsupported assurances, he may also be violating the anti-fraud provisions of the U.S. federal securities laws. (See *SEC v. Hanly,* 415 F.2d 589 [2d Cir. 1969].)

Example 4: Cullen Brokerage Services, Inc., uses radio advertisements that claim investors can increase their return by investing in money market funds rather than municipal bonds. The advertisements do not mention that the current after-tax yield on most money market funds is less than that on municipal bonds for investors in the highest personal tax brackets.

Comment: The advertisements are misleading to a large class of potential investors because they predict performance for all investors and do not distinguish the impact on investors in high tax brackets.

Procedures for Compliance

Unintentional misrepresentations concerning the services an analyst or investment manager or firm is capable of performing, or the qualifications of an analyst or his firm, can be prevented if each employee of a firm and each analyst/manager understands the limits of the firm's or the individual's capabilities and the need to be accurate and complete in presentations.

Firms can provide guidance for employees who make written or oral presentations to clients or potential clients by providing a written list of the firm's available services and a description of the firm's qualifications. This written list should suggest ways of describing the firm's services, qualifications, and compensation that are both accurate and suitable for client or customer presentations. Registered investment advisers in the United States are required to deliver a written description of these matters under the brochure rule of the Investment Advisers Act (Rule 204-3). In certain instances, a report of disciplinary actions taken against the firm or an employee and any precarious financial condition must be provided to clients and prospective clients.[7]

Individual analysts should make certain that they understand the services the firm can perform and its qualifications, whether or not the firm provides guidance. In addition, each analyst can prepare an inventory of his own qualifications and a list of the services he is personally capable of performing as a basis for accurate presentations to clients or customers. Use of a written list or inventory is suggested because it will help the analyst focus on the firm's and his own strengths and limitations.

Misrepresentations about the expected performance of an investment are best avoided by compliance with Standard III A. If an analyst has a reasonable basis for investment recommendations, he will not make unsupported statements about the recommendations, and he is less likely to make misleading statements.

There is a substantial body of law relating to disclosure and use of information about a firm's capabilities and performance and the past and expected performance of securities. This emanates from several sources, including the SEC, state and provincial securities commissions, stock exchanges, and the National Association of Securities Dealers. Among these are disclosures about "exit fees" and an SEC no-action letter stating that if sales literature is disseminated in a language other than English, a prospectus must also be available in that language.[8] A firm should have procedures for the preparation and review of this information, which almost invariably will involve the firm's legal or compliance departments.

Footnotes

1. *Morrill-Stanfill & Co.*, [1978] Fed. Sec. L. Rep. (CCH) ¶81,682 (April 13, 1978).
2. *In re Melhorn*, SEC Administrative Proceeding File No. 3-7165 (March 31, 1989); see also *In re Investors Portfolio Management, Inc.*, SEC Administrative Proceeding File No. 3-6729 (June 26, 1990).
3. *In re Investors Portfolio Management, Inc.*, SEC Administrative Proceeding File No. 3-6729 (June 26, 1990) (advertisement failed to disclose that high yield product was based on an unusually risky investment strategy); *In re Security Evaluation, Inc.*, [1971–2] Fed. Sec. L. Rep. (CCH) ¶78,786 (May 8, 1972) (failure to describe limitations of "device" whereby firm performed statistical analysis of clients' portfolios); *In re Spear*, SEC Rel. No. IA-188, [1964–66] Fed. Sec. L. Rep. (CCH) ¶77,216 (March 25, 1965) (advertisement claiming ability to forecast securities prices failed to disclose the inherent difficulty thereof). For further elucidation of the constraints on advertising, see *In re Bridwell & Co.*, SEC Rel. No. IA-180, [1964–66] Fed. Sec. L. Rep. (CCH) ¶77,183 (December 18, 1964); SEC Private Letter Ruling, A.R. Schmeidler & Co., Inc.
4. *In re Grillo*, SEC Administrative Proceeding File No. 3-7292, (December 21, 1989).
5. See Securities and Exchange Commission, *Statement of Staff Interpretive Position* on "Applicability of the Investment Advisers Act to Financial Planners, Pension Consultants, and Other Persons Who Provide Investment Advisory Services as a Component of Other Financial Services," particularly at 14-19, Application of Antifraud Provisions, on duty to disclose material facts, Rel. No. IA-1092 (1987).
6. *Marbury Management, Inc. v. Kohn*, 629 F.2d 705 (2d Cir. 1980). *In re Paul K. Peers, Inc.*, SEC Rel. No. IA-177, [1964–66] Fed. Sec. L. Rep. (CCH) ¶77,222 (March 22, 1965).
7. Securities and Exchange Commission, *Financial and Disciplinary Information that Investment Advisers Must Disclose to Clients*, Release No. IA-1083 (September 25, 1987).
8. SEC no-action letter, October 16, 1989, addressing American Funds that if sales literature or advertisements are distributed in another language, a prospectus is also needed in that language.

Standard III E
Reference Material

1. Investment Advisers Act of 1940, Rule 206(4)-1; Rules 204-2 and 204-3.
2. (Ontario) Securities Act, R.S.O. 1980, c. 466, §1(1)24, Misrepresentation.
3. Canadian Interim National Policy Statement No. 42, "Advertising of Securities on Radio and Television," 1988 and Draft National Policy No. 43, "Advertisement of Securities," (1989).
4. Securities and Exchange Commission, *Guide to Broker–Dealer Compliance: Report of the Broker–Dealer Model Compliance Program Advisory Committee*, Chapter VI, "Advertising and Sales Literature" (November 13, 1974).
5. Securities and Exchange Commission, *Advertising by Investment Companies*, rules adopted effective May 1, 1988, Release Nos. 33-6753; IC-16245; (February 2, 1988); *Record Keeping by Investment Advisers*, rules adopted effective October 20, 1988, Release No. IA-1135, amended, July 27, 1989; and SEC *Staff Interpretive Letter* "Regarding Mutual Fund Advertising Rules" (May 13, 1988).
6. National Association of Securities Dealers, *Rules of Fair Practice*, Article III, §19(a), Customers' Securities or Funds, Improper Use, and 35, Communications with the Public.
7. New York Stock Exchange, Rules 352, Guarantees and Sharing in Accounts, 435 (5), Miscellaneous Prohibitions, Circulation of Rumors, 472, Communications with the Public, and 791, Communications to Customers.
8. "Is Beta Dead?" *Institutional Investor* (July 1980).
9. Roll, "Return to Simpler Methods," *Pensions & Investments* (August 18, 1980).

III. RESEARCH REPORTS, INVESTMENT RECOMMENDATIONS AND ACTIONS

F. Performance Presentation Standards

1. The financial analyst shall not make any statements, orally or in writing, which misrepresent the investment performance that the analyst or his firm has accomplished or can reasonably be expected to achieve.

2. If an analyst communicates directly or indirectly individual or firm performance information to a client or prospective client, or in a manner intended to be received by a client or prospective client ("Performance Information"), the analyst shall make every reasonable effort to ensure that such Performance Information is a fair, accurate and complete presentation of such performance.

3. The financial analyst shall inform his employer about the existence and content of the Association for Investment Management and Research's Performance Presentation Standards (See Appendix A), and this Standard III F, and shall encourage his employer to adopt and use the Performance Presentation Standards.

4. If Performance Information complies with the Performance Presentation Standards, the analyst shall be presumed to be in compliance with III F 2 above.

5. An analyst presenting Performance Information may use the following legend on the Performance Information presentation, but only if the analyst has made every reasonable effort to ensure that such presentation is in compliance with the Performance Presentation Standards in all material respects:

"This report has been prepared and presented in compliance with the Performance Presentation Standards of the Association for Investment Management and Research."

Purpose of the Standard

The purpose of this standard is to state the responsibility of AIMR members and nonmember holders of, and candidates for, the CFA designation to avoid misrepresentation with regard to investment performance of the member or his firm. The overall philosophy underlying this standard is the need for full disclosure of investment performance data to clients and client prospects. Certain statistics and presentation data have been delineated as basic requirements. Nevertheless, the standard is a performance *presentation* standard, not performance *measurement* standard. Therefore, the central theme is that investment managers may present any reasonable statistics provided that their derivation, and particularly any exclusions therefrom, are highlighted and made abundantly clear. **The standard takes effect on January 1, 1993.**

Conduct Affected by the Standard

An analyst must give a fair and complete presentation of performance information whenever communicating data with respect to the performance history of individual accounts, composites of groups of accounts, or composites of the analyst's or the firm's results. Accordingly, misrepresentations of past performance or reasonably expected performance are prohibited.

If such performance information complies with the AIMR Performance Presentation Standards (See Appendix A), the analyst shall be presumed to be in compliance with this standard. Care should also be exercised in observing Standards III E and II A.

Each analyst must inform his employer of the content of the AIMR Performance Presentation Standards and encourage their adoption.

Application of the Standard

An analyst presenting performance information may use the following legend in the presentation thereof, but only if such presentation is fully in compliance with the Performance Presentation Standards in all material respects: "This report has been prepared and presented in compliance with the Performance Presentation Standards of the Association for Investment Management and Research."

The following is an example of the application of Standard III F 1 and 2.

Example 1: Taylor Trust Co. represents to its potential clients that "you can expect steady 25 percent annual compound growth of the value of your investments over the year," pointing to the performance of its common trust fund over the past two years. Although Taylor's common trust fund increased at the rate of 25 percent per year for one year in which the entire market increased by about that amount, it never averaged that growth for more than one year, and the average rate of growth of all of its trust accounts for five years was 5 percent per year.

Comment: Taylor's statement is materially misleading and in violation of Standard III F in two respects. First, it should have disclosed that 25 percent growth occurred only in one year and, second, it did not include client accounts other than in its common trust fund. Additional details about the performance of both categories of accounts should have been supplied as well as caveats that no growth rate can be assured and that risks are involved in virtually all investments. To the extent Taylor's statement was delivered in the context of recommending a specific investment or investments, it violated Standard III A 3 as well.[1]

Misrepresentations about the investment performance of the firm can be avoided if the analyst maintains data about the firm's investment performance in written form and understands the classes of investments or accounts to which that data applies and the risks and limitations inherent in using such data. In analyzing information about the firm's investment performance, the analyst should ask:

1. How many years' past performance does this information reflect? Does it reflect performance for the prior year only, after several years of poor performance? An average of several years' performance? Has the performance been measured in accordance with AIMR standards? (See Appendix A.)

2. Does investment performance vary widely among different classes of funds or accounts? If so, the analyst must consider describing investment performance by classes and not by an overall average figure, accurately explaining what the performance figures represent.

This standard's requirement for full disclosure in presenting portfolio performance is embodied in the Performance Presentation Standards. Generally, the approach is based on time-weighted total returns (before management fees but with the omission always noted when presenting data) for each year (for no fewer than ten years if possible) of operation (see Appendix A).

On related matters, the Investment Advisers Act establishes conditions on various types of communications and prohibits others. If past recommendations are used, they must meet several criteria; the use of hypothetical portfolios is discouraged.

Procedures for Compliance

Analysts should refer to the Report of the Performance Presentation Standards Implementation Committee, forthcoming in early 1993, published by AIMR. This comprehensive report contains the performance presentation standards, implementation guidelines, extensive explanations of their application, a summary of applicable legal standards, performance calculations, a checklist, and sample performance tables, among other materials. Appendix A to this *Handbook* contains a summary of the mandatory requirements and disclosures of the revised performance presentation standards and related materials. The 1993 report updates the Implementation Committee Report of December 1991, and will contain the revised performance presentation standards.

Footnotes

1. Securities and Exchange Commission, *Advertising by Investment Companies,* rules adopted effective May 1, 1988, Release Nos. 33-6753; IC-16245; February 2, 1988, and amended July 27, 1989.

Standard III F
Reference Material

1. Association for Investment Management and Research, *Answers to Common Questions about AIMR's Performance Presentation Standards* (Charlottesville, Va., September, 1992).
2. Association for Investment Management and Research, *Report of the Performance Presentation Standards Implementation Committee* (Charlottesville, Va., December, 1991, revised May 1992).
3. Institute of Chartered Financial Analysts and the Financial Analysts Federation, *Performance Measurement: Setting the Standard, Interpreting the Numbers* (Charlottesville, Va., January/February, 1989).
4. Association for Investment Management and Research, *Performance Reporting for Investment Managers: Applying the AIMR Performance Presentation Standards* (Charlottesville, Va., 1991).
5. Financial Analysts Federation, *Report of the FAF Committee for Performance Presentation Standards*, (Revised August 2, 1990).
6. Investment Counsel Association of America, Inc., *The Standards of Measurement and Use for Investment Performance Data*, (1972); reprinted 1985.
7. Beebower and Kantor, "A Look at Performance-Based Fees," 3 *SEI Research Reports* 2 (April 1987).
8. "Broker Made Promises Firm Could Not Keep, Reparations Award Upheld," *Securities Regulation & Law Report* (Bureau of National Affairs May 29, 1987).
9. Ferguson, "Performance Measurement Doesn't Make Sense," *Financial Analysts Journal* (May/June 1980).
10. McConnell, "Can Phony Performance Numbers Be Policed?" *Institutional Investor* (June 1989).
11. Murphy, "Why No One Can Tell Who's Winning," *Financial Analysts Journal* (May/June 1980).
12. Treynor, "The Future of Performance Measurement," *Financial Analysts Journal* (July/August 1980).

III. RESEARCH REPORTS, INVESTMENT RECOMMENDATIONS AND ACTIONS

G. Fair Dealing with Customers and Clients

The financial analyst shall act in a manner consistent with his obligation to deal fairly with all customers and clients when (1) disseminating investment recommendations, (2) disseminating material changes in prior investment advice, and (3) taking investment action.

Purpose of the Standard

The purpose of this standard is to state the responsibility of AIMR members and nonmember holders of, and candidates for, the CFA designation to treat all clients, customers, and the public fairly when disseminating investment recommendations or material changes in prior investment advice or when taking investment action. Only through the fair treatment of all parties will the confidence of the investing public be maintained in the profession of financial analysis and investment management.

Conduct Affected by the Standard

This standard covers the manner in which investment recommendations or material changes in prior recommendations are disseminated to customers or clients. As the issuance of an investment recommendation can affect the market value, this standard states the obligation of each financial analyst to ensure that information is disseminated in such a manner that all customers or clients have a fair opportunity to act upon such recommendations.[1]

The standard covers the conduct of two broadly defined groups of financial analysts. The first includes financial analysts whose primary function is the preparation of investment recommendations to be disseminated either externally or internally for the use of others in making investment decisions. Most financial analysts employed by brokerage firms are included in this group; however, it also includes financial analysts employed by other organizations such as investment counseling or advisory firms, banks, and insurance companies, if their primary responsibility is the preparation of recommendations to be acted upon by others in their organizations, including those who take investment actions for clients.

The second group includes those analysts whose primary function is taking investment action (portfolio management) based on research recommendations prepared internally or received from external sources. Investment action, like an investment recommendation, can affect market value; consequently, this section of the standard states the obligation of each member when taking investment action to ensure that all customers or clients are treated fairly in light of their investment objectives and circumstances, notwithstanding the fact that the member may have discretionary power over certain accounts and not over others.

In the case of either group, the fairness in the handling and execution of customer/client orders ahead of the interests of the firm or its employees cannot be overemphasized[2] (see Standard IV).

Application of the Standard

Customers or clients must be treated fairly. In an era of expanding institutional financial power, every effort to treat all customers fairly and impartially must be maintained. A customer may have multiple relationships with an institution. For example, a bank may hold many positions for a customer, such as corporate trustee, pension fund manager, manager of funds for individuals employed by the customer, loan originator, creditor, and the like. Care must be exercised to treat all clients fairly including those with whom multiple relationships do not exist. The term "fairly" was consciously chosen to express the principle that the financial analyst must take care not to discriminate against any customers or clients when disseminating investment recommendations or taking investment action. It does not say "equally," as it would be physically impossible to reach all customers or clients simultaneously whether by mail, telephone, computer, facsimile transmission, or wire. In addition, not all recommendations or investment actions are suitable for all clients and customers.

To comply with this standard, financial analysts should be certain that procedures are established to ensure fair treatment of all customers. Good business practice dictates that initial recommendations be made available to all customers if they indicate an interest. Although a recommendation need not be communicated to all customers, the selection process by which customers receive it should be based upon suitability and known interest and not upon any preferred or favored status. A common practice is to communicate recommendations within the firm and to customers simultaneously.

An investment recommendation is any opinion expressed by a financial analyst in regard to purchasing, selling, or holding a given security or other investment. This opinion can be disseminated to customers or clients through an initial detailed research report, a brief update report, by addition to or deletion from a recommended list, or simply by oral communication. Because it is so difficult to determine what type of communication is for general distribution rather than internal use only, a workable guideline is to consider that any recommendation is disseminated if it is distributed to anyone outside the organization that initiated the investment recommendation.

Whenever a material change in an investment recommendation has been made, it is the financial analyst's responsibility to ensure that this change is disseminated on a basis that is fair to all customers and clients. Although the definition of material change is subjective in nature, and reasonable persons may have different opinions, a financial analyst should err on the conservative side and, if there is any doubt, the change should be treated as material.

It is very likely that the duty to customers is more critical when a firm changes its recommendation than when it makes an initial recommendation. For example, in its *Guide to Broker–Dealer Compliance* (see note 2 in Reference Material below), the Securities and Exchange Commission stated:

"Material changes in the broker–dealer's prior investment advice arising from subsequent research should be communicated to all current clients who the broker–dealer knows have purchased and may be holding securities on the basis of its earlier advice, at least under circumstances where to do so would not impose an unreasonable hardship on the broker. Persons placing orders contrary to a current firm recommendation should ordinarily be advised of the recommendation before the order is accepted."

A material change in a firm's recommendation is one that could be expected to affect the investor's judgment or motivate an informed buyer or seller to take investment action. This definition is similar to the definition of material information in the inside information rule (see Standard II C). Material change includes changes in recommendations based on opinions reasonably certain to have a substantive impact on the market value of the investment when disclosed. A change of recommendation from buy to sell and sell to buy would generally be material.

Example 1: Ames, a well-known and respected analyst, follows the mainframe computer industry. In the course of his research, he finds that a small, relatively unknown company whose shares are traded over the counter has just signed significant contracts with a few of the companies he follows. After doing a considerable amount of investigation, he decides to write a research report on the company and recommend purchase. While the report is being reviewed by the company for factual accuracy, Ames schedules a luncheon with a few of his best clients to discuss the company. At the luncheon, he mentions the purchase recommendation scheduled to be sent early the following week to all the firm's clients.

Comment: Ames violated Standard III G by disseminating the purchase recommendation to the clients with whom he had lunch a week before the recommendation was sent.

Example 2: Eliot is an analyst with a brokerage firm. The firm has a large investment advisory department that manages four mutual funds as well as a large number of other discretionary and non-discretionary accounts. Eliot has been recommending purchase of Harris Co. as an excellent long-term investment for a number of years. Many of her firm's brokerage and advisory clients, as well as three of the mutual funds, had purchased shares in the company on the basis of her recommendations. Two days before the firm's monthly research list, which includes buy, hold, and sell recommendations, was to be sent to the printer for distribution to all clients, Eliot learned from Harris's largest customer that it would not renew a significant service contract with Harris that was scheduled to expire in six months. She deduced that the loss of this contract would eventually have a material impact on the company by interrupting Harris's long-term revenue and earnings growth trend. However, since she did not have time to write a follow-up report on Harris, she decided only to change her recommendation from buy to hold. Because she had on earlier occasions switched her rating from buy to hold, albeit based on relative price considerations, she did not feel compelled to broadcast this latest change. Nevertheless, on the day the research list was delivered to the brokerage firm for mailing to customers, one of the mutual fund managers called to inquire if her change was due to price considerations or a change in fundamentals. She replied, "A change in fundamentals." She gave the same answer to a joint meeting of the research and investment management departments later that week. Immediately upon hearing the reason, but still before broad distribution of the monthly research list, the fund manager and the other account managers sold all the shares held in their performance-oriented clients' portfolios over which they had complete discretion.

Comment: Eliot should have disclosed the reason for her change in investment recommendation by a summary report to be released with the research list. She should not have disclosed that information selectively to the mutual fund manager and the research and investment management departments. Even if she had made such a report, the mutual fund manager should not have acted until after the report was disseminated.

This is a difficult area for brokers and advisers because of the practical problems and differences in communicating with various types of customers and clients on a uniform basis. Two safeguards should help. An equitable system should be designed to prevent selective discriminatory disclosure, and customers and clients should know what kind of communication they will receive.

Example 3: The president of a corporation, Rivers, moves his company's growth-oriented pension fund to a bank primarily because of the excellent investment performance achieved by the bank's commingled fund over the prior five-year period. A few years later, Rivers compares the results of his pension fund with those of the bank's commingled fund. Even though the two accounts had the same investment objectives and similar portfolios, he was startled to learn his company's pension fund had significantly underperformed the bank's commingled fund. Questioning this at his next meeting with the pension fund's manager, Rivers was told that whenever a new security was placed on the recommended list, the bank, as a matter of policy, would first purchase the security for the commingled account and then purchase on a *pro rata* basis for all other pension fund accounts. Similarly, when a sale was recommended, the security would be sold first from the commingled account and then sold on a pro rata basis from all other accounts. One other factor the pension fund manager thought might have contributed to the better performance of the commingled fund was the bank's policy to use new issues in only the commingled account because the bank could not get enough shares (especially the "hot" ones) to be meaningful to all of the pension fund accounts. As Rivers didn't seem completely satisfied or pleased by the explanation, the pension fund manager was quick to add that non-discretionary pension accounts and personal trust accounts had a lower priority on purchase and sale recommendations than discretionary pension fund accounts. Furthermore, the manager stated that the company's pension fund had the opportunity to invest up to 5 percent in the commingled fund if the president so desired.

Comment: The bank's policy did not treat all customers fairly, as it gave priority to the growth-oriented commingled fund over all others and priority to discretionary accounts over non-discretionary accounts. The violation of the standard might have been avoided if the bank's policy had been described in writing as one of administrative convenience and made known to Rivers before he transferred his account.

Procedures for Compliance

Even though a specific individual may not be responsible for the distribution of investment recommendations, each financial analyst has the obligation to inform his employer of the Code of Ethics and Standards of Professional Conduct (see Standard I). Consequently, compliance procedures should be established to govern all employees of the financial analyst's firm who disseminate investment recommendations or take investment action, to ensure that all customers and clients are treated fairly.

The formality and complexity of such compliance procedures depend upon the nature and size of the organization and the type of security involved (whether it be a small over-the-counter security or a U.S. Government long-term bond). An investment adviser who is a sole proprietor and handles only discretionary accounts does not disseminate recommendations to the public. Nonetheless, he should have a formal procedure to ensure that all clients receive fair investment action.

In order to ensure that all customers and clients are treated fairly, the following points should be considered in establishing compliance procedures. Although they are primarily designed for brokerage firms preparing recommendations for external distribution to customers, the procedures are also applicable to firms preparing recommendations solely for their own internal use.

■ *Limit the number of people involved.* Every effort should be made to limit the number of people who are privy to the fact that a recommendation is going to be disseminated. Establishment of a Chinese Wall (as described in footnotes 37 and 42 of Standard II C) is appropriate.[3]

■ *Shorten the time frame.* Every effort should be made to limit the amount of time that elapses between the decision to make an investment recommendation and the time the actual recommendation is disseminated. If a detailed, long institutional recommendation is in preparation that might take two or three weeks to publish, a short summary report including the conclusion might be published to shorten the time frame. In an organization where both a research committee and investment policy committee must approve a recommendation, the meetings should be held on the same day if possible, rather than several days apart.

The process of reviewing, printing, and mailing reports, or faxing or distributing them by electronic mail, necessarily involves the passage of time, sometimes long periods of time. In large firms with more extensive review processes, the time factor is usually not within the control of the analyst who prepared the report. Thus, many firms and their analysts communicate to customers and firm personnel the new or changed recommendations by a "flash." (The communications technique varies, including fax, electronic mail, wire, or short written report.)

■ *Publish personnel guidelines for pre-dissemination.* It is essential that guidelines be established for personnel who have prior knowledge of an investment recommendation, prohibiting them from discussing or taking any action on the pending recommendation prior to its dissemination. Such guidelines are discussed under Standard IV.

■ *Develop procedures for dissemination.* Procedures should be established for dissemination of investment recommendations so that all customers or clients are treated fairly, i.e., they are informed at approximately the same time. For example, if a new recommendation is going to be communicated, supervisory personnel should time the announcement of the recommendation to avoid placing any clients or group of clients at unfair advantage relative to other clients insofar as acting on the new information is concerned. A communication to all branch offices should be sent at the time of the general announcement. It is appropriate to accompany the announcement of a new recommendation with a statement that trading restrictions for the firm's employees are now in effect. (See the next paragraph and Standard IV.)

■ *Establish control over trading activity.* Procedures should be established to control and monitor the trading activity by firm personnel to ensure that transactions on behalf of customers and clients take precedence over transactions that will benefit the firm, its officers, partners, or employees. (See Standard IV.) This fair dealing standard is concerned primarily with treating all customers fairly in disseminating investment advice and taking action as contrasted with Standard IV, which requires that client transactions are completed before action is taken for the firm or its employees. In summary, however, so-called "front running" (firm trading for its account before trading for customers) violates the policies of the exchanges, which prohibit the activity as inconsistent with fair trading principles and rules.[4]

Because dissemination and assimilation of procedures to ensure fair dealings take time, an appropriate waiting period should be established during which broker–dealer and investment firm personnel should be prohibited from executing orders for the firm, their own accounts, and those of their immediate families.   Such a waiting period will vary according to circumstances. Supervisory personnel should consider such relevant factors as the liquidity of a security being recommended, because "thinness of trading" is likely to influence the amount of time that must pass before a firm can successfully consummate all transactions on its clients' behalf. While a waiting period of a few days may seem appropriate for a brokerage firm, it may be considerably longer in the case of trading activity by members of an investment counseling firm. Restrictions in addition to those based on the length of the waiting period should also be considered.

As the fair treatment of all customers and clients necessarily means that their interests have priority over individual transactions by a financial analyst, procedures should be integrated with those required for compliance with Standard IV.

■   *Maintain a list of investment recommendations.* A change in a list of current investment recommendations should be considered material. Under normal circumstances, a change from buy to buy/hold would not be considered material, whereas a change from buy to sell would be considered a material change and should be disseminated in a manner fair to all customers and clients.

■   *Establish procedures for determining material change.* A procedure should be established to determine whether a change in an investment recommendation is considered material.   One individual could have responsibility for such a determination, but it is preferable to involve more than one person so that different points of view are considered. This is sometimes a complex issue not always conducive to an easy solution; to the extent written guidelines for employees can be established, they should be.

■   *Maintain a list of holders.* To notify customers or clients of a change in an investment recommendation, a list should be maintained of all customers or clients and the securities or other investments each holds.

To make certain that all clients and customers are treated fairly when investment actions are taken on their behalf, compliance procedures should be established by which employees of the financial analyst's firm can fulfill this obligation.

■   *Maintain a list of holdings.* A list including telephone and fax numbers should be maintained of all securities or other investments and the clients holding each. If the security or other investment is to be sold, this list can be used to ensure that all holders are treated fairly in the liquidation of that particular investment.

■   *Execute orders on a systematic basis.* When orders are placed to purchase or sell a given security or other investment for more than one client, every effort should be taken to execute those orders on a *pro rata* basis so that all customers are treated fairly.

■　*Establish systematic account review.* A procedure should be established so that each account is reviewed on a regular basis by a supervisor to make certain that no client or customer is being given preferential treatment and that the investment action taken for each account is suitable for the account's objectives.

■　*Evaluate contra-action.* There may be good reason for buying a given security or other investment in one account while selling it in another account, because investments should be based on individual needs and circumstances. However, a review procedure should be established to detect whether one account is being used to bail a favored account out of a bad investment or whether the accounts are being churned.

■　*Disclose levels of service.* If an organization offers two or more levels of service to clients on the same or a differing fee structure, this should be disclosed to all clients. For example, if an advisory service is offered on both a discretionary basis and a nondiscretionary basis, it should be indicated that action may be taken for the discretionary accounts prior to taking the same action for nondiscretionary accounts because of the differences inherent in such accounts. However, this is an area of potential pitfalls, and care should be taken to treat different types of customers and clients in an equitable manner notwithstanding disclosure.

Footnotes

1.　*In re Butcher & Sherrard*, SEC Rel. No. 34-9894, [1972–73] Fed. Sec. L. Rep. (CCH) ¶79,135 (December 11, 1972).
2.　New York Stock Exchange Rule 472, Communications with the Public.
3.　Pitt and Groskaufmanis, "A Second Look at Corporate Codes of Conduct," *Director's Monthly* (November 1989). See section on Chinese Walls, pp. 4-5.
4.　Securities and Exchange Commission, *The October 1987 Market Break: A Report of the Division of Market Regulation*, at 3-30 (February 1988); see also *In re E.F. Hutton & Company Inc., Now Known as Shearson Lehman Hutton Inc.*, on "Improper Handling of Customer's Limit Order," which found that the company did not disclose that it would give its own position priority, SEC Administrative Proceeding File No. 3-6490 (July 6, 1988).

Standard III G
Reference Material

1. Securities and Exchange Commission, *Guide to Broker–Dealer Compliance: Report of the Broker–Dealer Model Compliance Program Advisory Committee,* Chapter X, "Research and Recommendations" (November 13, 1974).
2. Securities and Exchange Commission, *Statement on the Future Structure of the Securities Markets,* 137 1BNA Sec. Reg. & L. Rep. Pt. II at 6 (February 2, 1972).
3. Securities and Exchange Commission, *Report of Special Study of Securities Markets* (1963).
4. Securities and Exchange Commission, *The October 1987 Market Break: A Report by the Division of Market Regulation* (February 1988).
5. New York Stock Exchange, Rule 472, Communications with the Public.
6. New York Stock Exchange, *Expanded Policy on Timely Disclosure* (July 18, 1968).
7. Fleischer, Mundheim, and Murphy, "Disclosure of Investment Advice," 6 *Review of Securities Regulation* 16 (September 27, 1973).

IV. Priority of Transactions

The financial analyst shall conduct himself in such a manner that transactions for his customers, clients, and employer have priority over transactions in securities or other investments of which he is the beneficial owner, and so that transactions in securities or other investments in which he has such beneficial ownership do not operate adversely to their interests. If an analyst decides to make a recommendation about the purchase or sale of a security or other investment, he shall give his customers, clients, and employer adequate opportunity to act on this recommendation before acting on his own behalf.

For purposes of these Standards of Professional Conduct, a financial analyst is a "beneficial owner" if he directly or indirectly, through any contract, arrangement, understanding, relationship or otherwise, has or shares a direct or indirect pecuniary interest in the securities or the investment.

Purpose of the Standard

The purpose of this standard is to state the responsibility of AIMR members and nonmember holders of, and candidates for, the CFA designation to give the financial interests of their customers, clients, and employers priority over their own personal financial interests. The standard is designed to prevent any potential conflict of interest or even the appearance of a conflict of interest with respect to an analyst's personal transactions.

Conduct Affected by the Standard

This standard covers the activities of every investment professional who has knowledge of pending or prospective transactions that may be made on behalf of his customers, clients, or employer. Because an analyst often acts in a fiduciary capacity or other capacity with similar duties, this standard, in effect, prohibits him from disclosing such information to inappropriate persons and specifically states that transactions for customers, clients, and employer have priority over personal transactions.

The standard applies to transactions in which the financial analyst is deemed to be a beneficial owner—that is, personal transactions, and in other circumstances explained below. This occurs, as described in the standard, if the analyst has a direct or indirect pecuniary interest in the securities or the investment, and includes:

- Transactions for the analyst's own account.
- Transactions for family accounts including spouse, children and other members of the analyst's immediate family, and family equivalents, sharing the same household.
- Transactions for accounts in which the financial analyst has a direct or indirect pecuniary interest (such as a trust or retirement account in which he has a beneficial interest).

These transactions must be subordinate and not adverse to transactions for clients, customers and employers.

Transactions for family members who are not clients or customers must be effected only after client, customer and employer transactions.

Moreover, if the analyst has investment discretion over family accounts of which he is not the beneficial owner, and which are clients or customers, transactions for these accounts must not be given preferential treatment.

This standard prohibits the analyst from conveying information about a recommendation or investment action to inappropriate persons (other than clients, customers or an employer) including those persons whose relationship makes the analyst a beneficial owner of their securities. Finally, for those accounts of which the analyst is the beneficial owner, action may be taken only after clients have had an adequate opportunity to act on the recommendation.

The definition of "beneficial owner" appears in the second paragraph of the standard. This definition is based on, but is interpreted more broadly than that adopted by, the Securities and Exchange Commission Rule 16a-1(a) (2) under Section 16 of the Securities Exchange Act. (SEC Rel. No. 34-28869, February 8, 1991). The SEC also uses that definition for purposes of required reporting and the prohibition of certain personal securities transactions under Rule 204-2(a) (12) of the Investment Advisers Act and Rule 17j-1 of the Investment Company Act. (SEC Interpretive Letter, Investment Company Institute, July 31, 1992).[1]

Application of the Standard

This standard clearly states that the interests of customers, clients, and employer must have priority and take precedence over the financial interest of the financial analyst/investment manager who is making a recommendation or taking investment action.[2] However, this standard also applies to individuals who have access to information during the normal preparation of research recommendations or the taking of investment action.[3] (See Standard II A, Standard II C, and Standard II D.)

Although it is obvious that an investment professional should not buy or sell securities or other investments on his own behalf before taking action for customers, clients, or an employer, this standard also applies to other personal financial transactions that might act to the detriment of the client's interests. It is not possible to list all of the situations in violation of this standard, but the following examples are representative.

Example 1: Jacobs, a research analyst, fails to change a recommendation from buy/hold to sell because she wants to sell a personal holding and does not want to wait until all clients have the opportunity to sell first.

Comment: Jacobs violated Standard IV. Her decision not to change her recommendation until her own financial goals had been served resulted in losses to her clients due to the subsequent decline in the value of that particular holding.

Example 2: A research analyst, Long, fails to recommend purchase of a given common stock for his employer's account because he wants to purchase the stock personally and does not want to wait until the recommendation was approved and the stock was purchased by his employer.

Comment: Long violated the standard by taking advantage of his knowledge about the stock's value before allowing his employer to benefit from that information.

Example 3: Young, a portfolio manager, personally owns a large block of a thinly traded stock. With the general stock market declining rapidly, she wishes to sell her position but knows the order could not be executed without seriously affecting the stock's market price. Consequently, she sells the block of stock to one of her institutional clients over whose account she has discretionary control. The stock declines, and the client is adversely affected.

Comment: Young violated Standard IV by using the client's funds for her personal financial benefit, and she breached her fiduciary duty by not acting in the client's best interests. She should have disclosed to the institutional client her holding in the stock (as specified in Standard V) and the fact that she acted as a principal in the transaction.

Example 4: A cash tender offer is announced by a company whose stock is held by Smith's (an analyst) employer as well as Smith's father. Under the terms of the offer, the first 1 million shares tendered would be accepted in full at $28 a share, and the next 1 million shares on a *pro rata* basis also at $28 a share (which is 20 percent above the existing market). Smith immediately calls his father with the news but waits a few days to tender his employer's holding.

Comment: Smith violated Standard IV by placing his father's financial interests above his employer's. As a result, Smith's father might have received $28 a share for all his shares, whereas it is possible that only a portion of Smith's employer's holding would be purchased because of the delay.

Example 5: Baker, the portfolio manager of an aggressive growth mutual fund, maintains accounts in his wife's maiden name at several brokerage firms with which the fund and a number of his other individual clients do a substantial amount of business. Whenever a new "hot" issue becomes available, he instructs the brokers to buy it for his wife's account. Because such issues normally are scarce, Baker often acquires shares while his clients are not able to participate.

Comment: Under Standard IV, Baker should have acquired shares for his mutual fund and only thereafter for himself, even though this might have prevented him from participating in new issues. Under Standard V, he should have disclosed the trading for his wife's account, as this was a conflict of interest.

Example 6: Michaels is an entry-level employee who holds a relatively low-paying job serving both the research and investment management departments of an active investment management company. She purchases a sports car and begins to wear expensive clothes after only a year of employment with the firm. The director of the investment management department has responsibility for monitoring the personal stock transactions of all employees. Upon the director's investigation, she discovers that Michaels has parlayed a bank loan of $1,000 into a tidy sum of money by buying stocks just before they were put on the firm's recommended purchase list. Michaels regularly was given, but declined to complete, the firm's quarterly personal transaction form.

Comment: Michaels violated Standard IV by placing personal transactions ahead of client transactions and thus should have been subject to disciplinary action. In addition, her supervisor violated Standard II D by permitting Michaels to continue to perform her assigned tasks without first having signed the quarterly personal transaction form.

Another point that must be considered is the supervisor's responsibility under Standard II D to establish and implement procedures to prevent violations of law. As the employee in this case violated both the Investment

Company Act of 1940 and the Investment Advisers Act of 1940 by trading on information before it was released to clients, this brings into question the adequacy of the supervisor's actions. If the firm had discharged its responsibilities by establishing rules and procedures, reviewing them with employees, and monitoring employees' compliance on a regular basis, the supervisor's duties would very likely have been satisfied and thus neither the firm nor the supervisor would have been subject to disciplinary action.

If Michaels had communicated information about the firm's recommendations to a person who traded the security, this would be a misappropriation of the information and a violation of Standard II C and the insider trading rules.

Example 7: A brokerage's insurance analyst, Wilson, makes a closed-circuit report to the firm's branch system. During the broadcast, he includes negative comments about a major company within the industry. The following day, Wilson's report is printed and distributed to the sales force and public customers. The report recommends that both short-term traders and intermediate investors take profits. Seven minutes after the broadcast, the firm's trading department closes out a long call position in the stock. Eight minutes later, a sizable put position is established. The firm took this action, it claimed, to facilitate anticipated sales by institutional clients.

Comment: The brokerage firm expected that both the stock and option markets would respond to the sell recommendation, but it did not give customers an opportunity to buy or sell in the options market before the firm itself did. By taking action before the report was disseminated, the firm could have depressed the price of the calls and increased the price of the puts. A conflict of interest would have been avoided if the firm had waited until its clients had an opportunity to receive and assimilate Wilson's recommendations before it traded for its own account. The firm's action was inconsistent with just and equitable trading principles.

Under certain circumstances, the use of nonpublic recommendations could be in violation of Rule 10b-5 under the Securities Exchange Act of 1934. If Wilson had participated in the firm's trading action, he would be in violation of Standard IV. If another person subject to the Code and Standards participated in management's action, that person would also be in violation of the standard.[4] It is also clear that Wilson could violate securities laws and the standard by engaging in transactions in securities he was recommending for his firm's clients before his clients had an opportunity to do so.[5]

While the foregoing examples are situations or actions that clearly must be avoided, others that are uncertain should be discussed with and cleared by a person in a supervisory capacity. The ultimate test of any situation is whether full disclosure of the facts would indicate that the interests of the customer, client, or employer have been best served rather than those of the financial analyst.

Procedures for Compliance

An individual code of ethics and compliance procedures should be established and distributed to all firm personnel so that they are aware of the obligation to place the interests of customers, clients, and their employer above their own personal financial interests.

Although many organizations for which members work (such as most broker–dealers and investment advisers to investment companies)[6] are required by law to have a code of ethics or compliance procedures, these should be established by all firms for the protection not only of the investing public but also for the protection of the firm's employees.[7]

The form and content of such compliance procedures depend upon the size and nature of each organization and the laws to which it is subject. However, because a violation of this standard in most instances also will involve a violation of Standard III G, the compliance procedures for Standard III G should be considered as supplemental to the following typical procedures for organizations involved in the investment process.

■ *Define personal transactions.* It is essential that all employees be aware of what constitutes a personal transaction. Although a minimum definition is included in this chapter, it might also be appropriate under certain circumstances to include a stricter standard as a matter of firm policy.

■ *Define investment.* The definition of investment for these purposes is any medium by which placement of funds generally occurs with the expectation of preserving value and earning a positive return. The definition of investment is set forth so that it includes not only bonds, common stocks, and related securities (including convertible bonds, preferred stocks, warrants, options, puts and calls, and financial futures) but also such diverse vehicles as interests in real estate, oil and gas and other natural resources, commodities, currencies, and tangible property such as works of art and other collectors' items.

■ *Define access person.* The definition of an "access" or "covered" person (i.e., any person who might have knowledge of pending or actual recommendations or actions) should be broad enough to cover all those persons involved. As operational procedures may be changed or personnel reassigned, it is appropriate to have a systematic review (at least annually) of which personnel are included as access or covered individuals.

■ *Limit the number of access persons.* Effort should be made to limit the number of people who have knowledge of a pending investment recommendation or action. Implementing the concept of the Chinese Wall (as described in footnotes 37 and 42 to the discussion of Standard II C) may be appropriate in certain organizations to limit the number of persons so classified.[8]

■ *Define prohibited transaction.* Prohibited transactions should be defined clearly so that employees completely understand their obligations to customers, clients, and employer. Restrictions should specify the time period during which employees are prohibited from engaging in trading activity on their own or their firm's behalf. The period could vary. For example, many broker–dealers have procedures requiring employees to adhere to prohibitions against trading for specific time periods both before and after a research recommendation is made. An investment counseling firm might restrict employees from purchasing (or selling) a given investment until all accounts have been reviewed. Organizations with multiple branches might require more elapsed time than single offices to disseminate information fully.

■ *Establish reporting and prior clearance requirements.* A reporting system for all personal transactions should be established. The Comptroller of the Currency has issued specific regulations for employees of national banks. These regulations are usually viewed as the norm for state-chartered banks as well. Rule 204-2(a) (12) under the Investment Advisers Act sets out requirements for employees of investment advisory firms. In both cases, quarterly reporting is mandated for personnel. The record should include the date and nature of the transaction, the price, and the name of the broker, dealer, or bank through which it was effected. Both exclude transactions in U.S. Government securities, and the Comptroller those in mutual funds and transactions involving in the aggregate $10,000 or less during the calendar quarter.

Equally important is the need to review all personal transactions against those of customers, clients, and the employer to ensure that employees have complied with the provision of this standard as well as Standard II C, Standard II D, and Standard III G. New York Stock Exchange Rule 342.21(a) is not specific with regard to reporting requirements, but it mandates that member firms have review procedures in place "to be reasonably designed to identify trades that may violate the provisions of the Securities Exchange Act of 1934, the rules under that act, or the rules of the Exchange prohibiting insider trading and manipulative and deceptive devices." The actual reporting procedures in place at member firms are extensive.

Depending upon circumstance, monthly reporting or other more stringent requirements might be desirable. As noted above, procedures requiring prior approval for all personal investment transactions by employees prevent any employee from unknowingly allowing a personal transaction to take precedence over those for his customers, clients, or employer. Procedures of this nature are becoming more common. Of course, such requests and all reports should be maintained on a confidential basis.

■ *Enforce procedures.* Normally, authority to enforce firm procedures is the responsibility of a compliance officer; however, in a small organization, it might rest with the director of research, the head of the investment management department, the head of a trading department, or a combination of all three. The person or persons granting approval should, in turn, have a third party approve their personal investment transactions.

■ *Develop disciplinary procedures.* In fairness to all employees, and as a deterrent to infractions of this standard, a method of taking disciplinary action should be established and enforced by the firm. Rule 342.21(a) of states that an internal investigation should be promptly conducted into any trade referred to above.

Footnotes

1. SEC Rel. No. 34-28869 (February 8, 1991).
2. *In re Farrer*, SEC Rel. No. IC-13131, [1982–83] Fed. Sec. L. Rep. (CCH) ¶83,332 (March 31, 1983).
3. *SEC v. Sarzynski* (S.D.N.Y.), SEC Rel. No. LR-10763 (May 22, 1985). (Individuals who traded directly or indirectly, or aided and abetted in such trading, on the basis of material inside information obtained by virtue of one individual's employment with a financial printer.)
4. *SEC v. Smith Barney, Harris Upham & Co., Inc.*, SEC Rel. No. 21242 (August 15, 1984).
5. *In re Butcher & Sherrerd*, SEC Rel. No. 34-9894, [1972–73] Fed. Sec. L. Rep. (CCH) ¶79,135 (December 11, 1972).
6. See, for example, Rule 17j-1 under the Investment Company Act.
7. The Insider Trading and Securities Fraud Enforcement Act amended the Securities Exchange Act by adding §15 (f), and amended the Investment Advisers Act by adding §204A, referring brokers and investment advisers, respectively to establish, maintain and enforce written policies and procedures reasonably designed to prevent the misuse of material nonpublic information. In addition, the NASD *Rules of Fair Practice* §40 prohibits various "private" transactions of registered representation without the consent of the employer.

8. See also Securities and Exchange Commission, *Broker–Dealer Policies and Procedures Designed to Segment the Flow and Prevent the Misuse of Material Nonpublic Information, A Report by the Division of Market Regulation* (March 1990).

Standard IV
Reference Material

1. Investment Company Act of 1940, Section 17(j) and Rule 17j-1 thereunder.
2. Investment Advisers Act Rule 204-2(a)(12).
3. "Comptroller of the Currency, Laws, Regulations and Rulings 12 CFR 12.6 (Section 1002.3)"
4. (Ontario) Securities Act, R.S.O. 1980, c. 466, §39, disclosure of financial interest of advisers and dealers.
5. Securities and Exchange Commission, *Guide to Broker–Dealer Compliance: Report of the Broker-Dealer Model Compliance Program Advisory Committee,* Chapters VII, "Investment Advisory Services," IX, "Proprietary Trading," and X, "Research and Recommendations" (November 13, 1974).
6. Securities and Exchange Commission, *The October 1987 Market Break: A Report by the Division of Market Regulation,* Chapters III, "The Effects of Derivative Products at 3-30-34, Frontrunning," IV, "Exchange Specialists," and XII, "Investor Complaints" (February 1988).
7. New York Stock Exchange, *Supervision and Management of Registered Representatives and Customer Accounts* (1973) pgs. 12,13,26.
8. Frankel, 2 *The Regulation of Money Managers,* Chapter XIII (1978).
9. Frankhauser and Frye, "Frontrunning," *Review of Securities & Commodities Regulation* (October 19, 1988).
10. Fleischer, Mundheim, and Murphy, "Disclosure of Investment Advice," 6 *Securities and Commodities Regulation* 16 (September 27, 1973).
11. Gillis, "Codes of Ethics for Investment Companies," *Financial Analysts Journal* (March/April 1981).
12 Marton, "Drawing the Line on Front-Running," *Institutional Investor* (December 1987).
13. Pickard and Axe, "Frontrunning: Regulators Mount New Attack on Intermarket Abuse," 3 *Insights* 10 (October 1989).
14. Russo and Lobel, "Frontrunning and Block Trading," *The Review of Securities and Commodities Regulation* (April 25, 1990).
15. Sandler, "Brokers' Practice of Trading for Own Accounts Before Filling Customer Orders Irks Investors," *The Wall Street Journal* (February 17, 1988).

STANDARD V
V. DISCLOSURE OF CONFLICTS

The financial analyst, when making investment recommendations, or taking investment actions, shall disclose to his customers and clients any material conflict of interest relating to him and any material beneficial ownership of the securities or other investments involved that could reasonably be expected to impair his ability to render unbiased and objective advice.

The financial analyst shall disclose to his employer all matters that could reasonably be expected to interfere with his duty to the employer, or with his ability to render unbiased and objective advice.

The financial analyst shall also comply with all requirements as to disclosure of conflicts of interest imposed by law and by rules and regulations of organizations governing his activities and shall comply with any prohibitions on his activities if a conflict of interest exists.

Purpose of the Standard

The purpose of the standard is to state the responsibility of AIMR members and nonmember holders of, and candidates for, the CFA designation to serve customers and clients with unbiased and objective advice based on thorough investigation and professional analysis. Anything less is unacceptable. This standard is designed to protect the client and customer by requiring full disclosure of all conflicts of interest. Once full disclosure of conflicts is made, the financial analyst's clients and customers have all relevant data necessary to evaluate the objectivity of the financial analyst's recommendation.

Employers should also be informed of any areas of potential conflict so that the assignment of responsibilities to the financial analyst or investment manager can be made on a fully informed basis.

Conduct Affected by the Standard

This standard requires the financial analyst and other investment professionals to issue advice that is objective. Can the analyst meet this requirement if, on behalf of his firm, he obtains or assists in obtaining fees for services other than research? Can he meet the requirement if he owns stock in the company being analyzed, or if he has a close personal relationship with its management? That customers' and clients' interests take priority is an essential principle that must not be ignored.

In the real world, analysts and portfolio managers face myriad situations in which their advice may become tainted. Indeed, a potential conflict of interest exists whenever an analyst makes buy/sell recommendations.

For instance, a sell-side analyst working for a broker–dealer may be encouraged, not only by members of his own firm but by corporate issuers themselves, to write research reports about particular companies. Because research is expensive, the broker–dealer will want a hand in deciding which industries and companies are to be covered by research reports. Nonetheless, responsibility for buy/sell recommendations should remain purely with the broker–dealer's research department. The buy-side analyst is likely to be faced with similar conflicts, as banks progressively exercise their underwriting and securities dealing powers. The same practices should therefore be followed. The potential for conflict of interest is increased by the recent emergence of broker-sponsored limited partnerships formed to invest venture capital. Increasingly, analysts are expected not only to follow issues from these partnerships once they are offered to the public but also to promote the issues in the trading market after public offerings. Analysts and employers should carefully examine situations presenting the threat of conflict of interest and resolve them in accordance with the principles set forth in this standard and, if in the near term, Standard IV.

On the buy side, investment activities such as those resulting from a change in asset allocation or sector weightings may affect the price of a security or group of securities, particularly in large investment organizations. To ensure that clients' interests receive priority on all occasions, a special effort should be made to monitor and, if necessary, control an analyst's personal investment transactions. The analyst is under a duty to inform his employer of any special relationships or investment holdings he has, so that the employer can make an informed judgment as to whether a conflict exists. Other pressures may exist. For example, the marketing division may ask an analyst to recommend the stock of a certain company in order to obtain business directly from that company.

In determining whether a conflict of interest is present, the analyst should also consult applicable federal and state securities laws and rules, as well as the rules and regulations of self-regulatory organizations such as stock exchanges and the National Association of Securities Dealers.

Application of the Standard

There are circumstances where a conflict, or the perception of a conflict, cannot be avoided in today's environment. These must be disclosed to the customer and client so investment decisions can be based on all the factors involved. The most obvious conflicts of interest that should always be disclosed are special relationships between the analyst or the analyst's firm and an issuer (including directorships and consultancies; underwriting and financial relationships; broker–dealer market-making activities; and material beneficial ownership).

Example 1: Analyst Ball, a partner in his firm, is on the board of a public company. He fails to disclose this fact when recommending securities of that public company. (See Standard VII B.)

Comment: Ball is in violation of the standard. Even though confidential, there could be a perception by the public that information not available to the public might be communicated to a director's firm whether it be a broker, investment adviser, or other type of organization. This holds true for any officer, director, partner, or employee of an investment firm.

Example 2: Weiss is a research analyst with Farmington Co., a broker and investment banker. Farmington's merger and acquisition department has represented Bestco, a conglomerate, in all of its acquisitions for 20 years. Farmington officers from time to time sit on the boards of directors of various Bestco subsidiaries. Weiss is writing a research report on Bestco.

Comment: Weiss should disclose Farmington's special relationship with Bestco. Broker–dealer management of and participation in public offerings should be disclosed in research reports. The New York Stock Exchange rule requiring disclosure where the broker–dealer has been the manager or co-manager of a public offering for the issuer within the past three years illustrates this policy. Because the position of underwriter to a company presents a special past and potential future relationship with a company that is the subject of investment advice, it should be disclosed.

Example 3: The investment management firm of Dover & Roe sells a 25 percent interest in its partnership to a multinational bank holding company, First of New York. Immediately thereafter, Dover & Roe changes its recommendation of First's common stock from sell to buy and adds First's commercial paper to its approved list for purchase.

Comment: Dover & Roe should disclose the new relationship with First to all its clients. This relationship should also be disclosed to clients by its portfolio managers when making specific investment recommendations or in taking investment actions with respect to First's securities.

Example 4: The marketing division of the Jones Investment Co. would like one of its analysts to recommend that clients buy stock in Xavier, Inc. Jones hopes to be selected as an investment manager of the company's employee benefit plans.

Comment: Even if the purchase recommendation has no influence on Xavier's selection of an investment manager, it may adversely affect client investment decision. Thus, the recommendation should have remained purely in the hands of the Jones research department.

Example 5: The underwriting affiliate of Cox Bank and Trust would like the trust department's common trust fund to purchase the remnants of a municipal offering it has not been able to place directly.

Comment: Even if these bonds were deemed to be of investment grade, it is illegal for the trust department's common fund managers to buy any securities directly from the underwriting affiliate.

Broker–Dealer Market-Making Activities. Disclosure of broker–dealer market-making activities alerts the customer and client that a purchase or sale might be made from or to the broker–dealer's principal account and that the firm has a special interest in the price of the stock. The New York Stock Exchange rule on disclosure of this activity again illustrates this policy.

Material Beneficial Ownership. If material beneficial ownership exists for an analyst recommending a security or other investment or the analyst's firm for its investment account, it should be disclosed. For the purposes of this standard, an analyst beneficially owns a security or other investment that he or a member of his immediate family owns or that is in trust for the analyst or his immediate family. Immediate family is usually defined as the spouse, children, and dependent relatives.

An analyst's or firm's beneficial ownership of a security or other investment is material for the purposes of this standard if the analyst or firm is unable, or appears to be unable, to render unbiased and objective advice. The question of what is material is as difficult in this context as it is in most others. It includes factors relating to the individual's circumstances, such as being a significant portion of his net worth. If the total amount would be considered significant in any typical investor circumstance, it likely would also meet the definition.

Example 6: Barton, a research analyst who follows firms producing small copiers, has been recommending purchase of Kincaid because of its innovative new line of copiers. Barton then inherits $3 million of Kincaid stock from a distant aunt; this comprises 85 percent of his net worth. He has been asked to write a follow-up report on the company.

Comment: Barton should disclose his ownership of the stock at the time of the follow-up report. It is a very high percentage of his net worth and the total amount of its value is very significant by any typical investor standard.

Example 7: In his own account, Barton speculates in penny stocks and purchases 100,000 shares of Drew Mining, Inc. for 30 cents a share. He intends to sell these shares on the sign of any substantial upward price movement of the stock. One week later, he is asked to write a report on penny stocks in the mining industry to be published two weeks later. Whether or not he owned Drew stock, he would have recommended it as a buy. This would likely have resulted in a surge of the price of the stock to the $2 range.

Comment: Although it could be argued that this holding was not material, Barton should have disclosed it because the potential for substantial gain was high if the market had responded strongly to his recommendation. The fact that he had recently purchased the stock also gave the appearance that he was not entirely objective.[1]

Example 8: Jacobs is a portfolio manager for several non-discretionary pension funds at Trenton Trust Co. His wife is comptroller, treasurer, and 20 percent shareholder of Miller Machine Parts, Inc., formerly a closely held corporation. Miller has been aggressively pursuing and winning foreign business and made a public offering to finance plant expansion one year ago. The market value of Mrs. Jacobs's holdings rose from $500,000 before the offering to $5 million one year after the offering. Trenton's research department recommends the stock to its trust officers and pension fund portfolio managers.

Comment: For purposes of this standard, Jacobs beneficially owns his wife's stock. He should disclose her ownership to his supervisor and to the trustees of all the pension funds he manages before buying Miller stock.

General. The most persistent conflict relating to this standard pertains to the analyst's ownership of stock in companies he recommends. The predominant acceptable solution is for the analyst to disclose his ownership so that his clients, customers, and employer have sufficient information to determine whether the analyst's impartiality has been impaired. Clearly, the easiest method for preventing a conflict is to prohibit the analyst from owning any of the securities he recommends. However, it could be argued that this approach discriminates against the analyst. A more acceptable approach would be to require that all employees of the analyst's firm comply with a strict set of outlined procedures regarding limits to their personal investment in securities their firm recommends.

It is significant that this standard refers to *material* beneficial ownership and *material* conflict of interest. Determining materiality is often a matter of judgment. The key is whether the member is free of the kind of conflict that would make it impossible for him to render unbiased and objective advice.

The analyst must also be aware of material ownership in his firm's investment account, market-making activities, corporate finance relationships, and directorships, all of which must be disclosed to clients and customers.

There are many potential additional areas of conflict that should be disclosed. In this day of working spouses, it is conceivable that the spouse of an analyst might derive a significant portion of annual income from business with a company whose securities are recommended by the analyst. When the analyst loses his ability to render unbiased and objective advice, disclosure of conflicts of interest should be made.

Instead of being made cautious by the disclosures, the investor might conclude that a close relationship with an issuer makes recommendations particularly well informed and insightful. One of the analyst's responsibilities is to caution the investor, if this interpretation of the conflict-of-interest disclosures overpowers mature judgment.

The intent of disclosure is to protect the investor, but disclosure also protects the analyst and the employer.

Procedures for Compliance

The financial analyst must hold himself responsible for disclosing material conflicts. Since materiality is a rather general term, it is suggested that a second financial analyst, department head, compliance officer, or key executive of the firm be consulted to determine when disclosure is expected and required. Investment recommendations, written or oral, should disclose all of the items discussed above. The chapter on Standard II D contains a checklist for supervisors reviewing research reports.

With respect to stock ownership, each firm should have its own established procedures. Prevention of an undisclosed conflict can usually be accomplished by an analyst obtaining approval before making an investment.

This also prevents a trade against the firm's recommendation or in anticipation of a research report by another analyst of which the member may not be aware.

One major area of conflict is covered by Standard VI C, which governs employees who receive compensation from persons other than their employer. This should be reviewed.

Many firms require employees to report all transactions by employees and their families for purposes of detecting conflicts of interest, trading on material non-public information (Standard II C), and employees giving personal transactions priority over client transactions (Standard IV). If a firm does not have such a procedure, the financial analyst should report to his employer any material beneficial interest he has in investments about which he is asked to make a report or take investment action as well as any corporate directorships or other special relationships. Such disclosures should be made whenever an analyst wishes to make recommendations or take actions concerning the investments in which he has a material beneficial interest or potential conflict. Such disclosures should be made before the analyst makes any recommendations about the investments to customers or clients.

Footnotes

1. *See In re Dow Theory Letters, Inc.*, SEC Rel. No. 1A-571 (March 7, 1977), where the publisher of a newsletter was subject to sanctions for purchasing stocks just prior to publication of recommendations. He agreed to disclose in the future any purchases made within three months before a recommendation.

Standard V
Reference Material

1. (Ontario) Securities Act, R.S.O. 1980, c. 466, §39, disclosure of financial interest of advisers and dealers.
2. Securities and Exchange Commission, *Guide to Broker–Dealer Compliance: Report of the Broker–Dealer Model Compliance Program Advisory Committee*, Chapters VII, "Investment Advisory Services," IX, "Proprietary Trading," and X, "Research and Recommendations" (November 13, 1974).
3. Securities and Exchange Commission, Uniform Form ADV, *Uniform Application for Investment Adviser Registration*, Part II, 9, "Participation or Interest in Client Transactions."
4. National Association of Securities Dealers, *Rules of Fair Practice*, Article III, §1, Business Conduct of Members.
5. New York Stock Exchange, Rule 472, Communications with the Public, and supplementary material.

VI. COMPENSATION

A. Disclosure of Additional Compensation Arrangements

The financial analyst shall inform his customers, clients, and employer of compensation or other benefit arrangements in connection with his services to them which are in addition to compensation from them for such services.

Purpose of the Standard

The purpose of the standard is to state the responsibility of AIMR members and nonmember holders of, and candidates for, the CFA designation to provide complete disclosure of the sources and nature of their compensation or other benefits received for services rendered, including compensation by the client or customer directly, and any incremental compensation or other benefit received by separate agreement or indirectly from third parties. The client, customer, or employer is entitled to have full knowledge of compensation or other benefit arrangements to assess the true cost of the service properly. In addition, because compensation or other benefit arrangements may have a material impact on loyalties and objectivity and thus are potential conflicts of interest, the information is necessary to evaluate the actions and motivations of the analyst or investment manager.

Compensation and other benefit disclosure requirements should also discourage the use of devices such as compensation in kind by products or services and reimbursement of expenses that conceal compensation received by the financial analyst or investment manager.

Conduct Affected by the Standard

The standard requires that each investment professional inform his customers, clients, and employer about additional compensation or other benefit agreements.[1] To inform means to advise in writing of the full circumstances as well as any subsequent modifications within a reasonable period of the effective date. "Employer" means immediate supervisor.

Application of the Standard

The following are examples of violations of this standard:

Example 1: White, a portfolio analyst for Adams Trust Co., manages the account of Cochran, a client. White is paid a salary by his employer, and Cochran pays the trust company a standard fee based on the market value of assets in his portfolio. One day, Cochran proposes to White that "any year that my portfolio achieves at least a 15 percent return before taxes, you and your wife fly to Florida at my expense and use my condominium during the third week of January." Cochran is insistent. White does not inform his employer of the arrangement and vacations in Florida the following January as Cochran's guest.

Comment: White violated Standard VI A by failing to inform his employer of this supplemental, contingent compensation arrangement. The nature of the arrangement could have resulted in partiality to Cochran's account, which could have detracted from White's performance with respect to other accounts he handled for Adams Trust.

Example 2: Snead, a portfolio manager for Thomas Investment Counsel, Inc., specializes in managing defined benefit pension plan accounts, all of which are in the accumulative phase and have long-term investment objectives. Recently, Snead's employer, in an attempt to motivate and retain key investment professionals, introduced a bonus compensation system that rewarded portfolio managers on the basis of quarterly performance relative to their peers and certain benchmark indices. One year later, an officer of Griffin Corporation, one of Snead's pension fund clients, asked why the corporation's portfolio seemed to be dominated by high beta stocks of companies that often appeared among the most actively traded issues. No change in objective or strategy had been recommended by Snead during the year. Snead avoided answering the officer's question.

Comment: Snead violated Standard VI A by failing to inform her clients of the changes in her compensation arrangement with her employer. The pressure to achieve short-term performance goals was in basic conflict with the objectives of her accounts. A supervisory failure may also have been involved as there apparently was no review of either the accounts involved or trades. (See Standard II D.)

Example 3: Hi-Tech Corporation manufactures products by means of a number of processes that are proprietary but only partly protected by patents.

As a leader in its industry, it has other trade secrets that its competitors would like to obtain. Jones, an analyst employed by a broker–dealer, follows the industry and is aware of some of the corporation's processes and trade secrets. He is approached by the Milton Company and offered a consulting arrangement that will pay him fees for his knowledge. He realizes that the only knowledge he has that Milton would use would be considered proprietary by Hi-Tech.

Comment: Because Jones has acquired his knowledge as a result of his employment as an analyst, he is obligated to disclose any such consulting arrangement to his primary employer. In addition, the analyst's obligation under the Code is to "conduct himself with integrity and dignity." Standard IX emphasizes the analyst's responsibility to act in a professional manner as well as with personal integrity, because analysts' actions reflect not only upon their personal reputations and that of their employer but also upon the investment profession as a whole.

Example 4: Rome, a trust officer for Paget Trust Company, was promoted to that position two years ago. Smith, his supervisor, is responsible for reviewing both Rome's trust account transactions and his monthly reports of personal stock transactions.

Rome has been using Black, a broker, almost exclusively for trust account brokerage transactions. Where Black makes a market in stocks, he has been giving Rome lower prices for personal purchases and higher prices for sales than he gives to Rome's trust accounts and other investors. Rome has been filing monthly reports with Smith only for those months in which he has no personal transactions, which is about every fourth month.

Comment: Rome violated Standard VI A by not disclosing to his employer the preferential treatment given for his personal stock transactions. He also violated his fiduciary responsibility to the bank's trust accounts (see Standard VII C) and probably violated banking laws. If the bank were a registered investment adviser, Rome would also have violated the Investment Advisers Act and other securities laws.[2]

If the bank were a registered broker and a member of the National Association of Securities Dealers, Rome would have violated NASD's free-riding provisions.[3]

Smith, the supervisor, violated Standard II D in failing to provide reasonable procedures for supervising Rome properly in his trading for trust accounts and to detect his failure to report personal stock transactions.

Procedures for Compliance

Information concerning a financial analyst's compensation should be provided to the financial analyst's customers, clients, and employer in writing.

The financial analyst also should make an immediate written report to his employer specifying any compensation he proposes to receive (in addition to salaries or other compensation received from the employer) for services rendered for the employer or the employer's customers or clients. This written report should state the terms of any oral or written agreement under which the financial analyst will receive additional compensation, such as the nature of the compensation, the amount of compensation, and the duration of the agreement. No arrangement should be entered into without the employer's approval because inherent conflicts of interest may exist in such circumstances.

The financial analyst also should disclose in writing any compensation he receives from an issuer or other person other than his employer, including payments in cash or in kind for services he renders to his customers or clients. This written statement should describe the compensation, such as fees for referring brokerage or for recommending an issuer's securities; identify the person or firm paying the compensation; and describe the conditions under which the compensation will be earned. If an employer or a financial analyst manages a portfolio for which the fee is based on a share of capital gains or capital appreciation (a performance fee), this should be disclosed to other customers or clients.[4]

The investment professional also should disclose, with the approval of his employer, special compensation arrangements with the employer that might conflict with client or customer interests, such as bonuses based on short-term performance criteria, commissions, incentive fees, performance fees, and referral fees. Information on the analytical compensation packages could be included in the company service promotional literature.

The financial analyst should keep a record of the written reports given to each customer or client. If the financial analyst's compensation for services to the customer or client from sources other than the customer or client changes materially, he should advise the customer or client in writing within a reasonable period of time. If the change affects a small number of clients, a reasonable period might be one or two weeks. If the change affects a large number of clients, a longer time period would be reasonable. An increase or decrease in salary is not a material change. Similarly, addition of bonuses based on length of service or other criteria not measured by employee performance is not a material change.

Footnotes

1. For cases discussing the duty of disclosure for investment professionals generally, see *U.S. v. Hibler* (C.D.Cal.), SEC Rel. No. LR-9490 (November 2, 1981); *In re Cortes*, SEC Rel. No. IA-743(January 7, 1981); *In re Pitts*, SEC Rel. No. 34-17274 (November 6, 1980); *In re Gatliff and Martinson*, SEC Rel. No. 34-16680 (March 20, 1980); *SEC v. Miller Advisory Services*, SEC Rel. No. LR-IA-705 (November 5, 1979).
2. See *In re Langfield*, SEC Rel. No. 34-13766, [1977-78] Fed. Sec. L. Rep. (CCH) ¶81,241 (July 19, 1977). See also Securities and Exchange Commission, Uniform Form ADV. *Uniform Application for Investment Adviser Registration*, Part II, 12, "Investment or Brokerage Discretion," and 13, "Additional Compensation," and *In re Patterson Capital Corp., and Joseph B. Patterson*, SEC Administrative Proceeding File No. 3-7349 (June 25, 1990), which describes required disclosure of soft dollar arrangements in Form ADV.
3. NASD, *Rules of Fair Practice*, Article III, §1, Business Conduct of Members, Board of Governors Interpretation on Free-Riding and Withholding.
4. Securities and Exchange Commission, *Exemption to Allow Registered Investment Advisers to Charge Fees Based Upon a Share of Capital Gains Upon or Capital Appreciation of a Client's Account*, Rel. No. 1A 996 (November 14, 1985).

Standard VI A
Reference Material

1. Securities Act of 1933, §17(b).
2. Securities Exchange Act of 1934, §9(a)(5).
3. National Association of Securities Dealers, *Rules of Fair Practice*, Article III, §10, Influencing or Rewarding Employees of Others, and 11, Payment Designed to Influence Market Prices, Other than Paid Advertising.
4. New York Stock Exchange, Rule 353, Rebates and Compensation.
5. Securities and Exchange Commission, *Interpretive Release Concerning the Scope of Section 28(e) of the Securities Exchange Act of 1934 and Related Matters*, SEC Rel. No. 34-23170 (April 23, 1986).
6. Securities and Investment Board of the United Kingdom, *Soft Commission Arrangements in the Securities Markets, a Policy Statement;* includes proposed core rules (July 1990).
7. Krikorian, "Introduction to Soft Dollars," *Fiduciary Standards in Pension and Trust Fund Management,* (Butterworth Legal Publishers 1989).
8. Gillis and Kern, "New Soft Dollar Rules," *Financial Analysts Journal* (September/October 1986).

VI. COMPENSATION

B. Disclosure of Referral Fees

The financial analyst shall make appropriate disclosure to a prospective client or customer of any consideration paid or other benefit delivered to others for recommending his services to that prospective client or customer.

Purpose of the Standard

The purpose of the standard is to state the responsibility of AIMR members and nonmember holders of, and candidates for, the CFA designation to inform customers and clients of fees paid or other benefit received for referrals of customers and clients. Such disclosure should help the customer or client evaluate any possible partiality shown in any recommendation of services as well evaluate the full cost of the services.

Conduct Affected by the Standard

Appropriate disclosure means advising the customer or client before entry into any formal agreement for services "of any consideration paid or other benefit delivered to others for recommending his services."[1] In addition, the nature of the consideration or benefit should be disclosed, e.g., flat fee or percentage basis, one-time or continuing, or based on performance or provision of research or other noncash benefit, together with the estimated dollar value. Consideration includes all fees, whether paid in cash, soft dollars, or in kind.

Application of the Standard

Example 1: Brady Securities, Inc., a broker–dealer, has established a referral arrangement with Lewis Corp., an investment counseling firm. Under this agreement, Brady refers all prospective tax-exempt accounts, including pension, profit-sharing, and endowment accounts, to Lewis. In return, Lewis makes available to Brady on a regular basis the security recommendations and reports of its research staff, which registered representatives of Brady use in serving customers. In addition, Lewis conducts monthly economic and market reviews for Brady personnel and directs all stock commission business generated by referral accounts to Brady. Lewis calculates that the incremental costs involved in functioning, in effect, as the research department of Brady amount to $20,000 annually; that referrals from Brady last year resulted in fee income of $200,000; and that directing all stock trades through Brady resulted in additional costs to Lewis clients of $10,000.

White, a partner of Lewis Corp., is contacted by Ross, the chief financial officer of Maxwell Corp. Ross states that he is seeking an investment manager for the corporation's profit-sharing plan and that "my friend Hill at Brady Securities recommended your firm without any qualifications, and that's good enough for me. Do we have a deal?"

White accepts the new account, but does not disclose his firm's referral arrangement with Brady Securities.

Comment: White violated Standard VI B by failing to inform the prospective customer of the referral fee payable in services and commissions for an indefinite period to Brady Securities. Such a disclosure could have caused Ross to reassess Hill's recommendation and make a more critical evaluation of Lewis Corp.'s services.

White may also have violated Standard II A if he were required to register as an investment adviser with the SEC or one or more states and did not disclose the information as required in Part II of the Uniform Form ADV.[2] (See also Standard VII C.)

The practice of Lewis raises other ethical and legal questions including whether the client referred, knew of, and consented to the use of Brady for all of its portfolio business. The SEC has raised various issues in connection with the use of brokerage for referrals.

Moreover, if cash were to be paid by Lewis to Brady Securities, that action would violate Investment Advisers Act Rule 206(4)-3, which prohibits cash referral fees in many circumstances unless certain specific steps are taken involving, among other things, extensive prior disclosure of the arrangement.

On a related issue, the New York Stock Exchange Rules prohibit rebates by registered representatives, among others, for business sought or procured by them (Rule 353, Rebates and Compensation), and both the NYSE and the National Association of Securities Dealers prohibit payment of compensation, or gratuities over a specified sum, to various persons outside the organization (Rule 350, Compensation or Gratuities to Employees of Others, and Article

III, Section 10, Influencing or Rewarding Employees of Others, respectively). The NYSE also prohibits an employee of a member firm from being employed or compensated by another person without the member firm's written consent (Rule 346, Limitations-Employment and Association with Members and Member Organizations).

Procedures for Compliance

The following checklist includes actions all financial analysts should follow.

■ *Disclose all agreements.* Disclose the existence and terms of any referral fee agreement to any prospective customer or client orally or in writing as soon as the analyst learns that the prospective customer or client has been referred pursuant to such an agreement.

■ *Describe the nature of the consideration and the estimated dollar value of the consideration.*

■ *Put it in writing.* Give a prospective customer or client a written disclosure statement no later than the time the person enters into a formal agreement for services. This written disclosure can be incorporated into the written disclosure of compensation paid by persons other than the customer or client for the analyst's services to the customer or client, which is required by Standard VI A.

■ *Consult a supervisor and legal counsel concerning any prospective arrangement regarding referral fees.*

■ *Follow the instructions of legal counsel in complying with Investment Advisers Act Rule 206(4)-3,* if the financial analyst works for an investment adviser.

Footnotes

1. *Rolf v. Blyth, Eastman Dillon & Co., Inc.*, 424 F.Supp. 1021 (S.D.N.Y. 1977), *aff'd* 570 F.2d 38 (2d Cir. 1978), *cert. den.* 439 U.S. 1039, 99 S.Ct. 642 (December 4, 1978); *In re Stein Roe & Farnham, Inc.*, SEC Administrative Proceeding File No. 307303 (January 22, 1990).
2. Securities and Exchange Commission, Uniform Form ADV, Uniform Application for Investment Adviser Registration, Part II, 12, *Investment or Brokerage Discretion* and 13, *Additional Compensation.*

Standard VI B
Reference Material

1. Investment Advisers Act Rule 206(4)-3, SEC Rel. No. IA-688, [1979] Fed. Sec. L. Rep. (CCH) ¶82,128 (July 12, 1979).
2. Securities and Exchange Commission, *Interpretive Release Concerning the Scope of Section 28(e) of the Securities Exchange Act of 1934 and Related Matters,* SEC Rel. No. 34-23170 (April 23, 1986).
3. SEC Rel. No. IA-318, Fed. Sec. L. Rep. (CCH) ¶78,776 (May 9, 1972).
4. National Association of Securities Dealers, *Rules of Fair Practice,* Article III, §10, Influencing or Rewarding Employees of Others.
5. New York Stock Exchange, Rules 353, Rebates and Compensation, 350, Compensation of Gratuities to Employees of Others, and 346, Limitations-Employment and Association with Members and Member Organizations.
6. Securities and Investment Board, London, *Soft Commission Arrangements in the Securities Markets, a Policy Statement;* includes proposed core rules (July 1990).
7. Krikorian, "Introduction to Soft Dollars," *Fiduciary Standards in Pension and Trust Fund Management* (Butterworth Legal Publishers 1989).
8. Gillis, "Regulation of Investment Managers and Federal Securities Laws," at 628–43 for discussion of relationships with brokers, *The Investment Manager's Handbook* (Dow Jones-Irwin 1980).
9. Casey, "Finders Fee Compensation to Brokers and Others," 31 *The Business Lawyer* 707 (January 1976).
10. Fleischer, Mundheim, and Murphy, "Disclosure of Investment Advice," 6 *Review of Securities Regulation* 16 (September 27, 1973).
11. Gillis and Kern, "New Soft Dollar Rules," *Financial Analysts Journal* (September/October 1986).
12. Lybecker, "Advisers Act Developments," 8 *Review of Securities Regulation* 931 (April 23, 1975).
13. Quinn, "Eliminating Soft Dollars: A Win–Win Argument," *Financial Analysts Journal* (September/October 1988).
14. Ricks and White, "Regulators Stew Over 'Soft Dollars,'" *The Wall Street Journal* (April 4, 1989).

STANDARD VI C
VI. COMPENSATION

C. Duty to Employer

The financial analyst shall not undertake independent practice
which could result in compensation or other benefit in competition
with his employer unless he has received written consent from
both his employer and the person for whom he undertakes
independent employment.

Purpose of the Standard

The purpose of the standard is to state the responsibility of AIMR members
and nonmember holders of, and candidates for, the CFA designation to abstain
from covert competitive activity that could disadvantage or damage an
employer or client. Written consent by both employer and outside client is
necessary to permit independent practice that could result in compensation.

Conduct Affected by the Standard

Each financial analyst must receive written consent from the employer and
outside client before engaging in independent practice that could result in
compensation or other benefit. "Practice" means any service that the employer
currently makes available for remuneration. If the independent practice is
undertaken—that is, actually begun rather than only making preparations to
begin such practice while employed—the standard is applicable. The standard
also applies to activity being conducted that could result in compensation and
the actual receipt of compensation is not required.

In addition, if an investment professional plans to leave his current
employer, he has a fiduciary duty of loyalty to the employer to act in the best
interest of his employer and not to do anything that would conflict with this
duty to his employer until his resignation is affected.

Application of the Standard

Example 1: Boggs, a portfolio manager for ABC Trust Company, was asked by a neighbor, Gray, to "take a look at the pension fund portfolio of my small manufacturing company." Gray, as president of the company, acts as trustee of the pension plan and has invested the funds based on his own limited financial knowledge. He has not sought the services of Boggs's employer or any other professional investment manager, because he believed the plan was too small to interest anyone.

Boggs reviewed the portfolio on Saturday and developed a number of recommendations, which he discussed with Gray on Sunday at Gray's house. Boggs was surprised at the size of the fund, which would be ranked as large as ABC Trust's other retirement accounts. Gray was impressed with Boggs's thorough analysis and asked if he would do a similar review again in three months. As a gesture of appreciation, he sent Boggs an expensive gift, which Boggs accepted. After the next review and meeting, Gray insisted that Boggs accept a check for an amount that was in excess of the quarterly fee ABC Trust would have charged an account of this size.

This arrangement was mutually satisfactory, and quarterly meetings continued for a number of years. Boggs did not inform his employer of the service he was performing for Gray.

Comment: Boggs violated Standard VI C by not seeking written consent to provide services for Gray. Because of the size of the account, Gray's willingness to pay for professional assistance, and Gray's request for continuous review, Boggs was clearly in competition with his employer. The fact that he performed these services on his own time (weekends) is not relevant. The written consent of both ABC Trust and Gray were the requirements for Boggs to accept compensation without violating Standard VI C.

Example 2: Adams, a registered investment adviser, does business as a sole proprietorship with four clients. He is interested in making an affiliation with a brokerage firm; he is offered and accepts a position as an employee with Star Brokerage Services in the advisory department. He continues to maintain his initial business as well.

Comment: Adams should obtain the written consent of his new employer to maintain and to be independently compensated by his old clients. Registration with various self-regulatory agencies supervising member brokers will also be required. Adams should also disclose in writing to each of his clients and prospective clients his employment by Star Brokerage Services.[1] (See Standard V.)

Example 3: Black is a representative registered with the SEC and the National Association of Securities Dealers (NASD) and employed by Drew Brokers, Inc. Black is also working with Acme, Inc., unbeknownst to Drew, to make a sale in a private transaction of a block of securities owned by the principal stockholder of Acme and has arranged for a buyer of those securities. Upon completion of the sale, Black is to receive a negotiated fee from the seller. The transaction has not been completed, however, nor any compensation paid to Black, at the time that Drew Brokers discovers the activity and alleges that it is in violation of Standard VI C as no consent has been obtained from Drew or Acme.

Comment: This conduct is a violation of Standard VI C. Black has not received consent from Drew and from Acme and the principal stockholder, and if completed, the transaction could result in compensation. It is clearly in competition with his employer, as Drew Brokers engages in the same business. This type of private transaction is also in violation of the NASD *Rules of Fair Practice* Section 40.

Investment professionals, officers of a corporation, and all employees occupy positions of trust with their employers. They have a duty of loyalty and a duty to protect the business of their employer.

An officer or professional employee has a higher standard of conduct. He must not only protect the interest of the corporation committed to his charge but must also refrain from doing anything that would injure the corporation, deprive it of profit, or deprive it of the advantage that his skills and ability bring to it.

In spite of high standards of conduct imposed on professional employees, they are not necessarily precluded from entering an independent business in competition. The departing employee is generally free to make arrangements or preparations to go into a competitive business before terminating his relationship with his employer, provided no unfair or wrongful acts are committed in the course of such preparations and that such preparations do not breach the employee's duty of loyalty.

Basic standards for those who plan to compete are difficult to define because the spectrum of potential activities is as broad as the facts of individual situations. Courts look at the total circumstances to separate permissible preparations from violations of duty, for which liability may be imposed.

Circumstances which might be a violation, especially in combination, include:

■   Misappropriation of trade secrets.
■   Misuse of confidential information.
■   Conspiracy to bring about mass resignation of employees by other

employees.

■ Solicitation of employer's customers prior to cessation of employment.

■ Planning involving a conspiracy or characterized by secrecy and deceit.

■ Self dealing (an employee may not appropriate for his own property a business opportunity or information belonging to his employer).

■ Misappropriation of customers or customer lists. (Some courts have made an exception to this rule when the departing employee originally brought the client to the employer.)

■ A change from the original understanding between client, employer, and employee.

In determining whether the employee has breached the fiduciary duty to his employer, courts conduct a thorough examination of the facts and circumstances of the particular case. If it is determined that the employee has violated his duty, the courts may either reduce or eliminate his pay during the period in which he is in violation.

Example 4: Magee manages pension accounts for Trust Assets, Inc., but is frustrated with the working environment there. After a lengthy job search, Magee is offered a position with Fiduciary Management. Before resigning from Trust Assets, Magee asks four big accounts to leave that firm and open accounts with Fiduciary.

Comment: Magee has a duty to Trust Assets as long as he is employed there. Soliciting its client relationships is unethical and violates Standard VI C.

Example 5: Marsh is a portfolio manager at Olsen & Co. She decides to start her own investment management business, and without the knowledge of her superiors at Olsen, quietly goes about the business of attracting new clients for her new firm. She succeeds in persuading several prospects to sign investment management agreements. Marsh had previously made presentations to these prospects on behalf of Olsen. Before she has the opportunity to announce her new venture, the principals at Olsen uncover her business plan from outside sources.

Comment: Marsh violated the fundamental agency law principle requiring every employee to act solely for her employer's benefit. Even though she had not solicited her existing Olsen clients, she nevertheless solicited prospects of Olsen for her new firm in competition with her current employer. Therefore, Marsh is in violation of Standard VI C.

Example 6: Hightower has been employed by Jason Investment Management Corporation for fifteen years. He began as an analyst and assumed increasing responsibilities and positions over the years and is now a senior portfolio manager and a member of the firm's investment policy committee. Hightower has decided to leave Jason and start his own investment management business. Hightower has been careful not to tell any of Jason's clients that he is leaving as he does not want to be accused of breaching his duty to Jason by soliciting Jason clients before his departure date. However, Hightower is planning to copy and take with him the following documents and information that he developed or worked on while at Jason: (1) the client list with addresses, telephone numbers, custodians, investment objectives and other pertinent client information; (2) client statements with a breakdown of assets held and cost data; (3) sample marketing presentations to prospective clients with Jason's performance record; (4) Jason's recommended list of securities; (5) computer program models for asset allocation with different objectives; (6) computer program models for stock selection; and (7) personal computer spread sheets for Hightower's major corporate recommendations with income and balance sheets and ratios which he developed when he was an analyst. Should Hightower copy and take copies of these documents?

Comment: The standards provide that an investment professional holds a position of trust and has a duty to his employer. This obligation is consistent with the common-law concept of duty of loyalty of employees to their employers. It is well established that except with consent of their employer, departing employees may not take property of their employer whether it be tangible property including books, records or other materials and may not interfere with their employer's business opportunity. The details of these requirements vary from state to state, and, in addition are often embodied in employee agreements which also have widely varying terms. Thus, a departing analyst should be alert that taking any employer records, even though prepared by him, may be a violation of the standard as well as local law (See Standards II A and V). In these situations, because of the widely varying circumstances and legal requirements, analysts are encouraged to seek advice of counsel.

Procedures for Compliance

The financial analyst should provide a written statement to his employer describing the type of services he would render the prospective independent client or customer, the expected duration of the services, and his compensation for services rendered. The financial analyst should not render services until he receives a written consent from his employer to all of the terms he has disclosed.

The financial analyst also should disclose to the prospective client or customer the identity of his employer, the fact that he is performing independently of his employer, and the fees or charges his employer would make for rendering the same services. The financial analyst should not render services until the client gives consent in writing, indicating that he has read and understood the member's written disclosure statement.

Footnote

1. *Yankee Management of Boston*, SEC no-action letter (June 5, 1974).

Standard VI C
Reference Material

1. National Association of Securities Dealers, *Rules of Fair Practice,* Article III, §10, Influencing or Rewarding Employees of Others, and §40, Private Transactions.
2. New York Stock Exchange, Rule 346, Limitations-Employment and Association with Members and Member Organizations.

VII. RELATIONSHIPS WITH OTHERS

A. Preservation of Confidentiality

A financial analyst shall preserve the confidentiality of information communicated by the client concerning matters within the scope of the confidential relationship, unless the financial analyst receives information concerning illegal activities on the part of the client.

Purpose of the Standard

The purpose of the standard is to state the responsibility of AIMR members and nonmember holders of, and candidates for, the CFA designation to preserve the confidentiality of certain types of information communicated by clients and to urge them to educate their firms about this responsibility.

Conduct Affected by the Standard

The investment professional must preserve the confidentiality of information received from a client if two criteria are met. First, the analyst/manager must be in a relationship of trust with the client who has engaged him, on the basis of his special ability to conduct a portion of the client's business or personal affairs. Second, the information the analyst or manager receives must result from or be relevant to that portion of the client's business that is the subject of the special or confidential relationship. However, if the information concerns illegal activities by the client, the financial analyst may have an obligation to consult with his supervisor and, in conjunction with legal counsel, decide whether to report the activities to the appropriate governmental organization. (See Standards II B and VII C.)

Application of the Standard

Example 1: Connor, a financial analyst employed by Johnson Investment Counselors, Inc., provides investment advice to trustees of City Medical

Center. The trustees have given her a number of internal reports concerning City Medical's needs for physical plant renovation and expansion. They have asked Connor to recommend investments that would generate capital appreciation in endowment funds to meet projected capital expenditures. Connor then is approached by a local businessman, Kasey, who is considering a substantial contribution either to City Medical Center or to another local hospital. Kasey wants to find out the building plans of both institutions before making a decision, but he does not want to speak to the trustees.

Comment: The trustees gave Connor the internal reports so she could advise them on how to manage their endowment funds. As the information in the reports is clearly both confidential and within the scope of the confidential relationship, Connor should refuse to divulge information to Kasey.

Example 2: Moody is an investment officer at the Lester Trust Company. He has an advisory customer who has talked to him about giving approximately $50,000 to charity to reduce his income taxes. Moody is also treasurer of the Home for Indigent Widows, which is planning its annual giving campaign. It hopes to expand its list of prospects, particularly those capable of substantial gifts. Moody recommends that the home's vice president, responsible for corporate gifts, call on his customer and ask for a donation in the $25,000–$50,000 range.

Comment: Moody violated the standard by revealing confidential information about his customer even though the attempt to help the home was well intended.

Example 3: The Internal Revenue Service and Department of Labor approach Jones, the portfolio manager for Maxwell Company's pension plan, to examine pension fund records, stating that Maxwell's corporate tax returns are being audited and the pension fund reviewed. Two days earlier, Jones learned in a regular investment review meeting with Maxwell officers that potentially excessive and improper charges are being made to the pension plan by Maxwell and that similar charges are yet to be made. Jones consults her employer's general counsel and is advised that Maxwell has probably violated ERISA tax and fiduciary regulations as well as state fiduciary law by these charges to the pension fund.

Comment: Jones should inform her supervisor of these activities, and the employer should take steps with Maxwell to remedy these violations. If that is not successful the firm may well have a duty to disclose the evidence in its possession of the continuing legal violations. Advice of counsel should be sought regarding appropriate steps to be taken. (See Standards II B and VII C.)

Example 4: Billings is a rating officer who follows beverage companies for a major rating agency. In the course of an annual update, one of the companies told him that a large division faced environmental problems that had not yet been disclosed. An appropriate reserve was estimated. In Billings's judgment, the reserve would significantly harm the company's already thin capital base, trigger debt covenants, and possibly put the company into play. Following the meeting, Billings wants to lower the company's ratings dramatically, but the action cannot be justified without disclosing the nonpublic information. Company management is furious and threatens to sue the rating agency, which it views as a "constructive insider" to which it could disclose the problem without risk of dissemination until the company is ready to make its announcement.

Comment: Rating agencies are in fact treated by most companies as insiders. Billings can urge the company to release the information publicly as soon as possible, but he could not disseminate the information without the company's consent.

Procedures for Compliance

The simplest, most conservative, and most effective approach is to avoid disclosing any information received from a client, except to authorized fellow employees who are also working for the client. This, of course, includes information that is conveyed in confidence by a client and information that, under the standards, may not be disclosed by a financial analyst.

There are some instances in which analysts may want to disclose information received from clients that is outside the scope of the confidential relationship and does not involve illegal activities. Before making such a disclosure the financial analyst should ask:

1. In what context was the information disclosed? If disclosed in a discussion of work being performed for the client, did the client indicate the information was relevant to the work?

2. Is it background information that will enable the analyst to perform services for the client more effectively?

3. If the analyst is contemplating disclosure of material nonpublic information in accordance with Standard II C, can he persuade the client to disclose the information? Does he have a fiduciary duty as described in Standard VII C to be discussed with his supervisor?

Standard VII A
Reference Material

1. National Association of Securities Dealers, *Rules of Fair Practice*, Article III, §9, Use of Information Obtained in Fiduciary Capacity.
2. American Bar Association, *Model Code of Professional Responsibility*, Canon 4, and Ethical Considerations and Disciplinary Rule thereunder (1980).
3. American Institute of Certified Public Accountants, *Code of Professional Ethics*, ET §301 (1990).
4. See Chapter on Standard II B generally and references therein.

VII. RELATIONSHIPS WITH OTHERS

B. Maintenance of Independence and Objectivity

The financial analyst, in relationships and contacts with an issuer of securities, whether individually or as a member of a group, shall use particular care and good judgment to achieve and maintain independence and objectivity.

Purpose of the Standard

The purpose of the standard is to state the responsibility of AIMR members and nonmember holders of, and candidates for, the CFA designation to maintain independence and objectivity in dealings with issuers so that their customers, clients, and employer will have the benefit of their work and opinions unaffected by any potential conflict of interest or circumstance adversely affecting their judgment.

Conduct Affected by the Standard

Investment professionals may be offered gifts or invited to lavish investor relations functions that could prejudice their opinions about a sponsor. These offers apply broadly to many different kinds of incentives: tickets, favors, job referrals, and future business transactions, and so on. Although modest gifts and entertainment are acceptable, at some point the line of propriety may be crossed.

Analysts may also come under pressure from their own managements to issue favorable reviews of certain companies. In a full-service investment house, the corporate finance department may be an underwriter for a company's securities and loath to antagonize that company by publishing negative research. Similarly, the commercial side of a bank may derive substantial revenues from its lending/deposit relationship with a company and attempts may be made to influence the work of analysts in the trust department. The situation may be aggravated if the CEO of the company sits on the bank's board and attempts to interfere in the trust department's decision-making process. Financial analysts acting in a sales/marketing capacity should be especially certain of their independence in selecting appropriate investments for their clients.

The investment professional must continuously be conscious of the need to maintain independence and objectivity. It is, therefore, the responsibility of the analyst/manager to take whatever action is necessary to maintain the appropriate balance with an issuer to retain independence and objectivity.

Common sense and logic should be used in contacts and relationships with issuers. The aim of the financial analyst is to prevent situations from arising that might be, or be perceived to cause, a loss of independence or objectivity in recommending investments.

An analogous situation concerns the relations between analysts and other financial intermediaries. Material gratuities and hospitality should not be accepted from financial intermediaries if they would influence an analyst's independence and objectivity (see Standard II D).

Application of the Standard

Special care should be taken by the analyst and investment manager to resist subtle and not-so-subtle pressures by issuers to promote their companies or recommend their stock. Investor relations programs organized by issuers are designed to obtain the broadest following possible and usually present a favorable picture of the company's prospects.

The following examples illustrate the financial analyst's need to maintain independence and objectivity:

Example 1: Tyler's, a mining analyst with Bullock Brokers, is invited by Precision Metals to join a group of his peers from across the United States in touring mining facilities in several western states. The company arranges chartered group flights from site to site and for accommodations in Spartan Motels, the only chain with accommodations near the mines, for three nights. Tyler allows Precious Metals to pick up his tab, as do the other analysts—with one exception, Adams, an employee of a large Boston trust company. Adams insists on following his company's policy and pays for his motel room.

Comment: The policy of Adams's company complies with the standard. If Tyler's firm has no policy, he could consult his supervisor about handling the room charge. Failing to receive a clear-cut answer, he could consult his conscience. In this instance, the trip was strictly business and he was not accepting irrelevant or lavish hospitality. Companies paid the transportation to the point of departure, which was not an inconsiderable expense. The arrangements were not at all unusual. The itinerary required charter flights, for which analysts could not be expected to pay. The accommodations were modest. Investment professionals must continually deal with questions of degree. In the final analysis, they must consider both whether they can remain objective and whether their integrity might be perceived to have been compromised in the eyes of their clients.

Example 2: Dillon, an analyst in the corporate finance department of her firm, is making a new business presentation including the promise of research coverage.

Comment: Dillon may agree to accept research coverage but must not commit herself to a favorable recommendation. Her recommendation (favorable, neutral, or unfavorable) must be based on an independent and objective investigation and analysis of the company and its securities.

Example 3: Fritz is an equity analyst with Hilton Brokerage, covering the mining industry. He concludes that the stock of Metals & Mining is overpriced at current levels. However, he is concerned that a negative research report would hurt the good relationship between Metals & Mining and the investment banking division of his company. In fact, he is aware of a proposal before the company to underwrite a debt offering.

Comment: Fritz's analysis of Metals & Mining should be objective and based solely on consideration of company fundamentals. Any pressure from other divisions of his company is inappropriate.

Example 4: As support to the sales effort of her corporate bond department, Wagner offers credit guidance to purchasers of fixed-income securities. Her compensation is closely linked to the performance of this department. Near the quarter's end, Wagner's company has a large inventory position in the bonds of Milton, Ltd., which the company had been unable to sell as a result of a recently announced operating problem. Salespeople have asked her to contact large clients to push the bonds.

Comment: Issues involving unethical sales practices are significant potential abuses. Wagner's opinion on the bonds of Milton, Ltd. should not be clouded by internal pressure or compensatory incentives. Wagner must be able to justify any recommendations first to herself and then to any client of her firm.

Example 5: Joe Clinrock is a securities analyst following airline stocks, and is a rising star at his firm. His boss has been carrying a buy recommendation on International Airlines and asks Joe to take over coverage of that airline. Joe is told that under no circumstances should the prevailing buy recommendation be changed.

Comment: Joe should be independent and objective in his analysis of International Airlines. If he feels that is compromised, he has two options: tell his boss that he doesn't feel he should cover the company under those constraints, or pick up coverage of the company, reach his own independent conclusions, and share them with his boss or other supervisors in his firm to the extent that they conflict with his boss' opinion.

Procedures for Compliance

Managements of securities firms are expected to establish a policy stating that any research reports on issues of corporate clients reflect the unbiased opinion of the analyst. Compensation systems should also protect the integrity of the investment decision process.

A sharing-of-expenses policy relating to gifts and entertainment should be adopted by each financial analyst as a general guideline, when feasible. This involves an economic decision by the financial analyst, and this cost-sharing action should eliminate the possibility for, and alleviate any perception by the public of, the financial analyst being subjected to undue influence by a corporate issuer. This subject is also treated in Standard II D and in Standard VI A, Standard VI B, and Standard VI C. This standard is applicable to the financial analyst, individually, or as a part of a group. This means analyst societies, splinter groups, or other groups of financial analysts should follow these guidelines when seminars, conventions, or other group activities are involved.

Exhibit A lists specific guidelines for compliance.

EXHIBIT A
GUIDELINES FOR COMPLIANCE

1. *Disclose all corporate relationships*, including whether any analyst, officer, partner, or employee of the securities firm is a director of the company and whether the securities firm underwrites the securities of the company and/or makes a market in them.

2. *Devise a restricted list.* If management is unwilling to permit dissemination of adverse opinions about a corporate client, remove the company from the research universe and put it on a restricted list setting forth only factual information.

3. *Restrict special cost arrangements.* When attending meetings at the issuer's headquarters, a financial analyst should pay for commercial transportation and hotel charges. This will offset the issuer's cost of meals and other activities. No corporate issuer should reimburse a financial analyst for air transportation. Issuers should be encouraged to limit the use of corporate aircraft to situations in which commercial transportation is not available or in which the efficient movement of a group of analysts could not otherwise be expedited. Likewise particular care should be taken when frequent meetings are held between an individual issuer and an individual financial analyst. The financial analyst should not always be hosted by an issuer. Alternate absorption of expenses is encouraged.

4. *Limit gifts.* Acceptance of gifts by financial analysts from issuers should be limited to token items. The National Association of Securities Dealers and the New York Stock Exchange have $50 and $100 limits, respectively. This is a good guideline for financial analysts. In cases where the wholesale value is clearly in excess of this amount, the gift should be returned to the issuer.

Standard VII B
Reference Material

1.   National Association of Securities Dealers, *Rules of Fair Practice,* Article III, §10, Influencing or Rewarding Employees of Others.
2.   New York Stock Exchange, Rule 350, Compensation or Gratuities to Employees of Others.

VII. RELATIONSHIPS WITH OTHERS

C. Fiduciary Duties

The financial analyst, in relationships with clients, shall use particular care in determining applicable fiduciary duty and shall comply with such duty as to those persons and interests to whom it is owed.

Purpose of the Standard

The purpose of the standard is to state the responsibility of AIMR members and nonmember holders of, and candidates for, the CFA designation to understand the nature of the fiduciary responsibility they assume with each client relationship and to apply that understanding appropriately to their professional conduct. A fiduciary, as defined by the American Bankers Association, is "an individual or . . . institution charged with the duty of acting for the benefit of another party as to matters coming within the scope of the relationship between them."[1] AIMR members need such knowledge in order to place the fiduciary obligation first in all dealings, thus avoiding potential conflicts of interest with that obligation and other inappropriate conduct. The duty required in fiduciary relationships exceeds that which is acceptable in many other business relationships.

Conduct Affected by the Standard

This standard relates principally to those members who have discretionary authority or responsibility for the management of a client's assets or who have other relationships of special trust.

The investment manager's fiduciary[2] responsibility to a client includes a duty of loyalty as well as a reasonable standard of care. The Employee Retirement Income Security Act of 1974 specifically imposes and defines fiduciary duties[3] and includes both requirements. Investment actions should be carried out for the sole benefit of the client and should not be compromised. An investment manager's duty is based upon this tenet and is a continuing responsibility. To the extent these conditions are met, within the confines of the law, a breach of fiduciary duty is avoided.

A necessary corollary of this duty is to determine what the responsibility is and to whom it is owed. In many instances, there is a difference between the party that hires the investment manager and the beneficiary of the fund. An employee benefit plan may be the most common example in which fiduciary responsibility is to the beneficiary of the fund as opposed to the company that employs the manager.

The appropriateness of a specific investment approach will depend on such factors as the nature of the manager–client relationship, what is represented, what is agreed to, and what others similarly situated would regard as appropriate. Fiduciary standards apply to a large number of persons in varying capacities, but the exact duties may differ in many respects. The duties are usually directed against conflicts of interest, utilization of opportunities for one's own benefit, and other forms of self-dealing. (See also Standard VI B, Standard VII A, and Standard VII B.)

Investment managers may, however, occasionally find themselves at odds with sponsors advocating investments on the basis of altruistic rationales. For instance, state and local governments and nonprofit entities may seek to invest pension funds in community projects. The managers must ensure that such investments do not impair the integrity of the funds in question or the financial security of the participants.

Application of the Standard

Situations involving potential conflicts of interest with respect to fiduciary responsibility can be extremely complex, as these situations often involve a number of competing interests and conflicts. The examples that follow serve to illustrate certain specific conflict areas.

Example 1: First County Bank serves as trustee for the Miller Co.'s profit sharing plan. Miller is the target of a hostile takeover attempt by Newton, Inc. In attempting to ward off Newton, Miller's management persuades Wiley, an investment manager at First County Bank, to purchase Miller common stock in the open market for the employee profit sharing plan. Miller's officials indicate that such action would be favorably received and would likely result in other accounts being placed with the bank. Although Wiley believes the stock to be fairly valued and would not have otherwise made the purchases, he does so to support Miller Co.'s management, to maintain its good favor, and to realize additional new business. The heavy stock purchases cause the market price to rise to such a level that Newton retracts its takeover bid.

At about the same time, Miller asks its shareholders to vote in favor of certain proxy proposals permitting changes in the corporate bylaws that would, if approved, virtually eliminate the possibility of a successful hostile takeover bid. Without giving the matter much attention, Wiley votes the proxy in favor of management.

Comment: The standard requires that a fiduciary, in evaluating a bid, act prudently and solely in the interests of plan participants and beneficiaries. This requires a careful evaluation of the long-term prospects of the company against the short-term prospects presented by the takeover offer and by the ability to invest elsewhere.[4]

In this instance, Wiley, acting on behalf of his employer, the trustee, clearly violated the standard by using the profit sharing plan to perpetuate existing management, perhaps to the detriment of plan participants and the company's shareholders, and to benefit himself. Wiley's fiduciary responsibilities should take precedence over ties to corporate management and any self-interest. A duty exists to examine such a takeover offer on its own merits and to make an independent decision. A guiding principle should be the appropriateness of the investment decision to the profit sharing fund in contrast to the benefit to the company's management, which hired Wiley, or to any personal interest.

With respect to the proxy solicitation issue, the investment manager has a duty to examine management's proposals and to take whatever action he deems appropriate to protect the plan's investments, particularly in situations where management actions appear improper and can be construed to be substantially unfair to shareholders.[5] By voting with management in this situation, Wiley did not meet the requisite standard of care.

Instances may arise, of course, in which management proposals serve the best interests of the corporation and its shareholders and, therefore, should be supported. In all proxy issues, the investment manager has a duty to make independent decisions and to view with objectivity that which is in the best interest of the client or beneficiary for whom the proxy is voted.[6]

Example 2: JNI, a successful West Coast investment counseling firm, serves as investment manager for the pension plans of several large regionally based companies. Its trading activity generates a significant amount of commission-related business. JNI uses the brokerage and research services of many firms, but most of its trading activity is handled through a large brokerage company, Thompson, Inc., principally because there are close personal relationships between the executives of the two firms. Thompson's commission structure is relatively high; JNI considers its research services and execution capabilities average. To express its gratitude for business, Thompson provides JNI with institutional investor performance analyses as well as pension fund liability and asset allocation studies. In addition, Thompson absorbs a number of JNI overhead expenses, including magazine subscriptions.

Comment: An investment manager, operating in a fiduciary capacity, often has discretion over the selection of brokers executing transactions. Accordingly, payment of brokerage commissions (soft dollars) represents a potential area for abuse, which the standard addresses. Conflict issues arise when an investment manager directs brokerage commissions in situations that might be considered inappropriate given the level of service received. Actions of this nature are contrary to ethical standards and could be in violation of the law.

In this situation, JNI executives breached a fiduciary duty by paying commissions that they knew did not measure up to the value of the brokerage and research services received. The firm should act in good faith in directing commission business to ensure that fairness and loyalty to the client are maintained. In addition, JNI has an obligation to ensure that brokerage services provided are for the express benefit of the client. Payment of operating expenses by Thompson essentially shifts part of the overhead burden to the client, who pays the investment management fee. JNI has failed to uphold its fiduciary allegiance and, therefore, violates the standard. Full disclosure of brokerage commission policies as well as actual commissions paid, together with client consent, serve as effective tools to mitigate such conflict-of-interest situations.[7]

Example 3: Edwards Brothers, a struggling East Coast independent investment advisory firm, serves as investment manager for the profit sharing plans of several widely dispersed companies. Recently, it was learned that one of its brokers, Scott Co., is close to consummating management agreements with prospective new clients for Edwards. Significantly, one of Edwards's important existing clients, Crayton Corp., has signed an agreement whereby Edwards is directed to place securities transactions for Crayton's account through Scott exclusively. However, to induce the Scott Co. to exert best efforts to land more new accounts, Edwards directs transactions to Scott not only from Crayton Corp.'s account but from other clients as well, without their knowledge.

Comment: Edwards Brothers has an obligation to ensure that brokerage services provided are for the express benefit of the client. The appearance of a conflict stems from the fact that the commissions more clearly benefit the investment adviser than the client. At the very least, Edwards had an obligation to disclose to the other clients the fact that commissions were being applied as referral fees to Scott in consideration for incidental marketing services. (See Standard VI B)[8]

Example 4: The named fiduciaries of Plan P retain Jones to manage part of the assets of Plan P. Jones directs the plan's brokerage transactions through Brown. In return, Brown provides research on tax-exempt securities to Jones. Although tax-exempt securities would not be a suitable investment for Plan P, Jones has determined that this research would be useful to his managed accounts as a whole.

Comment: Jones's arrangement with Brown is encompassed by Section 28(e) of the Securities Exchange Act. However, in retaining Jones, the named fiduciaries of Plan P are required under Section 404 (a) (1) of ERISA to periodically review the execution secured by Jones and ensure that the brokerage commissions paid by Plan P to Brown are reasonable.[9]

Procedures for Compliance

Compliance procedures should be established to govern the actions of financial analysts who are in positions of fiduciary responsibility to ensure that investment-related decisions are made on behalf of the client and others to whom the duty is owed. The firm needs to identify situations in which violations are likely to occur on an account-by-account basis and to develop procedures accordingly. Legal advice should be obtained as appropriate.

In establishing compliance procedures, the following factors should be considered:

■ *Follow all rules and laws.* Compliance procedures should incorporate requirements of federal, state, and provincial law, as well as relevant rules and regulations of regulatory agencies and applicable self-regulatory organizations. In addition, the investment manager should be aware of any specific laws affecting the client as well as the wishes of the client.

■ *Investigate fiduciary responsibilities.* The process of developing investment objectives for an account should include understanding fiduciary responsibility and identifying the individual or body to whom such responsibility is owed. An appropriate investment approach to achieve plan objectives can then be established.

■ *Disclose all conflicts.* A high degree of disclosure is essential, particularly as it pertains to potential conflicts of interest and costs incurred in managing an account. Investment professionals should consider making disclosure of soft dollar arrangements for such items as research services, data base access, quote/information services, and other similar services used in the decision-making process and potentially capable of affecting client transaction costs. The clients' express consent should be obtained before specific transactions or changes in procedure are made that potentially would present conflict of interest situations. In some circumstances, even such consent does not make certain actions permissible, and legal counsel should be consulted.

■   *Represent the best interests of clients.* With respect to proxy-related matters, an investment manager should deal responsibly with the issues and represent the best interests of the client and beneficiaries. The firm should establish written guidelines or procedures that reflect current law and provide adequate guidance to employees concerning what is permissible conduct in dealing with proxy issues.[10]

Footnotes

1.   The American Bankers Association (*Glossary of Fiduciary Terms* 1959).
2.   As interpreted by Eugene B. Burroughs, CFA, in *Pension World,* fiduciary under ERISA means "any person who (1) exercises any discretionary control over the management of a plan or the management or disposition of its assets, (2) renders investment advice for a fee with respect to the funds or property of a plan, or has the authority to do so, or (3) has any discretionary authority or responsibility in the administration of a plan."
3.   See also the implied definition of fiduciary, Investment Advisers Act of 1940, §206(1) and (2).
4.   See Department of Labor letter of February 23, 1988, footnote 4: ". . . Section 404(a)(1) (ERISA) requires, among other things, that a fiduciary of a plan act prudently, solely in the interest of the plan's participants and beneficiaries, and for the exclusive purpose of providing benefits to participants and beneficiaries. To act prudently in the voting of proxies (as well as in all other fiduciary matters), a plan fiduciary must consider those factors which would affect the value of the plan's investment. Similarly, the Department has construed the requirements that a fiduciary act solely in the interest of, and for the exclusive purpose of providing benefits to, participants and beneficiaries as prohibiting a fiduciary from subordinating the interests of participants and beneficiaries in their retirement income to unrelated objectives."
5.   Cottle, Murray, and Block, "Corporate Governance: Impact of Security Analysis," in *Security Analysis* (Fifth Ed. 1988) discusses the security analyst's responsibility to be concerned about corporate governance issues, including hostile takeovers, since they impact the valuation of securities and investment results. The third edition (1951) of Graham and Dodd, *Security Analysis* in Part VI on "Stockholders and Management" commented, "It may be just as important to do the wise thing while *being* a stockholder as it is to act wisely in *becoming* or *ceasing to be* a stockholder."
6.   For a discussion of a fiduciary's responsibility to a pension fund in the face of a forced takeover or tender offer, see Casey, *Ethics in the Financial Marketplace,* Chapters 4 and 7.
7.   See, for example, *In re Glass,* SEC Rel. No. IA-1003 (December 17, 1985).

8. See Casey, *supra*, Chapters 9 and 10 for discussion of execution versus soft dollars.
9. U.S. Department of Labor Welfare and Benefits Administration, *Statement on Policies Concerning Soft Dollar and Directed Commission Arrangements,* Technical Release No. 86-1 (May 22, 1986).
10. See, for example, Morton Klevan "Fiduciary Duty and Proxy Voting," *Annual Review of Banking Law* (1988) and Casey, *supra,* Chapter 5.

Standard VII C
Reference Material

1. Employee Retirement Income Security Act of 1974 (ERISA), §404(a)(1) (A),(B),(C), Fiduciary Responsibility.
2. Securities and Exchange Commission, *Interpretative Release Concerning the Scope of Section 28(e) of the Securities Exchange Act of 1934 and Related Matters*, SEC Rel. No. 34-23170 (April 23, 1986).
3. U.S. Comptroller of the Currency—Trust Banking Circular "Soft Dollar Purchases" March 13, 1980, and "Use of Commission Payments by Fiduciaries," June 19, 1986.
4. Securities and Exchange Commission, *Interpretations of Section 28(e) of the Securities Exchange Act of 1934: Use of Commission Payments by Fiduciaries*, SEC Rel. No. 12251 (March 24, 1976).
5. National Association of Securities Dealers, *Rules of Fair Practice*, Article III, §24, Selling Concessions.
6. U.S. Comptroller of the Currency, November 23, 1988, letter on obligation of ERISA fiduciaries with regard to proxy voting and other rights of stock ownership.
7. U.S. Department of Labor Welfare and Benefits Administration, *Statement on Policies Concerning Soft Dollar and Directed Commission Arrangements*, Technical Release No. 86-1 (May 22, 1986).
8. U.S. Department of Labor Pension Welfare and Benefits Administration, letter dated February 23, 1988, on fiduciary responsibility rules governing the conduct of plan officials and others.
9. U.S. Department of Labor Pension Welfare and Benefits Administration, letter dated January 23, 1990, on investment managers' responsibility to vote proxies, match proxies with holdings on the record date, and maintain a record of votes.
10. Department of Labor, Walker, address on fiduciary implications of proxy voting of plan assets (May 12, 1988).
11. Securities and Investment Board, London, *Soft Commission Arrangements in the Securities Markets, a Policy Statement;* includes core rules (July 1990).
12. Association for Investment Management and Research, *Establishing a Proxy Voting Policy for Professional Investors*, Charlottesville, Va. (1990).
13. Financial Analysts Research Foundation, *Broader Perspective on the Interest of Pension Plan Participants* (DeMong, Gray, and Milne, eds. 1985).
14. Financial Analysts Research Foundation, *Takeovers and Shareholders: The Mounting Controversy* (DeMong and Peavy, eds. 1985).
15. Toronto Society of Financial Analysts, "Soft Dollar Survey Results: More on Soft Dollars," *Newsletter* (March 5, 1985); also submission of the Toronto Society of Financial Analysts and the Montreal Society of Financial Analysts to the Quebec Securities Commission on soft dollar arrangements (1985).
16. Casey, *Ethics in the Financial Marketplace* (Scudder, Stephens & Clark 1988).
17. Heard and Sherman, *Conflicts of Interest in the Proxy Voting System* (Investor Responsibility Research Center, Inc., 1987).
18. Krikorian, *Fiduciary Standards in Pension and Trust Fund Management* (Butterworth Legal Publishers 1989).
19. Levine, *The Investment Manager's Handbook*, Chapters 21–23 (Dow Jones-Irwin 1980).
20. Longstreth, *Modern Investment Management and the Prudent Man Rule* (Oxford University Press 1986).

21. Williams, Reilly, and Houck, *Ethics and the Investment Industry* (Rowan & Littlefield Publishers, Inc. 1989).
22. Blanc, "Soft Dollars," 18 *Review of Securities and Commodities Regulation* 4 (February 20, 1985).
23. Gillis, "Soft Dollars and Investment Research," *Financial Analysts Journal* (July/August 1985).
24. Gillis and Kern, "New Soft Dollar Rules," *Financial Analysts Journal* (September/October 1986).
25. Gillis, "The Money Manager as Fiduciary," *Financial Analysts Journal* (March/April 1972).
26. Gillis and Weld, "Fiduciary Responsibility Under the 1974 Pension Act," *Financial Analysts Journal* (May/June 1975).
27. Mercer, "Conflicts of Interest," *Investment Management and the Law* (Boston Security Analysts Society, Inc. and The Financial Analysts Federation 1979).

STANDARD VIII
VIII. USE OF PROFESSIONAL DESIGNATION

The qualified financial analyst may use, as applicable, the professional designation "Member of the Association for Investment Management and Research," "Member of the Financial Analysts Federation," and "Member of the Institute of Chartered Financial Analysts," and is encouraged to do so, but only in a dignified and judicious manner. The use of the designations may be accompanied by an accurate explanation (1) of the requirements that have been met to obtain the designation, and (2) of the Association for Investment Management and Research, the Financial Analysts Federation, and the Institute of Chartered Financial Analysts, as applicable.

The Chartered Financial Analyst may use the professional designation "Chartered Financial Analyst," or the abbreviation "CFA," and is encouraged to do so, but only in a dignified and judicious manner. The use of the designation may be accompanied by an accurate explanation (1) of the requirements that have been met to obtain the designation, and (2) of the Association for Investment Management and Research and the Institute of Chartered Financial Analysts.

Purpose of the Standard

The purpose of the standard is to state the responsibility of AIMR members and nonmember holders of, and candidates for, the CFA designation to use their professional designations (or their candidacy for the designation) properly and in a manner that reflects credit on the holder and the organization and does not mislead the investing public or others.

Obtaining the CFA charter is a significant achievement. It signifies that the investment professional has successfully completed a program including three examinations covering a defined body of knowledge fundamental to the practice of investment management. It is important that employers, clients, customers, and the public recognize this achievement and the professionalism expected of a charter holder. Thus CFAs are encouraged to use the designation in a dignified and judicious manner. The same is true with the designation Member for a qualified member of the AIMR and the Financial Analysts Federation (FAF). The term Regular Member refers to those AIMR and FAF members who have met specific requirements such as passage of CFA Level I examination and/or possession of qualifying experience and successful completion of a Self-Administered Standards of Practice Examination. (See Appendix B for sample questions.) Affiliate FAF members have agreed to abide by the Code and Standards but do not possess the necessary requirements to be regular members. The term Member includes those who are regular and affiliate members. These standards are also intended to prevent uses of the designation that would mislead employers, clients, customers, and the public regarding the meaning and significance of the designation.

Conduct Affected by the Standard

This standard applies to the use of the words Chartered Financial Analyst, or the abbreviation CFA, and, for an AIMR and FAF member, to the word Member. The standard also applies to related explanations or descriptions in instances that include letterheads and business cards, directory listings, printed advertising and descriptive firm brochures, and oral statements to current or prospective customers or clients.

Application of the Standard

Example 1: Vaughan, an investment adviser registered with the SEC, is required to file annually with the Commission and with most states Uniform Form ADV, which sets forth, among other items of information, his education and business experience. In addition, Vaughan must deliver to prospective clients a brochure containing this information and must annually offer to deliver such information to clients.

Comment: While not required by the SEC or states, it would be appropriate under this standard to indicate on Uniform Form ADV, and in the brochure, that Vaughan holds the designation Chartered Financial Analyst or the designation Member of the AIMR or FAF. This disclosure may also be accompanied by brief descriptions of the requirements met to obtain the designation as well as descriptions of AIMR, ICFA, or FAF, as applicable.

Example 2: Jones and Whittle, portfolio managers in a bank trust department, are awarded the CFA designation. The bank wishes to place a newspaper advertisement recognizing their accomplishment.

Comment: An advertisement consistent with this standard should be limited to a statement of facts regarding the designation and/or the ICFA as the conferring organization. For example, the advertisement could indicate that Jones and Whittle were required to pass three examinations totaling 18 hours, covering the areas of ethical and professional standards, equity and fixed income securities analysis, portfolio management, economics, financial accounting, and quantitative techniques.

If the bank desires to use the term Member, it would follow the same approach regarding description of AIMR, FAF, and the local FAF society. For a Regular Member, the bank could describe the requirements to pass CFA Level I, a six-hour examination covering most of the above topics, and specify that three years' of experience also are necessary. An alternate requirement is to have six years' experience and to have passed a Self-Administered Standards of Practice Examination. (See Appendix B for sample questions.)

Example 3: An advertisement for ACA Investment Advisory Firm states that all principals hold the CFA charter and that they all passed the three examinations on the first try. They are an elite within an elite, having accomplished what few in the investment profession have done. Therefore, their clients may expect superior performance from the firm.

Comment: This reference to the designation clearly violates this standard. It is untruthful in that it does not recognize the growing number of CFAs. It is misleading to imply that holders of the Charter will achieve better investment results and inappropriate to infer that those who pass the exams on the first try will be more successful than those who do not. ACA's advertisement does not represent use of the designation in a dignified and judicious manner and exceeds the permissible explanation specified in the standard.

Example 4: Overby, investment counselor, states in his firm's written promotional material that he is a CFA candidate. He enrolled in the program five years earlier and has not taken an examination at any level.

Comment: Even though Overby's above statement is truthful, it can be construed as misleading and bordering on misconduct as covered in Standard IX because of the growing public awareness and acceptance of the CFA designation and the standard of conduct that the designation implies. The achievement of the CFA charter is significant, requiring a dedicated effort over a relatively long period of time. Using the designation CFA or a reference to the candidacy process implies achievement of, or a striving toward, a recognized level of competence and ethical behavior. Adherence to a high level of conduct benefits both practitioners and the investing public. Candidates who have successfully completed one or more levels are not prohibited from stating this accomplishment in promotional materials. However, the statement should be couched in terms that avoid potential for any misrepresentation.

Procedures for Compliance

On letterheads and business cards, and in directory listings, only the abbreviation CFA or the words Chartered Financial Analyst should appear after the name of the holder. The same rule applies to a Member of AIMR or FAF. It would be inconsistent with this standard for the designation to appear in type larger than that used for the holder's name.

Only those who have attained the CFA charter may utilize the abbreviation CFA or the words Chartered Financial Analyst after their names. There is no designation for those who have completed levels one or two of the CFA exam.

Although CFA candidates certainly may refer to their participation in the program in promotional literature or resumes, it is preferable to place emphasis on concrete results (i.e. passage of Level I or II). A self-declared candidate for a given level should be planning to take the examination within the year.

Any description or explanation of the designation either in printed media, electronic media, or in formal oral presentations to clients or others should be limited to a concise description of the requirements met to obtain the designation and/or a concise description of the conferring organization, AIMR, ICFA, or FAF.

It is appropriate under this standard for a firm's investment and research departments to inform their legal, compliance, public relations, and marketing departments in writing of the requirements for the CFA designation and a description of ICFA, the requirements for the Member of AIMR or FAF, and a description of AIMR or FAF. Each organization prints its Articles of Incorporation, Bylaws, and other information in the AIMR membership directory and publishes booklets with additional descriptive material. The research and investment departments should agree in advance on the appropriate use of the designation in communications to customers, clients, and the public, in print or by other means.

Standard VIII
Reference Material

1. American Bar Association, *Model Code of Professional Responsibility,* Canon, and Ethical Considerations and Disciplinary Rules thereunder (1980).
2. American Bar Association, *Model Rules of Professional Conduct,* Rule 7.2 (1984).
3. American Institute of Certified Public Accountants, *Code of Professional Ethics,* ET §291 (1988), 502 (1989), 505 (1988), and 591 (1989), and BL §250 (1988).
4. Association for Investment Management and Research, *Bylaws,* Article 2, §1, 2, 3, 5, 6; Article 9, §1, 2, 3, 4; Article 10, §1, 2, 3, 4 (1990).
5. Financial Analysts Federation, *Bylaws,* Article 2, §1, 4, 5; Article 9, §1, 2, 3, 4; Article 10, §1, 2, 3, 4 (1990).
6. Institute of Chartered Financial Analysts, *Bylaws,* Article 2, §1, 2, 3, 4; Article 9, §1, 2, 3, 4 (1990).

IX. PROFESSIONAL MISCONDUCT

The financial analyst shall not (1) commit a criminal act that upon conviction materially reflects adversely on his honesty, trustworthiness, or fitness as a financial analyst in other respects, or (2) engage in conduct involving dishonesty, fraud, deceit, or misrepresentation.

Purpose of the Standard

The purpose of the standard is to state the responsibility of AIMR members and nonmember holders of, and candidates for, the CFA designation to avoid committing criminal acts that display a lack of honesty, trustworthiness, or fitness to practice as investment professionals and to avoid other acts of dishonesty, fraud, deceit, or misrepresentation. The scope of the standard extends beyond technical compliance with employment-related regulation to cover behavior that reflects adversely on the entire profession.

Conduct Affected by the Standard

Other standards address specific areas of professional responsibility and the overall obligation to comply with the laws, rules, and regulations that govern their professional, financial, and business activities. Standard IX speaks to the essential matter of personal integrity, both as it relates to the member's reputation and as it reflects on the profession as a whole.

The first section of the standard applies to criminal convictions that call the member's honesty and trustworthiness into serious question. The clause also applies to convictions involving criminal conduct that suggest that individuals are not fit to practice.

Consistent with the bylaws of AIMR (Article 10, Section 3 (b)), any conviction of a crime deemed to be a felony under the law of the applicable jurisdiction can constitute a violation of the first clause of the standard. Disciplinary action under this clause may be pursued upon conviction by a trial, guilty plea, plea of *nolo contendere*, or otherwise; it is possible to impose sanctions despite an appeal.

The second section of the standard prohibits dishonest and other fraudulent conduct even if there has been no criminal conviction.

Application of the Standard

Potential violations of the standard include conviction of perjury or obstruction of justice that might not be considered a violation of a law or rule governing a member's professional, financial, or business activity. Embezzlement related to a purely private activity or a community or civic responsibility is another cause for applying the standard, as is smuggling or illegal drug activity.

Example 1: Hall, the chairman and chief executive officer of a large public company, also serves as director of several multinational corporations. He tells a close friend and professional investment counselor, Patterson, about several planned mergers and acquisitions. On the basis of this material nonpublic information, Patterson purchases sizable blocks of the stock and advises clients to do the same. Substantial profits are realized when the stock is sold after merger announcements make prices soar.

An investigation by the SEC ultimately focuses on the relationship between Hall and Patterson. While testifying under oath, Patterson asserts that he and Hall are merely business acquaintances and that he learned of the mergers from a "Mr. Jones" who was not associated with any of the companies involved and who had since left the country.

Later, it comes to light that Hall and Patterson are close friends, that Jones does not exist, and that before Hall's appearance before the SEC, Patterson urged him to say that he had not discussed the merger plans with anyone outside the companies. Patterson is successfully prosecuted on several counts of perjury and obstruction of justice, both federal felonies.

Comment: Patterson's conduct violated the first clause of Standard IX, as well as the AIMR bylaws. Even if the crimes he committed had not been characterized as felonies, Patterson still would have violated Standard IX, because lying under oath and hindering an investigation by law enforcement authorities reflect materially on his honesty and trustworthiness. If the SEC had taken civil or administrative action against Patterson for violation of the insider trading rules or brought criminal charges against him for such violations, Standards II A or II C could be applied.

Example 2: Foster is employed as an analyst with the investment counseling firm of Ruffner & Ford. He is arrested for erratic driving after a fifth-year college reunion. A search reveals three ounces of marijuana in his car.

Subsequently, he is charged with possession of a controlled substance—a misdemeanor under state law. This is the third time in a year that he has faced drug possession charges. The first arrest involved possession of a small amount of cocaine. He avoided trial by pleading guilty and paying a $1,000 fine. Charges in the second arrest, which also involved marijuana, were dropped after his mother, a prominent corporate lawyer, met with prosecutors. Because his third arrest could not be so easily resolved, he enters into a plea bargain and is sentenced to 30 days in jail and a $500 fine. Although the president of his company is far from pleased with Foster's conduct, he does not believe it affected his day-to-day work. He tells Foster he may continue to work at the firm provided that there are no such further "incidents."

Comment: Foster's conduct could violate the first clause of Standard IX because it would seem to reflect adversely on his fitness as a financial analyst. Although his supervisor did not consider that the conduct warranted discipline, the critical inquiry is whether reasonable members of the profession (as well as the investing public) would condone the conduct. Although no clear rule can be formulated to resolve all situations of this type, Foster's repeated and serious violations of laws prohibiting the use of substances that clearly can interfere with judgment and job performance could violate Standard IX. A contrary result would be indicated if Foster merely had failed to pay three traffic tickets or had been fined for speeding three times in a year. Nonetheless, even those infractions should not be condoned if committed with a frequency suggesting gross disregard for the law.

The second clause of Standard IX prohibits fraudulent and dishonest activity, such as the submission of false insurance vouchers in an attempt to defraud an insurance company. It also prohibits dishonest business schemes, such as an employee's unauthorized purchase of the employer's property at reduced prices or the sale of property to the employer at inflated prices. Such conduct would violate the clause even if it did not result in a criminal conviction.

Dishonest activities that for some reason do not lead to a criminal conviction (for example, because the government agrees to the entry of a consent decree or because the analyst's employer declines to seek prosecution) and thus do not fall within the first section of the standard may nonetheless violate it under the second.

Unless accompanied by a criminal conviction, conduct involving a breach of trust may be subject to discipline under Standard VII C, rather than under either clause of Standard IX.

The following are two examples of the type of conduct that violate the second clause of Standard IX:

Example 3: Hoffman, a security analyst at ATZ Brothers, Inc., a large brokerage house, submits reimbursement forms over a two-year period to ATZ's self-funded health insurance program for more than two dozen bills, most of which had been altered to increase the amount due. An investigation by the firm's director of employee benefits uncovers the conduct. ATZ subsequently terminates Hoffman's employment and notifies AIMR, of which she was a member.

Comment: Despite the absence of a criminal conviction, Hoffman violated Standard IX because she engaged in a pattern of fraudulent activity. Even a few altered medical claims might be grounds for discipline in view of the intentional and calculated nature of the act and its direct relation to the matter of Hoffman's honesty.

Example 4: Black, who writes research reports about the automotive industry, volunteers much of his spare time to local charities. The board of one of the charitable institutions decides to buy five new vans to deliver hot lunches to low-income, elderly persons. Black offers to donate his time to handle purchasing agreements. To pay a long-standing debt to a friend who operated an automobile dealership—and to compensate himself for his trouble—he agrees to a price 20 percent higher than normal, splitting the surcharge with his friend. The director of the charity ultimately discovers the scheme and tells Black that his services, donated or otherwise, are no longer required.

Comment: Black engaged in conduct involving dishonesty, fraud, and misrepresentation in violation of the second clause of Standard IX.

Procedures for Compliance

For the individual member, perhaps the most important compliance features of Standard IX are its clear statement that personal integrity is required and that dishonesty or fraudulent conduct are clearly inconsistent with this requirement.

The public and private regulatory framework provide additional disincentives to those who might be inclined to ignore the proscriptions of Standard IX. Employers registered as broker–dealers or investment advisers are subject to the registration and reporting requirements of such agencies as the SEC, the Ontario Securities Commission, stock exchanges, and other self-regulatory organizations. Such agencies require disclosure of a wide variety of information about employers and some of their employees. The existence of certain facts causes an employee to be statutorily disqualified from engaging in the securities business. Certain employees also must disclose detailed information, including the existence of legal proceedings against them, including claims alleging misrepresentation, prior convictions of criminal offenses, and existence of businesses that became insolvent or otherwise failed while the employee held an interest.

An employer might adopt a clear policy that dishonest or similar conduct will not be tolerated and will result in sanctions by the employer. Such a policy might require reporting dishonest or similar conduct involving any of its financial analyst employees to AIMR.

Standard IX
Reference Material

1. Securities and Exchange Commission Forms BD, ADV, and U-4.
2. American Bar Association, *Model Rules of Professional Conduct,* Rule 8.4 (1989 ed).
3. American Bar Association, *Model Code of Professional Responsibility,* Canon 1 and Disciplinary Rule 1-102 (adopted 1980).
4. American Institute of Certified Public Accountants, *Bylaws,* §7.3.1 (January 12, 1988).
5. Canadian Bar Association, *Code of Professional Conduct,* Chapter 1, "Integrity" (revised August 1987).
6. Institute of Chartered Accountants of Ontario, *Member's Handbook,* "Rules of Professional Conduct," Foreword, at 505–06, Rules 101, 102, 201, and 202 (June 10, 1985).
7. The Law Society of Upper Canada, *Professional Conduct Handbook,* Rule 1 (adopted May 19, 1978).

INTERNATIONAL APPLICATION OF THE CODE AND STANDARDS

Objectives

AIMR's goal is to ensure that membership in the organization is recognized internationally as representing compliance under all circumstances with the highest ethical and professional standards and to encourage, to the greatest extent feasible, the development of homogeneous international standards.

An International Regional Committee, reporting to the Professional Conduct Committee, has responsibility for the administration of the member disciplinary process relating to the Code of Ethics and Standards of Professional Conduct outside the United States and Canada.

Requirements

Standard II A requires members to comply with applicable governing laws and regulations and the Code and Standards. In accordance with this standard, members in all countries should comply at all times with the Code and Standards as well as with the laws and regulations of the countries in which they are domiciled. Members pursuing their profession outside their domestic markets should also comply with the local laws and regulations.

Standard III A requires a financial analyst to have a reasonable basis for his recommendations and to avoid any material misrepresentations. Standard III B 1, Standard III B 2, and Standard III B 3) require the use of reasonable judgment and the communication of the basic characteristics of investments in research reports. Standard III C requires that a financial analyst consider the appropriateness and suitability of an investment for a particular portfolio or client. In accordance with these requirements, members should take into account differences in various countries' accounting standards, disclosure requirements, the extent of compliance, local market liquidity, capital and currency controls, and other relevant factors in trading securities in foreign markets and in advising their clients with respect to foreign securities.

Conduct Affected by the Requirements

When there is an absence of specific local or other regulatory requirements, the Code and Standards should govern members' actions. When the Code and Standards impose a higher degree of responsibility or higher duty than local or other law or custom, the member is held to the Code and Standards. When required to do so, members must also comply with the laws and regulations of their home country while residing and working in foreign countries or trading foreign securities. For instance, the compliance requirements of the SEC apply equally to employees of U.S. companies working in other countries and when trading in U.S. securities abroad. In addition, members must comply with the local laws and regulations of foreign countries.

Accounting and disclosure differences among countries and variations in the scope and effectiveness of local securities regulation can sometimes lead to misunderstandings on the part of those participating in foreign markets about the nature and extent of the information available to make investment judgments and about the degree of protection afforded to public investors. Investment professionals should make investors aware of differences in the basis for providing accounting figures; international variations in the timeliness, depth, quality, and comprehensiveness of corporate disclosures; the degree of public protection provided by securities laws and regulations; the general extent of regulatory compliance with laws and regulations; the degree of liquidity of foreign markets; and such other relevant factors as capital or currency controls. It is incumbent upon investment professionals to identify differences in these areas, to consider them in their work, and to inform their clients of any relevant significant difference when discussing investments in foreign markets.

It would be unprofessional, for example, for a research analyst to compare financial ratios (such as return on equity, debt/equity ratio, and net profit margin) prepared with figures presented under different accounting standards without examining the significance of these differences and, where appropriate, making adjustments to ensure comparability.

It would also be unprofessional for a portfolio manager to fail to consider (and, when appropriate, inform his clients of) the risks associated with trading in a foreign securities market if there were no enforced local government, stock exchange, or corporate rules in place concerning the use by insiders of material nonpublic information.

Application of the Requirements

Members should take the necessary action to ensure that in addition to being fully informed of the Code and Standards and the securities laws and regulations of their home country, they also have appropriate knowledge of the laws and regulations of all countries in which they trade securities or provide investment advice to others and the place of domicile of the issuers of corporate securities analyzed or traded. Members should familiarize themselves with the accounting and disclosure standards, the extent of compliance, market liquidity, and other relevant characteristics of the home countries of the issuers of the corporate securities they analyze.

Members should communicate to clients any relevant significant differences in regulatory, accounting, and disclosure requirements; compliance; and other market characteristics when advising them about investments in foreign markets.

Example 1: Collins is an investment analyst for a major New York-headquartered stock brokerage firm. He works in a less-developed country with a rapidly modernizing economy and a budding capital market. Local securities laws are embryonic in form and content and include no punitive prohibitions against insider trading.

Comment: Collins should be mindful of the risks that a small market and the absence of a fairly regulated flow of information to the marketplace represent to his own ability to obtain information and make timely judgments. He should include this factor in formulating his advice to clients. In handling material nonpublic information that accidentally comes into his possession, he should follow the AIMR Code and Standards and the requirements of the SEC (See Standard II C.) Under no circumstances can he take advantage of such information for himself or his clients.

Example 2: Jennings is an international portfolio manager based in Boston. A client who had previously stipulated that all of his money be invested in North American blue chip securities requests that, in the future, Jennings manage his money on an international basis, with emphasis on securities in countries with high rates of economic growth.

Comment: As an international fund manager, Jennings must be aware of relevant differences among countries in accounting, disclosure, and compliance standards; market liquidity; capital controls; taxation; and other factors and must be capable of incorporating such considerations into her assessments of potential risks and returns. Her client may well be unaware of these factors and their potential influence on the amount and volatility of his future investment returns. Jennings should explain these factors to her client and allow her to consider them before altering his investment strategy.

International Application of the Code and Standards
Reference Material

1. Securities and Exchange Commission, *Regulation of International Securities Markets*, a policy statement (November 1988).
2. Securities and Exchange Commission, "International Release" series, a compilation of SEC statements, memoranda of understanding, studies, reports, no-action letters, proposals, and concept releases related to the internationalization of the securities markets, *SEC Docket* (March 31, 1989). Updated periodically.
3. Securities and Exchange Commission, *Internationalization of the Securities Markets*, a staff report to the Senate Committee on Banking, Housing and Urban Affairs and the House Committee on Energy and Commerce, July 27, 1987. Chapters IV, "Accounting and Auditing Standards in Relation to Multinational and International Issues of Securities," and VII, "Enforcement of the Securities Laws in an International Securities Market," are particularly useful.
4. Securities and Exchange Commission, *The Securities Markets in the 1980s: A Global Perspective* (January 26, 1989) (update of the SEC's 1987 internationalization report).
5. The Options Exchange, *Regulation of Options: Europe, Pacific Basin* (1987).
6. The Council of the European Communities, *Directive Coordinating Regulations on Insider Dealing* (November 13, 1989).
7. Securities and Investment Board of the United Kingdom, *Financial Supervision Rules 1990: the New Approach*, Rulebook, Amendments and Additions, Release 87 (June 28, 1990).
8. Securities and Investment Board of the United Kingdom, *The Proposed Core Rules on Conduct of Business, Consultative Paper 42* (July 1990).
9. Securities and Investment Board of the United Kingdom, *Soft Commission Arrangements in the Securities Markets, a Policy Statement* (July 1990) (includes proposed core rules).
10. United Kingdom Department of Trade and Industry, *Changes to the Law on Insider Dealing, a Consultative Document* (1989).
11. Canadian Institute of Chartered Accountants, *Financial Reporting in Canada* (18th Ed. 1989) (a survey of annual reports of 300 Canadian public companies for 1988, 1987, 1986, and 1985).
12. International Federation of Accountants, *Guideline on Ethics for Professional Accountants* (July 1990).
13. International Organization of Securities Commissions, *IOSCO*, (1988) (a brief description). IOSCO is based in Montreal, Canada.
14. European Board Commission, *The European Bond Markets: An Overview and Analysis for Issuers and Investors* (1989).
15. European Federation of Financial Analysts Societies, *European Stock Market Guide* (1989).
16. European Federation of Financial Analysts Societies, *Glossary of Terms in the International Bond Markets* (1990).
17. The Asian Securities' Analysts Council, *Securities Markets in Asia and Oceania* (Second Ed. 1988).

18. Davis, *Shareholder Rights Abroad: A Handbook for the Global Investor,* Investor Responsibility Research Center (1989).
19. See also footnotes and references to Standard II C, particularly footnote 29 related to memoranda of understanding and other information and regulatory agreements between the SEC and other national regulators.

PROFESSIONALISM AND SERVICE TO THE INVESTING PUBLIC

Objectives

AIMR's goal is to support fair treatment for the investing public and to encourage high ethical and professional standards in the investment industry.

The financial analyst who is in a position to represent his profession in dealings with representatives of corporations, governments, regulatory bodies, and industry groups should encourage fair treatment of the investing public and the adoption of high ethical and professional standards in the field of investment management and research. An ethical and proficient industry is in the best interests of the investing public that relies on the profession's advice and management services. It is also in the best interests of investment professionals who seek to compete fairly on the basis of their professional abilities.

Conduct Affected by the Objectives

During the career of an investment professional, he may be placed in a position to represent the views of investors or the investment profession to legislators, government departments or agencies, other regulatory or professional bodies, members of the press, or the general public. In these representations, he should encourage fair treatment for investors. The monetary policies of central banks, the economic policies and securities laws and regulations of governments, corporate disclosure standards, and financial accounting standards are all set with a view to achieving many objectives and involve balancing the varied interests of many parties. However, any appropriately balanced set of policies and rules that is socially just and economically sound should accord fair treatment to the providers of investment capital. Usually implicit in such fair treatment is the requirement that laws, regulations and practices of government, self-regulatory organizations, and corporations do not have the direct or indirect effect of misleading the investing public, confiscating the public's savings in whole or in part, precluding the receipt of an appropriate return for the risks incurred or preventing recovery of capital invested.

The financial analyst should be careful to ensure that, in his professional advocacy representations on these issues, he is acting in the best interests of the investing public and not merely in the narrow interests of the financial industry or those engaged in the profession of financial analysis.

The financial analyst should make it clear that his own interest lies in being able to compete openly and fairly for an opportunity to serve the public's need for investment advice and investment services.

The financial analyst who is placed in a position of representing his profession should be supportive, when feasible and appropriate, of representatives of governments, regulatory bodies, industry groups and other persons seeking to institute, adhere to or promulgate high ethical and professional standards in the field. Such support may take the form of (1) participating in the preparation or administration of corporate policies on ethics and standards of practice or (2) encouraging, endorsing, or assisting the actions of governments and their agencies, industry and professional bodies, or representative groups of public investors to improve ethical and professional standards.

Application of the Objectives

The following are examples of application of the requirements.

Example 1: Wilson, a highly ranked securities analyst specializing in high-technology companies, is asked by Smith, the chief financial officer of one of the public companies he analyzes, to exercise his influence in the financial community to oppose a proposed new Financial Accounting Standards Board rule presented in an exposure draft requiring more rapid write-off of certain research and development expenditures. Smith argues that the accelerated write-offs would sharply reduce earnings in his company's industrial sector, leading to lower share prices and higher costs of financing. Although Wilson believes the new accounting standard is more economically realistic and conveys a better measure of income, he does not wish to alienate a valuable contact at one of the public companies he follows by refusing the request. He agrees to Smith's request and prepares a response to the exposure draft condemning the proposed changes.

Comment: Wilson is not acting in the best interests of public investors who have a right to receive economically realistic information about their investments. He is acting in his own self-interest.

Example 2: Benson, a member of an advocacy committee on bondholders' rights, is approached by a group of lobbyists who are sponsoring efforts to propose legislation that would give to government issuers new financial flexibility by granting them the right to extend the term to maturity on any or all outstanding government bonds by any number of years desired. The politicians involved believe that this measure will help governments avoid having to refinance low-cost debt during periods of high interest rates. The lobbyists state that these measures are in the best interests of taxpayers. Benson sends a memo to his fellow committee members suggesting that the group publicly support this new legislation.

Comment: The lobbyists' objective of keeping debt costs (and hence taxes) low may well be a worthy one, but it should not be accomplished by retroactively changing the terms of government bonds purchased by the investing public on the basis of a contractual commitment by the government issuer to pay interest and principal on certain dates. Quite apart from the risk that such a measure could destroy confidence in the markets for government debt and thereby have the opposite effect of sharply increasing the cost of servicing government debt, Benson should be opposed to the proposals on the grounds that they do not treat the investing public fairly.

Example 3: A group of investment professionals approaches a financial analysts' organization to seek support for higher minimum levels of training in investment analysis and portfolio management for professional fund managers. Their proposals are sensitive to the burdens on the financial industry arising from introducing new requirements, call for phasing in the new requirements over a period of years as well as providing for the grandfathering of experienced practitioners, and suggest that an appropriate private, self-regulatory organization administer the requirements (the approach to be adopted being a matter for further discussion). The minimum levels of investment training proposed are in keeping with those standards required by responsible firms of their fund managers. The organization decides to oppose the investment professionals' efforts on the grounds that they could lead to less freedom of choice in recruiting new junior portfolio managers and could encroach on the time of some currently employed but inexperienced portfolio managers by requiring that they undertake certain courses of study.

Comment: The investment professionals' actions appear to be directed at enhancing professional standards in the field of investment management and, therefore, to be in the best interests of the investing public. If the details of the proposals are fair and reasonable, the financial analysts' organization should be willing to discuss the proposed requirements and their method of implementation (government regulation or industry self-regulation) in a constructive manner and should not be unduly influenced by the short-term inconvenience to some novice practitioners associated with the new educational requirements.

APPENDIX A
PERFORMANCE PRESENTATION STANDARDS

The Report of the Performance Presentation Standards Implementation Committee, issued in December 1991, contains the AIMR Performance Presentation Standards along with explanation, interpretation, and related materials. An updated Report, to be issued in early 1993, includes revised standards, which take effect on January 1, 1993. The following summary lists mandatory requirements, mandatory disclosures, strongly recommended guidelines and disclosures, and clarification of the treatment of balanced composites. The Securities and Exchange Commission's position on advertising performance also follows.

The Performance Presentation Standards are a manifestation of a set of guiding ethical principles intended to promote full disclosure and fair representation in the reporting of investment results. A secondary objective of these standards is to ensure uniformity in reporting so that results are directly comparable among investment managers. To this end, some aspects of the standards are mandatory. These are listed below. However, not every situation can be anticipated in a set of guidelines. Therefore, meeting the full disclosure and fair representation intent means making a conscientious good faith interpretation of the standards consistent with the underlying ethical principles. This may require doing more than meeting the minimum mandatory requirements and disclosures.

Mandatory Requirements

- Presentation of total return using accrual as opposed to cash basis accounting. (Accrual accounting is not required for stock dividends, nor is it required for retroactive compliance.)
- Time-weighted rate of return using a minimum of quarterly valuation (monthly preferred) and geometric linking of period returns.
- Size-weighted composites using beginning of period values to weight the portfolio returns. (Equal-weighted composites are recommended as additional information, but are not mandatory.)
- Inclusion of all actual, fee-paying, discretionary portfolios in one or more composites within the firm's management (no selectivity in portfolios, no simulation or portability of results within composites).

■ Presentation of annual returns at a minimum for all years (no selectivity in time periods).

■ Inclusion of cash and cash equivalents in composite returns.

Mandatory Disclosures

■ Prospective clients must be advised that a list of all of a firm's composites is available.

■ For each composite, disclosure of the number of portfolios, the amount of assets, and the percentage of a manager's total assets which are represented by the composite. For composites containing five or fewer portfolios, disclosure of composite assets and percentage of firm assets, and a statement indicating that the composite includes five or fewer portfolios.

■ Historical compliance is at the discretion of the manager. When the firm's historical performance record is presented, a disclosure must be made that identifies the in-compliance periods from the periods that are not in compliance. The firm must also disclose that the full historical performance record is not in compliance. If semi-annual or annual valuation periods are used to calculate returns and weight composites for retroactive compliance, this must also be disclosed.

■ Disclosure of whether balanced portfolio segments are included in single-asset composites and, if so, how the cash has been allocated between asset segments.

■ Disclosure of whether performance results are calculated gross or net of fees, and inclusion of the manager's fee schedule in either case.

■ Disclosure of whether leverage has been used in portfolios included in the composite, and the extent of its usage.

■ Disclosure of settlement date valuation if used in place of trade date.

■ Disclosure of any non-fee paying portfolios included in composites.

Strongly Recommended Guidelines and Disclosures

■ Revaluation of the portfolio whenever cash flows and market action combine to distort performance. (Cash flows exceeding 10 percent of the portfolio's market value often cause such distortions.) The methodology should be disclosed.

■ Dispersion of returns across portfolios in the composite.

- Standard deviation of composite returns across time or other risk measures as determined by the manager.
- Comparative indices appropriate to the composite's strategies.
- Presentation of returns on a cumulative basis for all periods.
- Median-size portfolio and portfolio-size range for each composite (unless five or fewer portfolios).
- Percentage of total assets managed in the same asset class as represented by the composite. For example, percentage of total *equity* assets managed.
- Trade date preferred; settlement date is acceptable but must be disclosed.
- If leverage has been used, results on an all-cash (unleveraged) basis are provided, where possible.
- Convertible securities which are not reported separately are assigned to an asset class (equities, under most circumstances) and cannot be shifted without notice being given to clients concurrently or prior to such shifts.
- Presentation of performance may be either gross or net of fee as long as the method is disclosed and the fee schedule is attached. AIMR prefers performance gross of fees.
- Accrual accounting for stock dividends and for retroactive compliance.
- Equal-weighted composites presented *in addition* to the mandatory presentation of asset-weighted composites.

Clarification of the Treatment of Balanced Composites

- When a manager uses the total return of a balanced composite to market a balanced account strategy, a cash allocation to each of the segments of the balanced composite does *not* need to be made.
- When a manager uses the total return of a balanced composite to market balanced account strategy, but wishes to present the segment returns of the balanced composite as supplemental information in presenting his balanced strategy, the segment returns can be shown *without* making a cash allocation as long as the returns for each of the composite's segments (including the cash segment) are shown along with the composite's total return.
- When the segment returns of a balanced composite are being used to *market* equity strategies, fixed-income strategies, or other single-asset

strategies, a cash allocation to each of the segments must be made at the beginning of the reporting period. For example, if a manager is using the equity-only returns of the equity segment of the balanced composite as an indication of expertise in managing equity-plus-cash portfolios, the manager must assign a cash allocation to the equity segment at the beginning of each reporting period. The segment can then be included on the firm's list of composites. For retroactive compliance, a manager must make a reasonable and consistent cash allocation to each of the composite segments, and must disclose the methodology used for assigning cash.

■ When the results of the balanced account segments are added to single-asset composites, a cash allocation needs to be made to each of the segments. This prevents a manager from mixing asset-without-cash-returns to asset-plus-cash-returns.

SEC Position on Advertising Performance

Activities of investment advisors as defined in the Investment Advisers act of 1940 are subject to the act and to the rules and regulations of the Securities and Exchange Commission (SEC). Whether or not investment advisors are registered with the SEC, their advertising of investment performance is subject to the SEC's scrutiny under Section 206 of the Investment Advisers Act—the general antifraud provisions—and Rule 206(4)-1. The term "advertising" is broadly defined in Rule 206(4)-1(b) as any written communication addressed to more than one person, or a communication in the media, relating, among other things, to securities investment services.

In a series of no-action letters beginning in 1986 with a letter involving Clover Capital Management, Inc. (publicly available October 28, 1986), the SEC staff has expressed its view of the requirements for investment advisor performance advertising. The requirements include disclosures in connection with the presentation of both actual and model results. Many of the disclosure requirements are contained in the Clover letter.

In a November 1989 letter (Securities Industry Association, publicly available November 27, 1989), the staff announced that for periods beginning May 27, 1990, all performance information must reflect deduction of an advisor's actual fees, but that for periods before that date, model fees that meet certain standards might be used.

In the second of two letters on the subject involving the Investment Company Institute (ICI, publicly available September 23, 1988), the SEC staff indicated that although performance information generally must be presented net of advisory fees, it is permissible in one-on-one presentations, as described in the letter, to present performance information without the deduction of advisory fees. The SEC staff defines one-on-one presentations as manager performance presentations to any client, prospective client, or affiliated group entrusted to consider manager selection and retention. Communications by managers can, therefore, be made to multiple representatives of a given prospect, even if there are several portfolios within the group. Any written performance presentation materials distributed to more than one client or prospect, in other than one-on-one presentations, must present performance results after deduction of management fees.

In presenting performance net-of-fees, however, a number of additional disclosure requirements must be met. These were stated in the SEC staff letter, and are in addition to other disclosure requirements, as follows:

> "We will not recommend any enforcement action to the Commission if an investment adviser provides prospective clients performance results for advisory accounts on a gross basis in a one-on-one presentation as described in your letter. *This position is expressly conditioned upon the adviser providing at the same time to each client in writing*: [Emphasis added.]
>
> (1) "disclosure that the performance figures do not reflect the deduction of investment advisory fees;
> (2) "disclosure that the client's return will be reduced by the advisory fees and any other expenses it may incur in the management of its investment advisory account;
> (3) "disclosure that the investment advisory fees are described in Part II of the adviser's Form ADV; and
> (4) "a representative example (e.g., a table, chart, graph, or narrative) which shows the effect an investment advisory fee, compounded over a period of years, could have on the total value of a client's portfolio.
>
> "We also would not recommend any enforcement action to the Commission if an investment adviser provides gross performance data to consultants as long as the adviser instructs the consultant to give the performance data to prospective clients of the adviser only on a one-on-one basis and the consultant provides the disclosure in (1) to (4) above.

"Finally, because this response is based upon your representations and is expressly conditioned upon an adviser or consultant providing the information set forth above, any different representations or conditions may require a different conclusion. Further, this response only expresses the Division's conclusions on the questions presented."

As quoted above, the SEC staff stated in the ICI letter that performance advertising that does not deduct advisory fees may be delivered to a consultant for the prospective client in a one-on-one presentation provided that the four disclosures specified above are made.

Managers should review the SEC pronouncements on performance presentation to determine their applicability and should be aware that certain additional disclosures in performance presentations are required by these pronouncements, especially in the Clover letter. Members should also consult their own legal or securities compliance advisors regarding applicable disclosure requirements.

APPENDIX B
SELF-ADMINISTERED
STANDARDS OF PRACTICE EXAMINATION

1. Sandra Johnson, CFA, is a research analyst with a brokerage firm. She decided to change her recommendation on the common stock of Gray, Inc., from buy to sell. She mailed this change in investment advice to all her customers on Thursday. The day after the mailing, one of her customers called with a buy order for 500 shares of Gray, Inc. In this circumstance, Johnson should:

    a. accept the order because she has complied with the standard on fair dealing with customers.
    b. advise the customer of the change in recommendation before accepting the order.
    c. not accept the order until five days have elapsed after the communication of the change in recommendation.
    d. not accept the order because it is contrary to the firm's recommendation.

2. Fred Brown, CFA, works for an investment counseling firm. Joan Simpson, a new client of the firm, is meeting with Brown for the first time. Simpson had used another counseling firm for financial advice for years, but she has switched her account to Brown's firm. After a few minutes of "get-acquainted" small talk, Brown explains to Simpson that he has discovered a highly undervalued stock that offers large potential gains. He recommends that she purchase the stock for her account. Brown has committed a violation of the AIMR standards. What should he have done differently?

    a. He should have determined Simpson's needs, objectives, and tolerance for risk before making a recommendation for any type of security.
    b. He should have questioned Simpson on the reasons that she changed counseling firms. If the discovery process indicated that she had been treated unfairly at the other firm, Brown has a responsibility to notify AIMR of any violation.
    c. He could have thoroughly explained the characteristics of the company to Simpson, including the characteristics of the industry in which the firm operates.

d. He should have explained his qualifications, including his education, training, experience, and the meaning of the CFA designation.

e. All of the above.

3. Which of the following are forms of plagiarism?

    I. Citing quotations said to be attributable to "leading analysts" or "investment experts" without specific reference.

    II. Presenting statistical forecasts by others with the sources identified but without the qualifying statements that may have been used by the originator.

    III. Using factual information published by a recognized financial statistics reporting service without acknowledgement.

    IV. Making a verbal comment at a meeting with associates giving the impression that the analysis is original when in reality it is attributable to another analyst.

a. I and III only

b. III and IV only

c. I, II, and IV only

d. I, II, III, and IV

4. Which of the following statement are consistent with AIMR's Performance Presentation Standards?

    I. Performance measurement may be time weighted or dollar weighted.

    II. Total return, including income and capital appreciation, must be presented.

    III. For a balanced account in which the investment manager has discretion over the asset mix, cash should be included in the performance computation for the asset class for which it is designated.

    IV. Performance results for accounts no longer under management may be deleted from the presentation of all composite performance results.

a. I and II only

b. II and III only

c. I, II, and IV only

d. II, III, and IV only

5. Joan Grey, CFA, recommended the purchase of a mutual fund that invests solely in long-term U.S. Treasury bonds. She made the following statements to her clients:

> I. "The payment of the bonds is guaranteed by the U.S. government; therefore, the default risk of the bonds is virtually zero."
>
> II. "If you invest in the mutual fund, you will earn a 15 percent rate of return each year for the next several years."

Did Grey's statements violate the standards?

	Statement I	Statement II
a.	Yes	Yes
b.	Yes	No
c.	No	Yes
d.	No	No

6. Edward Anderson, a portfolio manager for XYZ Investment Management Company—a registered investment organization that advises investment companies and private accounts—was promoted to that position three years ago. Bates, his supervisor, is responsible for reviewing Anderson's portfolio account transactions and his required monthly reports of personal stock transactions.

Anderson has been using Jones, a broker, almost exclusively for portfolio account brokerage transactions. For securities in which Jones's firm makes a market, Jones has been giving Anderson lower prices for personal purchases and higher prices for sales than Jones gives to Anderson's portfolio accounts and other investors. Anderson has been filing monthly reports with Bates only for those months in which he has no personal transactions, which is about every fourth month.

Based on the above, which of the following applies?

> I. Anderson violated Standards V and VI A (Disclosure of Conflicts and Disclosure of Additional Compensation Arrangements) in that he failed to disclose to his employer the preferential treatment given his personal stock transactions.
>
> II. Anderson violated Standard VII C by breaching his fiduciary duty to his firm's clients.

III. Anderson violated the Investment Advisers Act and the Investment Company Act by failing to report personal securities transactions, thereby violating Standard II A (Compliance with Governing Laws and Regulations).

IV. Bates violated Standard II D by failing to provide reasonable procedures for supervising and monitoring Anderson in his trading for his portfolio accounts and to detect his failure to report personal stock transactions.

a. I only
b. I and II only
c. I, II, and III only
d. All of the above

7. Which of the following statements does not apply to AIMR's international application of the Code and Standards?

I. The financial analyst should take into account differences in various countries' accounting standards and local market liquidity when trading securities in foreign markets and when advising their clients with respect to foreign securities.

II. When there is an absence of specific local or other regulatory requirements, the Code and Standards should govern the financial analyst's actions.

III. The financial analyst is required only to comply with local laws, rules, regulations, or customs even though the AIMR Code and Standards may impose a higher degree of responsibility or a higher duty to the client.

IV. Compliance requirements of the Securities and Exchange Commission apply equally to employees of U.S. companies working in other countries and trading in U.S. Securities abroad.

V. A financial analyst who trades securities in a foreign securities market where there is no enforced local government, stock exchange, and/or corporate rules in place concerning the use by insiders of material nonpublic information is not subject to compliance under Standard II C (Prohibition Against the Use of Material Nonpublic Information).

a. II and III only
b. III, IV, and V only

    c.   III and V only

    d.   All of the above

8.   Ward Henley, CFA, is scheduled to visit the corporate headquarters of Evans Industries. Henley expects to use the information obtained to complete his research report on Evans stock. Henley learns that Evans plans to pay all of his expenses including costs of meals, hotel room, and air transportation. Which of the following actions by Evans would be consistent with the guidelines provided by the standards?

    a.   Accept the expense paid trip and write an objective report.

    b.   Pay for all travel expenses including costs of meals and incidental items.

    c.   Share the expenses, with Henley paying for his tickets and room, but allowing Evans to pay for meals and other activities.

    d.   Either b or c will be in compliance.

9.   Which of the following statements apply to Standard VI C (Compensation—Duty to Employer)?

    I. AIMR members and candidates for the CFA designation are prohibited from undertaking independent practice in competition with their employers.

    II. Written consent by the employer is necessary to permit independent practice that could result in compensation.

    III. Written consent by the outside client is necessary to permit independent practice that could result in compensation.

    IV. The financial analyst is required to disclose to prospective clients or customers the fees or charges that his employer would make for rendering the same services to the prospective client or customer.

    V. Investment professionals subject to the AIMR Code and Standards are prohibited from making arrangements or preparations to go into a competitive business before terminating their relationship with their employer.

    a.   I, II, and IV only

    b.   II, III, IV and V only

    c.   II, III, and IV only

    d.   All of the above

10. Based on Standard VII A (Relationships with Others—Preservation of Confidentiality), the financial analyst must preserve the confidentiality of information received from a client if which two of the following criteria are met?

    I. Information must be material and nonpublic.

    II. Information the financial analyst receives must result from or be relevant to that portion of the client's business that is the subject of the special or confidential relationship.

    III. The financial analyst must be in a relationship of trust with the client.

    IV. Information could reasonably be expected to impair the analyst's ability to render unbiased and objective advice.

  a. I and II only
  b. I and IV only
  c. II and III only
  d. III and IV only

11. Stephanie Reagle, an investment counselor with ABC Inc., successfully completed the level one CFA examination three years ago. She has not enrolled for subsequent examinations. Reagle's firm is revising its promotional materials, and Reagle states in these materials that she is a "CFA 1." In light of the above, which of the following statements apply?

    I. Reagle's reference to "CFA" 1 does not violate the Standards.

    II. Reagle's reference violates Standard VIII. Only those individuals who have attained the CFA charter may utilize the abbreviation CFA or the words Chartered Financial Analyst after their names.

    III. Reagle's reference to "CFA" 1 would not be a violation of the Standards if she were currently enrolled in the level two program.

    IV. Candidates who have successfully completed one or more of the three levels of the CFA program are prohibited from stating this accomplishment in promotional materials until and if they are awarded the CFA designation.

  a. I only
  b. II only

c. II and IV only

d. III only

12. Jane Doe, an analyst with LMN Brokerage firm, has discovered that projections included in a research report she prepared on one of the companies she follows has been significantly revised upward by her supervisor. Which of the following alternatives is consistent with the AIMR Standards?

    a. Doe should insist that her projections be restored or that her name be removed from the report.

    b. Doe should take no action; only her supervisor may have violated the Standards.

    c. Doe should agree to have the report disseminated contingent on distribution of a follow-up report incorporating her original earnings estimates.

    d. Doe should hire legal counsel.

13. Nancy Green is in the process of completing an investment research report. Which one of the following is not required based on Standard III (Research Reports, Investment Recommendations and Actions)?

    a. The report should avoid inflammatory and promissory statements.

    b. All records pertinent to Green's investment decision should be maintained.

    c. Opinions should be expressed only with regard to the investment recommendation.

    d. The report should be reviewed by an associate with supervisory authority.

14. Which one of the following statements does not accurately describe the AIMR standard concerning the use of material nonpublic information?

    a. Substantial penalties apply to the receipt of material nonpublic information.

    b. An analyst may violate this standard by passing material nonpublic information to others, even when this information has not been secured from the company.

    c. An analyst may use material nonpublic information if it has been developed from a combination of non-material pieces of information.

    d. Material nonpublic information may be used when it has been secured from sources that have not breached their fiduciary duty.

15. Pursuant to the AIMR Bylaws and the AIMR Rules of Procedure, membership in AIMR and/or the right to hold and to use the CFA designation may be summarily suspended by AIMR's Designated Officer for the following misconduct:

    I. Conviction of a crime which is defined as a misdemeanor.
    II. Conviction of a crime which is defined as a felony.
    III. Indefinite bar from registration under the securities laws (even though reapplication may be made after a specific period of time).
    IV. Failure to complete and return a professional conduct statement for each of two successive years.

    a. I and II only
    b. II and III only
    c. I, II, and III only
    d. II, III, and IV only

16. Joe Dumas, CFA, has recently been employed in the mergers and acquisitions subsidiary (M&A) of a major investment banking firm. One of his clients is Crown Company.

    Last week, however, he became director of investment policy for the investment management subsidiary (Investment) of a regional bank holding company. In reviewing the research prepared by Investment, he realized that the buy recommendation on Crown Company is based on sales trends that he knows have been reversed in the last month. Dumas knows this because Crown had told him about the changes when it was a client of his at M&A.

    Dumas also discovered that Investment has been acquiring sizable blocks of Crown in the portfolio of a major new client to bring that portfolio's holdings up to Investment's recommended portfolio allocation. There are a number of standards that Dumas should consider to guide his actions.

    What is the standard that must be applied first?

    a. VII C (Relationships with Others—Fiduciary Duties).
    b. III C (Research Reports, Investment Recommendations and Actions—Portfolio Investment Recommendations and Actions).
    c. II C (Compliance with Governing Laws and Regulations and the Code and Standards—Prohibition Against Use of Material Nonpublic Information).

d. IV (Priority of Transactions).

17. A week after the initial analysis discussed in question 16, Crown puts out a press release confirming the information Crown had given Dumas. Specifically, sales had in fact been down in the past month instead of the steady rise Crown had previously shown. Dumas asks Mike Hansen, the analyst at Investment responsible for Crown, to review his recommendation of Crown in light of the press release and get back to him by noon. What is Hansen's best action?

   a. Quickly change his recommendation to sell.
   b. Tell Dumas that he cannot change his recommendation until he has talked to the president of Crown.
   c. Rely on the information the company provided in the press release, recalculate his sales and earnings estimates accordingly, and adjust his recommendation to reflect the new estimates.
   d. Discuss with Investment's major clients the effect of the press release on Hansen's recommendation before advising Investment's portfolio managers.

18. Dawn Vincent, a trustee for the pension plan of Mawyer Industries, has just received a commission schedule form XYZ Brokerage, a firm with which she is not currently trading. The schedule shows fees which are lower than those charged by ABC Brokerage, the firm Vincent currently uses for a majority of transactions. ABC also provides research data and performance measurement for the pension plan, services that XYZ is not equipped to handle. Vincent is concerned that she may be violating her fiduciary duty of loyalty by not using the lowest cost brokerage firm. Which of the following statements applies to Vincent's situation?

   a. If she doesn't immediately transfer her business to XYZ, she will clearly violate her fiduciary duty.
   b. She will not violate her fiduciary duty unless she personally profits from her relationship with ABC.
   c. The "safe harbor" in Section 28(e) of the Securities Exchange Act of 1934 allows fiduciaries to pay higher commission even if the services are not commensurate with the cost.
   d. She can continue to trade through ABC if she determines, in good faith, that the value of the services to plan beneficiaries is commensurate with the cost.

19. A noteworthy development pertaining to insider trading involved passage of the Insider Trading Sanctions Act in 1984. This law includes all of the following provisions except:

    a. Liability in transactions involving a put, call, straddle, option, privilege, or group or index of securities.
    b. A comprehensive definition of material nonpublic information.
    c. Monetary damages of up to three times the profit, or the loss avoided, on insider trading transactions.
    d. A five-year statute of limitations on judicial actions.

20. The idea behind Standard IV (Priority of Transactions) of the AIMR standards is that employees should not:

    a. Place their own personal interests above those of their customers or employer.
    b. Attempt to notify their best customers about critical investment information sooner than their other customers.
    c. Place a buy or sell order in non-discretionary accounts without the prior consent of the client.
    d. Give preferential treatment to one client over another in security transactions.

Answers

1. b. Advise the customer of the change in recommendation before accepting the order.

2. a. He should have determined Simpson's needs, objectives, and tolerance for risk before making a recommendation for any type of security.

3. c. I, II and IV only.

4. b. II and III only.

5. c. Statement I, no; statement II, yes.

6. d. All of the above.

7. c. III and IV only.

8. d. Either b or c will be in compliance.

9. c. II, III and IV only.

10. c. II and III only.

11. b. II only.

12. a. Doe should insist that her projection be restored or that her name be removed from the report.

13. c. Opinions should be expressed only with regard to the investment recommendation.

14. a. Substantial penalties apply to the receipt of material nonpublic information.

15. d. II, III and IV only.

16. c. II C (Compliance with Governing Laws and Regulations and the Code and Standards—Prohibition Against Use of Material Nonpublic Information).

17. c. Rely on the information the company provided in the press release, recalculate his sales and earning estimates accordingly, and adjust his recommendation to reflect the new estimates.

18. d. She can continue to trade through ABC if she determines, in good faith, that the value of the services to plan beneficiaries is commensurate with the cost.

19. b. A comprehensive definition of material nonpublic information.

20. a. Place their own personal interests above those of their customers or employer.

APPENDIX C
BASIC RESOURCES

The list below includes books or reports that are frequently cited in the references of the individual sections of the *Handbook* or that provide extensive background information on major issues discussed in the text.

1. *Ethics and the Investment Industry*, eds. Oliver F. Williams, Frank K. Reilly, and John W. Houck. Rowman & Littlefield Publishers, Inc., Savage, Md. 1989, $16.95.

2. *Ethics in the Financial Marketplace*, John L. Casey. Scudder, Stevens & Clark, New York, N.Y., 1988, $10.

3. *Fiduciary Standards in Pension & Trust Fund Management*, Betty Linn Krikorian. Butterworth Legal Publishers, Stoneham, Mass. 1989, $55.

4. *The Financial Analyst's Handbook*, ed. Sumner N. Levine, Pt. I, "Methods, Theory and Portfolio Management;" Pt. II, "Analysis by Industry," 1975. Parts I & II are out of print. Second edition (one volume) including additional as well as updating material, 1988. Dow Jones-Irwin, Homewood, Ill. $80.

5. *Financial Analysts Journal.* Association for Investment Management and Research, Charlottesville, Va., bimonthly, $150 U.S. for domestic addresses.

6. *Financial Planners: Report of the Staff of the United States Securities and Exchange Commission to the House Committee on Energy and Commerce's Subcommittee on Telecommunications and Finance.* Securities and Exchange Commission, Washington, D.C., 1988.

7. *Guide to Broker–Dealer Compliance: Report of the Broker–Dealer Model Compliance Program Advisory Committee.* Securities and Exchange Commission, Washington, D.C., November 13, 1974.

8. *Internationalization of the Securities Market: Report of the Staff of the U.S. Securities and Exchange Commission to the Senate Committee on Banking, Housing and Urban Affairs and the House Committee on Energy and Commerce.* Securities and Exchange Commission, Washington, D.C., July 27, 1987.

9. *Investment Advisers Guide.* Two volume publication relating to regulation of investment advisers by the SEC, under ERISA, and in all 50 states.

Investment Company Institute, Washington, D.C., initial subscription $300 for the general public with annual updates at $100; initial subscription for associates $75, annual updates $50.

10. *The Investment Manager's Handbook,* ed. Sumner N. Levine. Dow Jones-Irwin, Homewood, Ill., 1980. Out of print.

11. *Managing Investment Portfolios: A Dynamic Process,* eds. John L. Maginn, CFA, and Donald L. Tuttle, CFA. Warren, Gorham & Lamont, Inc., Boston, Mass., 1990. $125.

12. *Modern Investment Management and the Prudent Man Rule,* Bevis Longstreth. Oxford University Press, New York, N.Y., 1986, $36.

13. *The October 1987 Market Break: A Report of the Division of Market Regulation.* Securities and Exchange Commission, Washington, D.C., February 1988, $38.

14. *Report of the Presidential Task Force on Market Mechanisms,* U.S. Government Printing Office, Washington, D.C., 1988, $17.

15. *Ethics in the Investment Profession: A Survey*, E. Theodore Veit, CFA, and Michael R. Murphy, CFA. The Research Foundation of The Institute of Chartered Financial Analysts, Charlottesville, Va., $20.

16. *Report of the Task Force on the Body of Knowledge.* Association for Investment Management and Research, Charlottesville, Va., January 15, 1991.

INDEX

A

B

C

F

G

J

K

L

M

S